Women of Chiapas

Women of Chiapas
Making History
in Times of Struggle and Hope

Edited by
Christine Eber
and **Christine Kovic**

Foreword by June Nash

ROUTLEDGE
NEW YORK AND LONDON

Published in 2003 by
Routledge
29 West 35th Street
New York, NY 10001
www.routledge-ny.com

Published in Great Britain by
Routledge
11 New Fetter Lane
London EC4P 4EE
www.routledge.co.uk

Cover: Margarita Ruíz Pérez and Lucia Pérez Pérez of the weaving cooperative, Tsobol Antzetik (Women United)—see page 191 for full photo and caption. Weaving designs on the cover and chapter title pages are representative of those woven by contemporary Maya women.

Photo and weaving designs by Christine Eber.

Routledge is an imprint of the Taylor and Francis Group.

Printed in the United States of America on acid-free paper.

10 9 8 7 6 5 4 3 2 1

Library of Congress Cataloging-In-Publication Data

Women in Chiapas: a world where everyone fits / edited by Christine Eber and Christine Christine Kovic.
     p.cm.
  Includes bibliographical references and index.
  ISBN: 0-415-94556-9 (alk. paper)—0-415-94557-7 (pbk: alk. paper)
   1. Maya women—Mexico—Chiapas. 2. Women—Mexico—Chaipas—Social
     Conditions. 3. Chiapas (Mexico)—History—Peasant Uprising, 1994- I. Eber,
    Christine Engla. II. Kovic, Christine Marie.

F1435.3.W55W65 2003
305.4'0972'75—dc21

2003043127

Contents

Acknowledgments

This book owes its existence in great part to the dialogue on social justice in Chiapas that women and men of diverse backgrounds have established over the past two decades. We are grateful to the many individuals and organizations who have nurtured this dialogue in different cultures and places, often in the face of many obstacles. To name these people and organizations would require another book. We say to all batzi colavalik (thank you very much) for what you have given and risked and pas bu'uncutik perton (forgive us) for any errors we have made. Foremost in our minds and hearts has been to create a book that respects the words and actions of women in Chiapas. We hope that we have succeeded.

We wish to say a special thank you to June Nash for writing the foreword to this book and for her support throughout the years; to María Pilar Milagros Garcia, Jeannette Minnie, Beth Pollack, and Heather Sinclair for translating the Spanish material; to the reviewers who offered invaluable guidance in revising the manuscript; to Priti Gress who believed in this book when it was still searching for its identity; and to our husbands, Michael O'Malley and Francisco Argüelles, who have supported our work in myriad ways. Last, we thank the institutions where we work, the University of Houston–Clear Lake and New Mexico State University, and our friends and colleagues in Chiapas, the U.S., and elsewhere. Without your generous insights and steadfast encouragement we could never have understood, nor had the courage to write about life in Chiapas.*

*In recognition of the fully collaborative effort that this book represents, we list our names alphabetically as co-editors and reverse our name order for authorships of the introduction and part overviews.

Foreword
Activists, Poets, and Anthropologists in the Frontlines of Research

Contributors to this anthology are forging a new direction in anthropology as they engage in research on indigenous and mestiza women in the struggle for democracy in Chiapas, Mexico. They succeed in bringing together anthropologically informed and humanistic pieces that address some of the most important transformative changes of the times. Among these are the participation of women in the public domain, and simultaneously in revolutionary movements as formerly excluded ethnic and gender sectors of the population seeking their niche in civil society. Their struggles represent a break with sexist and racist traditions that have heretofore characterized the construction of the nation. Just as the women's struggles range from cultural to political and economic arenas, so do the contributors engage in multiple forms of expression, from poetry to narratives and from history to ethnography.

In the course of their documentation and analysis of current processes of change in Chiapas, the editors are introducing new forms of anthropological expressions. Among these are the participatory engagement with people caught up in the end of millennial movements for survival that some call activist anthropology. This involves not only a clear statement of the investigators' commitment to shared principles with subjects of investigation, but a willingness to criticize moments when practice contradicts ideological premises. Some of the texts are written by foreign activists, such as Heather Sinclair, a U.S. midwife and health educator who participated as a human-rights observer in the Las Cañadas and whose Letter from a Peace Camp (Chapter 7) records the fate of a people under siege. Others are Mexican mestizas, like Inés Castro and Yolanda Castro who helped indigenous women organize the weaving cooperative Jolom Mayaetik. Some of the literary texts were written by community members like Flor de Margarita Pérez Pérez and Margarita Pérez, a traditional healer, who distill their cultural commitments in poems, plays, songs, and prayers. Still others like Shannon Speed, Susanna Rostas, and the editors, Christine Eber and Christine Kovic, bring their own commitment to values of social justice and human rights in their research focusing on the struggles of the people to achieve these. Their background as activists—Christine Kovic worked for two years in the Center for Human Rights Fray Bartolomé de Las Casas and Christine Eber has helped women's artisan cooperatives find markets—informs their research but does not intrude on it.

Activist anthropology stems from some of the same values related to social justice that inspired Sol Tax to promote "action anthropology" a half century ago with the Fox Indians. While conducting a field research team with the Fox in 1948, he crystallized in a letter to the students some of his thoughts about introducing change for progress in the Fox reservation. In the process of carrying out the agreed-upon action with the Fox, he felt that the students would learn more about culture and personality, social structure and everything else. Action anthropology often meant specific involvement in projects usually conceived and managed by the anthropologist and carried out with Indians. Among those projects in the Fox Reservation were the production of Tama-Craft industry, organization of a community center and encouraging citizenship and active participation in democratic processes (Blanchard 1979). The Cornell Anthropology Department carried out a similar project in Vicos, Peru that was overtly directed toward overcoming the paternalistic codes of behavior in the feudal agriculture still persisting in highland Peru in the 1950s and 1960s. Yet because the initiatives were those of the anthropologists, who, in the words of one of the Vicos students, became the new *patrones,* the Fox and Vicos projects were often criticized as "paternalistic." Nonetheless they satisfied the "citizen interests" as Tax called it (Blanchard 1979) of the anthropologists in contributing to the society by generating artistic talents of the people they study and enabling them to earn much needed cash. Action anthropology was later called "applied anthropology" as development agencies expanded the range of their projects to rural and indigenous areas.

In contrast to the action and applied anthropologists who promoted the reproduction of a given status quo, activist anthropologists take their lead from the people they study, adapting their talents and resources to the needs and interests of the people they join as they become engaged in transformative actions for structural change. The activist approach permits greater access to privileged sources of information than strictly scientific ethnography, but this comes with greater risks in representing one's findings. No matter how hard one seeks balance, some doors are closed at the moment that others are opened since associations with those who are considered opponents will mitigate trust. It is rare to find an anthropologist like Charles Hale who was able to maintain a credible presence with protagonists of the Nicaraguan Revolution that found themselves on opposite sides of the table as the conflict moved from that between Sandinistas and national elites to one between Sandinistas and the Miskitu Indians (Hale 1994). Yet this tension between distinct perspectives within a common cause is the essence of uniting theory to practice since it generates the discussions and actions that make for an evolving process.

Activist anthropology grows out of the conflict situations that anthropologists encounter in field sites throughout the world where there is little tolerance for neutrality. Those who have engaged in it, as Barrie Thorne (1983) learned in her activist research with war resisters during the Vietnam War period, find that guilt mixes with euphoria as participation in events as an observer-collaborator often means sharing the excitement but not the full risk as others. Thorne found that she was suspected of being a federal agent there to detect illegal activities of the draft resisters. Nonetheless protagonists of activism often value the role of observers in such crisis situations for itself, as I discovered when I joined a march of Bolivian mine workers opposing the closing of national mines in 1986 (Nash 1992). Since there were no immediate journalists on the scene when the 10,000 marchers were surrounded by the army to prevent them from continuing on to La Paz, many came up to talk with me when they saw me with pen and paper recording the event. There is, as well, the anxiety as to what revelations would injure the movement once they were printed. As a participant activist, the ethnographer finds himself/herself an instrument of the research, reflecting on feelings and emotions raised by the events in which he/she was involved as a participant. In the process of assessing the personal risk involved in participatory action, the ethnographer is sensitized to greater awareness of the implications of those who make up the social movement.

Activist anthropology need not imply that the anthropologist renounces scientific criteria or the theoretical premises that informs the discipline. On the contrary, it means situating oneself in the field of social action, defining and often clarifying to oneself the particular perspective that conditions his/her research. I have seen greater transparency in the work of activist anthropologists than that of self-styled "objective" scientific researchers who have not felt required to divulge what motivates the choice of research topics or the relations with those who provide them with information. One of the ways in which activist research is developing is in collaborative work with the subjects of inquiry. This is not, as some assert, reducing fieldwork to social work, but rather searching for directions in an unfolding research project with the subjects themselves. Most seasoned researchers have always admitted that the elucidation of what became their central problematics are a response to informants who themselves become engaged in the inquiry. I recall one of my own epiphanies when I was working in Amatenango del Valle on their increasing homicide rate. My research assistant, Mariano López Lin, served as president of the town during a period of intense conflict in which the victims were primarily young men who served as curers and were suspected to be witches responsible for the death of their neighbors and relatives. When I convinced him that I was not satisfied with the conventional response to the question, "Why are they killing more men as witches?" which was, "People are losing our traditions," he began to cogitate on the 37 cases we were reviewing. Suddenly as we were returning from the burial of one of the victims, he told me to stop the car and write down what he had to say. He recounted the times when there had been no murders in town and how they began to increase in the 1950s. He recalled that the *krincipales*—those who had served in the civil and religious hierarchies and had become elder advisers to all the active officials—authorized the advent of a young curer—*ilol* or one who sees (we would probably say diviner). Then when the president of the town and his *sindico* were chosen from among indigenous residents rather than Ladinos from outside the town, people no longer took the *krincipaletik* seriously. The control by the elder curers over the new declined along with the prestige of elder authorities, and people no longer had faith that the curers used their power for the good of the community.

This kind of collaboration is cultivated as we enter into an intense dialogue with people of a distinct cultural perspective yet one that we are intent on sharing. Marco Tavanti, an Italian Catholic priest who worked collaboratively with the Tzotzil group who call themselves *Las Abejas*, developed collective discussions of the events that led up to the horrifying massacre of 45 members of the community. He would raise issues to the diverse assembly of men and women, young and old, Protestant and Catholic, and government party PRI adherents and Zapatistas, asking them to reflect on this in common. He would challenge them to take their collaborators seriously and question their own premises, much as is done in a focus group (Tavanti 2003:25–26). He maintains—and his monograph on the community that lived through this traumatic period and transformed the tragedy into a collective memorial proves—that positive advantages can be gained from such a collaborative research design. The goal as he points out is as follows:

> Experiencing and welcoming diversity creates new cross-cultural and "syncretic" standpoints that are essential for interpreting our globalizing society. The point here is not just that foreigners interpret society from a standpoint of foreigners and indigenous from a standpoint of indigenousness. Rather, it is the experience of moving across localities and identities that generate new perspectives.

Anthologies such as this one edited by Christine Eber and Christine Kovic succeed in such a collaborative project by going beyond the usual network of the ethnologist to provide a broader scope for inquiry into the dynamics of social change in process. This is particularly marked by their inclusion of creative works that allow the writers to explore their inner psyches and their relations with a collective group as they imagine alternative scenarios. Plays, songs, prayers, life histories, and testimonials embody the experience of indigenous life and struggle that goes beyond ethnographic representation. These creative texts draw upon everyday forms in which women express their sentiments and reflect on salient issues in their lives. Yet because the creativity involves imagination, the question of ethnographic validity arises. How do we know that they represent "the truth"? What are the criteria of validity when the canons of ethnographic authority are dismissed? These canons include long-term, intimate acquaintance with knowledgeable members of the group whose intelligent perceptions are probed in many different contexts. Those chosen as informants presumably are respected by their communities and their testimonies have stood up in many different occasions. Can we accept the texts on their own merit, or is the authority of the ethnographer still operating though not given authorship?

The editors answer some of these questions in the part overviews by providing the deeper layers of meaning for the texts. For example, prayers are the most commonplace yet most elaborated forms of speech in Mayan cultures. Certain stock phases, such as "flowery words" in reference to prayer itself reflects the belief that people are responsible for keeping the universe in flower. This, in turn, leads us to question the context for prayer or flowery words. What the Western world refers to as religion is not a separate category of existence. Prayers are spontaneously occurring expressions in many daily lived experiences. Robert Redfield (1930) was probably the first U.S. anthropologist to recognize the religious experience among the folk of Tepoztlán, Mexico as a boundless experience wherein a man's cultivation of the milpa was as religious an experience as praying in church, or a woman's weaving—and even washing of the clothing of the saints—was as sacred an act as prayer. Like prayer, hymns are unbounded expressions that allow women to connect with each other and to find a common voice to express their hopes for the future. Religion, which might sometimes serve as the "opiate of the people" dulling people's senses to the real conditions of life, is also "the heart of a heartless world" as Marx himself said following up his much quoted adage. As such, religion provides a common expression for indigenous people at this moment in time.

As they participate actively in the social movements occurring in Chiapas, the contributors excel in uniting their voices with those of the women's cooperatives, church groups, political parties, and nongovernmental organizations (NGOs) with whom they work. In these collective actions, women unite their strategic needs as wives and mothers with their desire for structural change of their position as doubly oppressed. I have noticed in the processions and demonstrations that women engage in a strong ritual and religious symbolism. This was particularly evident in the Women's Day March in 1995 when the women all carried white flowers and candles as they were accompanied by incense bearers; these are the quintessential elements of the traditional festivals in indigenous communities. Although the march was a highly politicized event, with strong claims for peace and against militarism since it occurred a month after the invasion of Zapatista communities in the Lacandon jungle, the context was enhanced by these symbols to evoke the peace and justice they claimed.

These symbolic references to the sacred and to the special relationship of women to the Mother Earth often alarm First World activists who join the ranks of indigenous people. Yet we have much to learn from the anxiety raised in both these contexts. Our cultivated distancing from the spiritual sources of collective behavior may prompt disdainful reactions when we find the conviction of mobilized people expressed in religious terms. Zapatistas draw upon these sources latent in the Christian Base Communities that thrived in the Lacandon rain forest during the ministering of Bishop Samuel Ruíz who drew from Liberation Theology in formulating his own theology of rebellion. Religion has always provided a powerful stimulus to the wretched of the earth, whether directing them to the world after death or before. Indigenous communities drew from passages of Exodus in the Bible—the message of liberation of the Israelis—and applied it to their own condition of liberation from the slavery of the plantations in which they worked (Leyva Solano 1996). In Acteal, the Chenalhó hamlet where paramilitaries trained and financed by the Institutional Revolutionary Party massacred 45 members of the Christian Base Community that call themselves Las Abejas (The Bees), religious faith fortified their commitment to resistance against the government (Tavanti 2003). The strength of conviction in the justice of their struggle fortifies their movement precisely because of the martyrdom. This was as prevalent in early Christianity when it appeared as the religion of slaves and poor people subjugated or dispersed by Rome as it was in the workers socialist circles in the nineteenth century (Engels 1959), and as it is today in Chiapas.

Just as the referential system of religion in the politics of indigenous peoples raises hackles with the sophisticated outside observer, so too does the self-referential language of motherhood and identification with the earth often used by the women in these movements. In the postmodern, deconstructive mode now fashionable in anthropology, the very category of women is decried as essentialist.[1] Certainly a reductionist view of Third World women as people with " 'needs' and 'problems' but no freedom to act" (Chandra Mohanty, cited in Escobar 1995:8) merits criticism, but the critique should not end with the statement of the problem. The editors of this anthology have gone beyond the critique to include women speaking for themselves not only about their problems, but also about finding dignity as they overcome the fear and self-repression related to their former subjugation at home and in public life of "traditional communities." We must go beyond deconstruction of the rhetoric to discover the incentives generating a common collective image among indigenous movements.

Warren's (1998) study of pan-Maya activists in Guatemala provides a case in point. By promoting the revitalization of Indian languages, cultural icons, and identification with territories, pan-Mayanists hope to transform their relations to the state and civil society. This represents only one of the many ways in which Mayas of Guatemala are reasserting their heritage in contemporary struggles. Communities of Populations in Resistance and Committees of Campesino Unity were other contexts in which indigenous people joined with mestizos to contest the genocidal attack on small plot farmers of the western highlands and the colonizers of the Ixcan during the 1980s. Like Guatemala Mayas, Chiapas Mayan women are confronting the structural factors deriving from neoliberal policies that reduce social welfare and expand military bud-

---

[1]Micaela di Leonardo (1998) derides women's "cultural tropes" as an escape from political and economic conditions in its appeal to superior morality.

gets. To do it as women whose special responsibility is the care and nurturance of children is not to diminish alternative positions, but to complement them. The task of the activist anthropologist is to discover and act on the alternatives posed by indigenous people themselves, not to deconstruct their language as they seek common cause with other women.

There is no doubt that activist anthropology involves us in greater risks as well as rewards. This may not be a matter of choice. In conditions of massive social upheaval, no neutrals are allowed for long-term participant observation. Collaboration promotes a creative tension that goes beyond the events to clarify the conflicts and resolutions that enter into transformative change. The editors have done us a favor in bringing to our attention this insightful array of testimonials of activists, creative expressions of artists and poets, along with ethnographic analyses of one of the greatest transformative changes of the twentieth century.

—June Nash
January 4, 2003

References

Blanchard, David, 1979. "Beyond Empathy: The Emergence of an Action Anthropology in the Life and Career of Sol Tax," in Robert Hinshaw, ed., *Currents in Anthropology: Essays in Honor of Sol Tax*. The Hague, Paris, New York: Mouton Publishers, pp. 419–444.

di Leonardo, Micaela, 1998. *Exotics at Home: Anthropologies, Others, American Modernity*. Chicago: University of Chicago Press.

Engels, Friedrich, 1959. "On the History of Early Christiniaty," in Marx and Engels: *Basic Writings on Politics and Philosophy*. Garden City, NY: Doubleday, pp. 168–194.

Escobar, Arturo, 1995. *Encountering Development: The Making and Unmaking of the Third World*. Princeton, NJ: Princeton University Press.

Hale, Charles R., 1994. *Resistance and Contradiction: Miskitu Indians and the Nicaraguan State, 1894–1987*. Stanford, CA: Stanford University Press.

Leyva Solano, Xochitl, 1996. *Lacandonia al Filo del Agua*. Mexico, D.F.: Fondo de Cultura Maya.

Nash, June, 1992. "Interpreting Social Movements: Bolivian Resistance to the Economic Conditions Imposed by the International Monetary Fund," *American Ethnologist* 19(2).

Redfield, Robert, 1930. *Tepoztlán, a Mexican Village*. Chicago: University of Chicago Press.

Tavanti, Marco, 2003. *Las Abejas: Pacifist Resistance and Syncretic Identities in a Globalizing Chiapas*. New York & London: Routledge.

Thorne, Barrie, 1983. "Political Activist as Participant Observer: Conflicts of Commitment in a Study of the Draft Resistance Movement of the 1960s," in Robert M. Emerson, ed., *Contemporary Field Research: A Collection of Readings*. Boston: Little Brown, pp. 216–234.

Warren, Kay B., 1998. *Indigenous Movements and Their Critics: Pan-Mayan Activism in Guatemala*. Princeton, NJ: Princeton University Press.

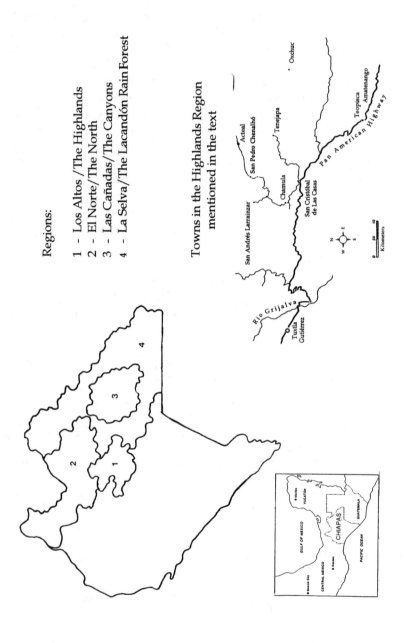

REGIONS of CHIAPAS

Regions:

1 - Los Altos / The Highlands
2 - El Norte / The North
3 - Las Cañadas / The Canyons
4 - La Selva / The Lacandón Rain Forest

Towns in the Highlands Region
mentioned in the text

# Introduction

CHRISTINE KOVIC
CHRISTINE EBER

We know that the struggle exists and takes time.
We want the struggle to stay in the memory, not just of one woman,
but of all women, so that they, too, can resist.
—Carmen, Tzeltal Mayan Woman
(from Hacía la Autonomía: Zapatista Women Developing a New World)

The chapters in this book highlight the concerns, visions, and struggles of women in Chiapas, Mexico. Images in the media of women defending themselves and their communities with their own hands have drawn attention to the conditions of life in Chiapas. Our book intends to deepen awareness of these conditions by exploring several issues that have taken center stage: poverty, discrimination, and violence; religious change and women's empowerment; and women organizing for social change. The chapters in this book are grouped into these themes.

Focusing on women's lives reveals the persistent inequalities of life in Chiapas. The life expectancy for women in Chiapas is two years less than for men, the reverse of what is found in most countries undergoing rapid economic development. Chiapas has the highest maternal death rate in Mexico (Freyermuth Enciso 2001). In rural communities, women's workloads have increased two to three times what they were before the 1980s (Rus 1990). Increasingly, women are the sole supporters of their families through selling agricultural or artisan products that they produce. The variety of activities women fulfill in subsistence and artisan production ensures the survival of peasant communities (Nash 2001).

In the midst of multiple stresses, it is remarkable that women have found the will and courage to work together to improve the conditions of life in their communities. Yet, by the 1960s women had already begun to form cooperatives to sell their artisan products and organize as midwives to attend to pregnancy and childbirth in their communities. Since the Zapatista uprising, some indigenous women have been fighting in the EZLN (the Zapatista Army of National Liberation) and defending their communities in civilian support bases for the Zapatistas.[1] Others have been involved in a range of civilian activities, protesting human rights abuses, and creating projects to expand options for autonomy and women's rights.

This introduction attempts to serve several purposes: to provide historical and cultural background for the diverse activities in which women of Chiapas have been involved since the 1970s; to situate the book's chapters in feminist scholarship about gender and women; and to explore points of divergence and alliance among the book's contributors. Separate overviews to the three parts of the book provide further framing of thematic and conceptual issues.

Opening New Spaces for Autonomy and Women's Rights: 1970s to Present

Chiapas has a population of 3.5 million people, 1 million of whom are indigenous. The majority of these people are of Mayan descent. Several native languages are spoken in the state, including Tzotzil, Tzeltal, Tojolobal, Ch'ol, and Zoque, among others. Chiapas has the highest level of poverty in the nation and within the state, indigenous communities are the poorest.

Although inhabitants of the state include mestizos (people of mixed indigenous and European descent) as well as indigenous peoples, we focus primarily on indigenous women in this introduction because most activities relating to women demanding their dignity have occurred in indigenous communities. Yet, it is important to bear in mind that mestizas and indigenous women, whether urban or rural, single or married, are united in their struggles to support themselves and their families, to curtail domestic violence and rape, and to be treated fairly in the judicial system.[2] Several chapters in this book take the perspectives of nonindigenous women and provide additional background on their experiences of the changes we relate here.

Indigenous women living in rural highland Chiapas assert their importance to their communities in a variety of publicly recognized roles, for example as midwives, healers, weavers of festival garments, and as coleaders of fiestas. The traditional religious cargo system rests on couples serving their communities, saints, and other powerful spiritual entities side by side in a year-long series of obligations. In San Pedro Chenalhó, women often receive the call to serve a cargo in a dream. Afterward they solicit their husbands' assis-

---

[1]Zapatista support bases are civilian support groups composed of men, women, and young people over 14 years of age, who provide material aid to EZLN combatants, implement Zapatista programs, and participate in consultations about EZLN actions.

[2]Most mestizas share with indigenous women the need to work very hard from childhood to support their families. *Mujeres de tierra fria: conversaciones con coletas* (*Women of the Cold Country: Conversations with Coletas*) by Diane Rus, is a collection of reflections by Coletas (mestizas from San Cristóbal de Las Casas) about their lives. The women describe helping to support their families and defending their rights as women in their households and neighborhoods. The women's stories show the complexity and singularity of their experiences as well as the many commonalities they share with indigenous women.

tance to fulfill the cargo (Eber 2000[1995]:90). In San Juan Chamula, a neighboring township to Chenalhó, Chamulas recognize that a cargo role belongs to
both spouses and that deities bless the couple for their participation (Rosenbaum 1993). Cargos underscore the complementarity and interdependence
between the genders and the significance of women's contributions to their
communities. Working long hours in the field, at home, and for communities
in cargos assures material as well as spiritual survival and is central to achieving the heat that signifies spiritual strength.[3] Women who take leadership roles
in Zapatista support bases often call these "cargos," evoking the service to a
larger good that is at the heart of both traditional cargos and the Zapatista
movement (Eber 1999:17). In contrast to these women, nonindigenous
women of Chiapas have scarce opportunities to enjoy public roles in support
of their communities.

Older indigenous women who have served as cargoholders stress the racism
and economic oppression that they share with their kinsmen rather than
gender oppression (Eber 1999; 2000[1995]; Rosenbaum 1993). In contrast,
younger women tend to stress gender oppression. The chapters in this book
offer abundant evidence from women of all ages of the disproportionate suffering of women. Women's accounts of marriage and childbirth provide com-
pelling evidence of the breakdown of notions of complementarity and
interdependence in daily life.

Several chapters refer to the marriage petition process in which a young man
chooses a girl to marry among the eligible young women in his community. The
tradition varies, but typically involves a young man, accompanied by a few relatives who speak on his behalf, making several visits to the parents of the girl he
would like to marry. On each visit the young man presents gifts of food to his
prospective in-laws. The wedding ceremony takes place at the last visit and centers around a feast that the young man provides and the words of advice and
support from the couple's parents, godparents, and other respected elders (see
Collier 1968; Eber 2000 [1995]: 67–68; Laughlin 1963; Nash 1973; Rosenbaum
1993). The bride petition is followed by a period of bride service, usually one to
two years, during which time the young husband works for his in-laws.

Young women and men in Chiapas have been transforming the marriage
process in a variety of ways, often without completely rejecting it (Collier 1999
[1994]:114–116; Flood 1994; Garza Caligaris and Ruíz Ortíz 1992; Siverts 1993).
For example, since the 1980s it has become common for couples to elope,
thereby announcing their decision to choose each other without their parents'
approval. But couples rarely stay away from home long. They often arrange to
make one formal visit during which time young men will bring food for a feast

---

[3]Indigenous conceptions of human growth and development in highland Chiapas hold
that humans acquire heat during the course of a life well-lived. Living well entails serving one's community and respecting one's fellow humans and the spiritual beings.

and money to compensate their in-laws for any grief they may have suffered and for the potential loss of the couples' labor, if they want to live in the city.

Although marriage is expected of both women and men, women have also asserted their wishes not to marry or to delay marriage. Women are able to choose singlehood more often than men because of the difficulty men have to survive without wives to provision the food that they raise and to help them in the fields, along with their children. Although the option for women not to marry or to delay marriage has existed for decades, the trend has intensified in recent years. The right to choose to remain single or to reject a suitor is a key demand of the Zapatista Revolutionary Women's Law (see Box 1, p. 23). However, women in a Zapatista civilian support base in a community of San Pedro Chenalhó list the bride petition process as one of the "good" traditions that they do not want to abandon (Eber 2001a). Other traditions they want to keep include weaving ancestral clothing, healing with prayer and herbs, and preparing ceremonial foods. The women juxtapose the good traditions with "bad" ones, such as men drinking and beating their wives and women not being able to go to school. These women's reluctance to abandon the bride petition may be partly a response to the loosening of bonds between kin that has resulted from increased migration and the economic crisis. Until the artisan cooperative movement and the expansion of civil society networks in the 1990s, relations with kin dominated women's social relationships. Women's desire to maintain the bride petition process may also be fueled by fear of the more independent way of life that attracts young people. This way of life devalues people's embeddedness in larger social wholes, which when well-balanced, protect their members in hard times.

The past few decades of planned economic change and the economic crisis of the 1980s have exacerbated tensions between men and women, and young and old people, and have led to increased impoverishment in rural and urban areas (Collier 1999 [1994]). Mexico's reinsertion into the global economy began under the presidency of Miguel de La Madrid (1982–1988) in response to the internal limits of import-substitution industrialization and also to the debt crisis and negotiations with the International Monetary Fund and the United States government. To "grow" itself out of its huge and mounting foreign debt, Mexican policymakers complied with mandates from international financial institutions to restructure and modernize (Benería 1992). Beginning in 1982 officials began implementing structural adjustment policies to achieve the agreed-upon measures for modernization, including: devaluations; privatization of parastatal firms; deregulation of markets and prices; reduction of trade barriers such as tariffs and import licensing; a policy of austerity (cutbacks in government social spending); and promotion of foreign investment and exports on the basis of export-oriented industrialization.

Several of these measures, such as the 1992 Agrarian Reform Law and changes in credit policies, favored large agribusiness operations and hurt peas-

ant farmers (*campesinos*) (Collier 1999 [1994]; Brown 1997).[4] Lacking sufficient land and cash to afford chemical and other inputs, poor farmers in Chiapas were hard-pressed to continue subsistence farming. Changes in the
agrarian economy have hurt both men and women. In the late 1980s and
1990s even short-term employment on plantations and in public-works projects that men had depended on to supplement subsistence farming became
difficult to find (Rus 1995). In this context, women's roles in household production became increasingly important to survival. In response, women intensified their household production. Comparing census data carried out in the
Chamula community of K'at'ixtik in 1977 and 1988, Diane Rus (1990) found a
dramatic increase in women's participation in income-generating activities,
namely, artisan production, agricultural day labor, and gathering firewood for
sale. Rus's findings challenged the assumption that the economic crisis did not
have a significant impact on rural producers.

In the face of crisis, women have found it increasingly difficult to respect
the ways of the ancestors while adapting to change. Although many young
women welcome the freedom to pursue more independent lives, their mothers
and grandmothers, who have lived their whole lives on ancestral lands, are
often saddened by the social upheaval of the past decades. As poverty deepened in the late 1980s and early 1990s, more and more women of all ages became involved in alternative social groups either through affiliating with
religious denominations or joining artisan or agricultural cooperatives.
Women in these groups say they are heartened by working with others to overcome economic hardships and to capture a degree of independence without
unduly disrupting household and community relations.

Artisan cooperatives were the first formal organizations of indigenous
women. In highland Chiapas these co-ops have served as important spaces for
women to earn small amounts of cash to support the family economy and also
as springboards for political mobilization. In 1977, Sna Jolobil (House of the
Weaver), one of the first cooperatives that involved indigenous women in its
governance, was established in San Cristóbal de Las Casas, the urban center of
highland Chiapas.[5] Previously, in the 1950s and 60s, the National Indigenous
Institute (INI) had organized cooperatives for indigenous handicrafts (see
Nash 1993; Eber and Rosenbaum 1993; Morris 1991; Vargas-Cetina 1999).
However, these cooperatives were controlled by representatives of the PRI

---

[4]Many indigenous and campesino organizations opposed the 1992 reform to Article 27
of the Mexican Constitution because the new law: (1) officially marked the end of
agrarian reform since the government claimed there was no more land to redistribute;
(2) allowed the once inalienable *ejido* lands to be bought and sold; and (3) was passed
without consultation with indigenous peoples and peasants, those who would be most
impacted by the reform.
[5]Sna Jolobil continues to be one the largest artisan cooperatives in Chiapas with hundreds of members.

(*Partido Revolucionario Institucional*, the Revolutionary Institutional Party), the political party that dominated politics in the state and nation for 71 years.

Although Sna Jolobil and the other early cooperatives were not created to be explicitly political, these cooperatives provided indigenous women their first opportunities to become connected to large groups of women beyond their local communities. Notwithstanding these benefits, early co-ops did not necessarily lead to changes in women's status or lessen their dependence on their kinsmen. Indeed, marital tension often increases when women become involved in cooperative work (Eber and Rosenbaum 1993; Rodriguez 2002). A powerful example of the limits of cooperatives is illustrated by the experiences of women in a pottery-making co-op in Amatenango del Valle that was established in the 1970s with the assistance of the PRI. Influenced by their collective experiences, women in this co-op began to participate in politics. Petrona López, president of the cooperative, ran for township president and was murdered during the political campaign. Although her killer was never tried, most people suspected that her running mate in the election, a former township president, hired him. Petrona paid with her life for challenging patriarchal family structures by organizing unmarried and single women in the cooperative (Nash 1993: 128–129). Recently, Rosalinda Santís Díaz, past president of Jolom Mayaetik, a weaving cooperative in San Cristóbal de Las Casas, was attacked in the streets by masked men who accused her of being a Zapatista. At a talk at New Mexico State University on March 11, 1999 Santís Díaz stated: "They are trying to frighten us because we are not only searching for markets, we are also participating in politics as women."

From the 1980s through the present, artisan cooperatives have provided both married and single women with economic alternatives to the exploitative markets controlled by nonindigenous shopkeepers and government development programs. Increasingly young women members of cooperative organizations are choosing to remain single (Rodriguez 2002). Cooperatives provide these young women alternative social and economic contexts within which to live more independently of their families and communities.

In the 1970s and 1980s, a number of new campesino organizations emerged in response to political and economic oppression (Harvey 1994). These organizations demanded land, wage increases for rural day laborers, higher prices for crops, and respect for human rights. Even as they faced government repression, these groups offered an alternative to the politics of the PRI that had dominated the state for decades.[6] Although men were the leaders

---

[6]During the 1980s, the Chiapas state government systematically co-opted or repressed the growing number of independent peasant organizations. From 1982–1987, there were 86 political assassinations in the state (Burguete 1987, cited in Gómez and Kovic 1994). In spite of this repression, the independent organizations continued to grow.

of these organizations, women participated in large numbers in marches, sit-ins, land takeovers, and other protests.

The Catholic Church played an important role in the 1970s by assisting young Catholics to critique the abuses that they endured at the hand of the state and powerful elites, both indigenous and nonindigenous. In 1974, Bishop Ruíz Garcia organized the first Indian Congress in San Cristóbal at the behest of the state governor. Women attended the congress along with men. The Congress marked the first time that indigenous people from throughout the state had spoken in public to each other about their experiences with oppression (Bermúdez 1995:311).

A pressing issue around which women began to organize in Chiapas in the 1980s was problem drinking. In Chenalhó in 1988, women followers of the Word of God (the name used in many indigenous communities to refer to the Catholic Church under Ruíz's direction) organized a movement to control alcohol sales (Eber 2000 [1995]: 229–231). Although the women favored pro-hibiting alcohol, their reasons were not narrowly moralistic. Their concern for conserving precious cash, as well as personal respect, was a primary motivation. They reasoned that legislation directed at prohibition would be a statement to powerful outsiders that indigenous people control their own affairs. Through their participation in meetings and rallies, women deepened their capacity to connect their personal troubles, such as problem drinking, to political issues. For example, although they criticized their kinsmen for drinking up precious cash, when they spoke out in public meetings, they also decried the injustice of their children going hungry while mestizo rum sellers strutted around in shiny boots with their fat stomachs leading the way. They also acquired leadership training, which those who later became involved in mixed groups in civil society drew upon to take their rightful places in these organizations.

In 1989 the Women's Group of San Cristóbal de Las Casas was established in response to the gang rape of a woman in the city and the irregularities and insen-sitivity of the judicial system in dealing with such cases. Initially, the Women's Group dedicated itself to the issue of violence against women. In time it became involved in other issues and members of the group came to see the necessity of feminist demands to change the underlying structures causing women's oppres-sion (Freyermuth Enciso and Fernández 1995). The Women's Group (known as COLEM since 1996) incorporates both mestiza and indigenous women, recog-nizing that they are united in resisting violence against women and unequal treatment in the judicial system. Although COLEM was the first nongovernmen-tal organization (NGO) to work specifically for women's concerns, a number of other NGOs have supported indigenous women, most notably Chi'iltak (Tzotzil for companions/friends), one of the oldest of such groups in San Cristóbal.

On January 1, 1994 the Ejército Zapatista de Liberación Nacional (Zap-atista Army of National Liberation or the EZLN), seized seven towns in Chiapas. The EZLN launched its uprising the same day that the North American Free Trade Agreement (NAFTA) went into effect. The uprising highlighted ethnic diversity in the Mexican nation and brought to national and international attention the exclusion of the majority of the Mexican population from discussions about development. The cry that went out from Chiapas on January 1 was "Enough is enough!" With these words the EZLN called for land, housing, jobs, food, health care, democracy, and justice and an end to the hundreds of years of exploitation and marginalization of indigenous peoples and peasants of Chiapas.

As soldiers and as civilian supporters, women have made their demands known and have gained important spaces within the EZLN. Zapatistas maintain that 30 percent of the soldiers in their army are women. One of the most visible woman military leaders is *Comandante* (Commander) Ramona, a Tzotzil woman who participated in the February 1994 peace talks in San Cristóbal de Las Casas and traveled to Mexico City to help establish the National Indigenous Congress on October 12, 1996. In addition, thousands of women make up the Zapatista support bases. Zapatista women were especially active in the "peace belts" that surrounded the buildings where the peace talks took place in 1995 in the township of San Andrés Sakam Ch'en de los Pobres (the autonomous township of San Andrés Larrainzar). Women along with men and their families traveled long distances and stood holding hands in the rain and sun for many hours to show their support for peace. Women also sacrificed time and resources to prepare for several international events and delegations. For example, at the Intercontinental Encounter Against Neoliberalism and For Humanity in July 1996, hundreds of foreigners gathered to show their support for Zapatista men and women and to participate in discussions about the implications of their movement. Zapatista women and their families donated food and firewood and helped build housing for the visitors at this event. In many cases, women used up all their available food and cash in these donations.

The Revolutionary Women's Law made public in January 1994, was drafted by Zapatista women in consultation with their communities (Hernández Castillo 1994a). The law affirms women's right to participate in the revolutionary struggle "without any discrimination based on race, creed, color, or political affiliation." The law also assures women the right to occupy leadership positions within the organization as well as many other rights, such as the right to education, to decide the number of children they will have, to participate in community affairs, and to be free from domestic violence. These laws echo the demands of many Mexican women, urban and rural, indigenous and mestiza (see Box 1, p. 23).

In addition to addressing women's political rights, the Zapatistas addressed the basic economic rights of women and children in one of the 34 points of their "Commitments for Peace," a set of demands formulated by the Zapatista delegation in the first peace talks between the Zapatistas and the federal government in February of 1994. These mention women's concerns and include demands for birth clinics and gynecological care; public programs ensuring sufficient food for children in rural communities; child-care centers, preschools, and infant-care centers; community corn mills and tortilla presses; the development of projects for farming, banking, and crafts; technical training schools for women; and improved transportation for bringing products to markets. (The 34 points appeared in *La Jornada* in March of 1994 and are reprinted in English in Womack 1999: 269–275).

Not surprisingly, the public demands for women's rights on the part of the EZLN did not automatically translate into improved conditions for Zapatista women or for broader groups of indigenous and mestiza women. Female Zapatista commanders voice their ongoing struggles to change gender roles within both the EZLN and their communities (Stephen 2002, Chapter 7). In Zapatista bases, women struggle to adapt the Zapatista agenda to their daily lives. For example, in a Zapatista base in Tzabalhó, Chenalhó, women decided that only single women could be Zapatista base representatives because married women had too many responsibilities and their husbands were not willing to take over more of the housework (Eber 1999). Both single and married women face constraints to participate in public meetings based on a gender ideology in indigenous communities that associates women with proximity to the home and with household-based labor (Rosenbaum 1993). Most women with children face formidable obstacles to attend meetings, from providing for child care, to paying for transportation, to exhaustion from adding organizing work to housework, child care, fieldwork, and weaving for household use or for sale (Eber and Tanski 2001).

An important aspect of the indigenous rights movement in Chiapas has been the demand for autonomy—that is—the right of indigenous people to govern themselves according to their own customs and traditions. In this movement, dozens of communities, and even whole townships, have declared themselves "autonomous" (Rus, Mattiace, and Hernández Castillo 2001). In autonomous townships, members elect their leaders according to their own traditions. The San Andrés Accords on Indigenous Rights and Culture support the demand for autonomy through redefining and expanding specific cultural, territorial, and political rights for indigenous peoples that relate to Article 4 of the Mexican Constitution. The EZLN and government representatives signed the San Andrés accords during the 1996 peace talks between the EZLN and the federal government.

Women play an important role in the autonomy movement. In both all-women's groups and in communal assemblies of both men and women, women are insisting that their views on traditions be heard. As we mentioned in relation to women's views on the bride petition, women are carefully weighing which traditions they want to keep and which they cannot defend (K'inal Antzetik 1995).[7] As Hernández Castillo (1997: 110) points out, indigenous women "do not completely reject either Mexican nationalism or autonomous indigenous discourses. Instead, they assert themselves as simultaneously Mexicans and indigenous." For example, in May of 1994 several nongovernmental organizations (NGOs) convened a workshop on women's rights and customs in San Cristóbal de Las Casas.[8] Over 50 indigenous women attended the event, and the document *El Grito de la Luna* (The Cry of the Moon) was prepared for presentation at a public forum for discussion on constitutional reform regarding indigenous rights. The women affirmed the positive values in customs, including the respect for land, language, and traditional medicine practices. However, women criticized several aspects of customs:

> The customs that we have should not do harm to anyone. We do not like the custom when the authorities make crooked deals and they are the ones who decide how to distribute the land. The authorities do what they want and we cannot always defend them.

Women denounced the use of "custom" to justify gender discrimination. They noted that at times only men inherit land and that donations given by the community for sick people are only collected for males. They criticize that women are forced to marry against their will, and that domestic violence and alcohol abuse are tolerated. A workshop participant stated:

> Some say that it is custom to force us to marry even when we don't like the man. Sometimes, it is custom to exchange a cow for a woman. It is custom that men hit their wives and pay a fine of a day's work and then come back to hit them again for complaining.
>
> (Quoted in Hernández Castillo 1994b: 51).

In July of 1994, hundreds of indigenous and mestiza women from throughout Chiapas attended the first Women's Convention in San Cristóbal de Las Casas. The women discussed issues of health, democracy, and family life, among others. In their summary document, the women demanded the right to be respected by men, to inherit property, to decide how many children to bear, and to be able to choose their marriage partner (Rojas 1994). This important meet-

---

[7]A pamphlet, "Mujeres Indígenas de Chiapas: Nuestros derechos, costumbres y tradiciones," resulted from workshops on women's rights and traditions that K'inal Antzetik (Women's Earth) organized in collaboration with Chi'iltak, Conpaz, CODIMUJ, Unión Regional de Artesanos J'pas Joloviletik, La Organización Independiente de Mujeres Indígenas (OIMI), the Organization of Indigenous Doctors of the State of Chiapas (OMIECH), and La Cooperativa de Alfereras J'pas Lumetik.

[8]The Women's Group of San Cristóbal de Las Casas, OMIECH, the Artisan Union J'paz Joloviletik, and the Women's Commission of CONPAZ organized the event.

ing was held in preparation for the National Democratic Convention (CND) organized by the EZLN. At this convention, thousands of Mexicans, along with international participants, met in the Lacandon rain forest in August of 1994 to discuss civil society's involvement in Mexico's transition to democracy.

The first National Congress of Indigenous Women took place in August 1997 in Oaxaca, Mexico. Indigenous women from throughout the nation united to share their experiences, denounce violence, and propose national and regional changes (Marcos 1997). They discussed issues such as rape, the abuses of the military, indigenous traditions, and access to education for women and girls. A number of women from Chiapas attended the congress, including a Zapatista delegation led by Commander Ramona. Emphasizing the importance of women working together to affect change, Ramona stated, "We have to unite more, to organize more, to network more. . . . Women lack the courage to speak, to organize, to work. But we women can work with much affection for our pueblos" (quoted in Marcos 1997: 16).

In the wake of the Zapatista uprising, the Mexican government accused the Zapatistas of giving birth to violence and sent the army to Chiapas to restore "peace." By stationing troops in Chiapas, the government established a constant military presence that discourages dissent and autonomy. On February 19, 1995 President Ernesto Zedillo broke the truce with the EZLN established in the days following the uprising by sending thousands of troops to the Lacandon rain forest to detain Zapatista leaders. This offensive was carried out as part of what came to be known as "a low-intensity war," a military strategy to counter popular organizations by instilling fear through misinformation and psychological and military tactics (Global Exchange 1998; SIPAZ 2002).

Following the failure of the February 1995 military offensive against Zapatista sympathizers, paramilitaries stepped up their activities. Key objectives of paramilitary groups have included terrorizing and displacing populations sympathetic to the EZLN (Centro de Derechos Humanos Fray Bartolomé de Las Casas 1996, 1998[a]). Over a dozen armed groups have been known to operate in the state (Hidalgo 2000). The state's relationship to paramilitary groups has ranged from tolerating them to training and maintaining them. Paramilitary groups have been especially active in areas where the government has found it expedient to displace local populations in order to protect strategic natural resources and to isolate the military (Centro de Investigaciones Económicas y Políticas de Acción Comunitaria 1998; Global Exchange 1998). Using paramilitary groups as a smoke screen, the military and police protect themselves from indictment for human rights violations.

From 1997 through the fall of 2001, over one-third of Chenalhó's 30,000 population lived in refugee camps. The effects of massive displacements and paramilitary activities throughout the state resulted in thousands of people being unable to harvest their crops, both for subsistence and cash (Centro de

Investigaciones Económicas y Políticas de Acción Comunitaria 1997). In addition to having their livelihoods threatened and living in temporary camps, people living in heavily militarized and paramilitarized areas have had to carry out their daily routines under surveillance, and at the risk of harassment, intimidation, and violence. With militarization, violence toward women increased. For example, in July 1994, three Tzeltal women on their way to market were raped by a group of soldiers at a military checkpoint in Altamirano. In addition to stopping women on roads, soldiers have invaded the places along the rivers where groups of women gather to wash clothes and bathe themselves and their children. While the men drink beer, they wash their tanks and jeeps and take baths with prostitutes who accompany them. In many cases soldiers force women and girls to wash their clothes and feed them. They also draw local women into prostitution, a previously rare practice within indigenous communities. Prostitution has had far-reaching implications for women, including increasing family violence, increased confinement of women by fearful kin, and health problems (Balboa 1997). Health workers in Chiapas have noted a dramatic rise in the number of cases of cervical cancer. They fear an epidemic of cervical cancer and other sexually transmitted diseases (Graciela Freyermuth Enciso, personal communication). Communities denounce the military invasion, particularly the prostitution and alcohol abuse.[9]

The military and paramilitary buildup resulted in numerous cases of violence in the Zona Norte (Northern Zone, a region of northeast Chiapas); San Juan Libertad (El Bosque); and in Acteal, San Pedro Chenalhó. In the Zona Norte, over 100 people were killed in the violence between PRD (Party of the Democratic Revolution) supporters and paramilitaries from August 1995 to September 1996 (Centro de Derechos Humanos Fray Bartolomé de Las Casas 1996). The massacre of 21 women, 9 men, and 15 children on December 22 at Los Naranjos, a refugee camp in Acteal, was the most alarming case of violence. It was committed by 60 men belonging to La Mascara Roja (The Red Mask). The shooting lasted from 11:30 in the morning until 4:30 in the afternoon. The residents of the refugee camp attempted to flee or hide in a canyon, but they were surrounded on all sides and a total of 45 indigenous people were killed. The attorney general declared that the massacre was the unfortunate result of family feuding or community strife. But investigations revealed that high-ranking military officers were complicit in the massacre. Retired Brigadier General Julio César Santiago Díaz was stationed from 1:00 until 4:00 in the afternoon at the entrance to Acteal, 200 meters from where the massacre occurred. He was accompanied by 40 state police and 4 state police comman-

---

[9]The 1996 book *Militarización y violencia en Chiapas* (Coordinación de Organismos No Gubernamentales por la Paz, et al.) includes a number of human-rights reports that describe the impact of militarization on communities of the Lacandon rain forest.

ders, all of whom listened to the rapid succession of gunfire for over 3 hours and did nothing to stop it (Marín 1998).[10]

Women have been at the forefront of protesting the Acteal massacre and other killings. They have joined marches and pilgrimages; one woman traveled to present her testimony of the Acteal massacre at the United Nations in Geneva, Switzerland; and in X'oyep, Chenalhó, women joined hands in a human chain to obstruct the entrance of soldiers into their communities.

In March 1999, 5,000 civilian supporters of the Zapatistas traveled throughout Mexico to conduct a consultation on the San Andrés Accords, the agreement that the Zapatistas and government representatives had forged from the peace talks that were suspended on August 29, 1996. Most women members of the delegation left their communities or the state of Chiapas for the first time in their lives. Flor de Margarita Pérez Pérez, a contributor to this book, left Chiapas for the first time in her 42 years on the delegation that traveled to Oaxaca. In the places where they traveled throughout Mexico, the women delegates talked with both indigenous and nonindigenous people about their concerns and struggles. In one of a number of public consultations (*consultas*) convened by Zapatista supporters, 3 million Mexicans cast ballots in favor of the San Andrés Accords.

In February 2001, male and female Zapatistas left their homes again to speak to their nation. Following the election of Vicente Fox in 2000, the Zapatistas announced that they would march to Mexico City to speak with the government and civil society. Fox's election broke the PRI's 71-year monopoly on political power in Mexico, giving hopes to diverse sectors of the Mexican population that democracy would finally be possible. So, on February 24, 2001, the Zapatista delegation departed from La Realidad in the Lacandon rain forest and began a 17 day journey to Mexico City. Thousands of supporters greeted the delegation as they traveled through 12 states. The delegation participated in dozens of events with students, trade unionists, writers, and other fellow citizens.

The Zapatista delegation hoped to address the congress to discuss the urgent need for the passage of the San Andrés Accords. Yet, a number of members of congress rejected the idea, stating that the entrance of Zapatistas would violate the "sacred" space of congress. These members were led by Senator Diego de Fernández de Cevallos of the PAN (The National Action Party) who threatened to resign if the Zapatistas entered the congressional chambers. Members of the PAN and the PRI proposed that a delegation of 10 legislators

---

[10]For an overview of events in 1997 leading up to the massacre at Acteal, see *Camino a la masacre: Informe Especial de Chenalhó*, Centro de Derechos Humanos Fray Bartolomé de Las Casas, 1998. For a women-centered account see Hernández Castillo, ed. 2001(a).

meet the Zapatistas outside the congress, but the Zapatistas rejected the proposal and instead announced their decision to meet with members of the European Parliament and return to Chiapas. With this pressure, a number of parties maneuvered so that the congress finally agreed to receive the Zapatista delegation. The narrow margin of the vote—220 in favor and 210 opposed—expressed the extreme reluctance of the elected government officials to allow a group of indigenous men and women to address the congress.

On March 28 a group of 23 comandantes of the EZLN, their faces covered with ski masks, their weapons in Chiapas, entered Mexico's *Palacio Legislativo* (National Congress). Commander Esther, an indigenous women dressed in the traditional clothing of Huixtán, led the delegation and addressed the congress. Subcommander Marcos—a mestizo, poet, national hero, and spokesman for the EZLN—traveled with the delegation to Mexico City, but did not enter the congress. For once, the members of congress were forced to listen to an indigenous voice, the voice of an indigenous woman. When the Zapatista delegation entered the congress on March 28, it was half empty. A group of PAN senators along with some PRI-istas refused to listen to the voices of a group of indigenous peoples from Chiapas. Their absence was in stark contrast to the visits of politicians to Tzotzil highland communities during presidential or gubernatorial campaigns. On these visits, politicians don the clothing of local people and promise to respect their traditions. They offer money and handouts to encourage local people to turn out for their speeches. Indigenous people have learned that politicians make these gestures to buy votes from "good little indians" who "know their place."

Speaking to the half-empty congress, Commander Esther took all of this in stride, commenting that those who were absent refused to listen to the words of an indigenous woman. In her speech, she condemned the racism of Mexican society and the structural violence experienced in everyday life. She spoke of customs and traditions, insisting, "We [women] know which are the good and which are the bad." She called for justice, liberty, and democracy and an end to the colonial and post-colonial practices of treating indigenous peoples as if they are children in need of protection:[11]

> In this fragmented country, we Indians live condemned to be ashamed because of the color that we are, the language we speak, the clothes that we wear, the music and dances that speak of our sadness and happiness, our history.
>
> . . . We suffer from indifference because no one remembers us. They send us to live in the corner of the mountains of the country so that no one will arrive to visit or see how we live.
>
> . . . Meanwhile we do not have services of potable water, electricity, schools, dignified housing, roads, clinic, not even hospitals, while many of our sisters, women,

---

[11]Esther's speech is printed in full in *La Jornada*, March 29, 2001, "Queremos ser indígenas y mexicanos."

children, and elders die of curable illnesses, malnutrition, and childbirth, because there are neither clinics nor hospitals where they can be taken care of.

. . . My voice doesn't lack respect for anyone, but we didn't come to ask for handouts. My voice comes to seek justice, liberty, and democracy for all the indigenous peoples.

During his presidential campaign of 2000, Vicente Fox provoked anger and resentment by stating that he could resolve the conflict in Chiapas in "15 minutes." The Zapatistas had set three conditions necessary for reinitiating dialogue with the government: (1) the withdrawal of thousands of troops stationed in Chiapas; (2) the liberation of Zapatista prisoners; and (3) the passage of the San Andrés Accords. When the Zapatista delegation arrived in Mexico City, it seemed possible that these conditions could be met. However, at this writing in October 2002, the situation seems less hopeful. Troops have been pulled out of some areas, yet a strong military presence remains in many communities. According to data from the activist research center CIEPAC, the Mexican Army is positioned in 232 locations in Chiapas with 32 permanent checkpoints (*La Jornada*, May 4, 2002). Flyovers of army planes are common occurrences in many communities. Some Zapatista prisoners have been released, but many remain in jail. A stalemate persists between the congress and the EZLN over a watered-down law on indigenous rights and culture passed by congress that does not offer the support for indigenous autonomy provided by the San Andrés Accords.

Following the 2000 elections, Pablo Salazar Mendiguchía, of a multiparty coalition, became the first non-PRI governor of Chiapas. This change opened the possibility that the state government would punish the intellectual authors of the Acteal massacre, dismantle the paramilitary groups, and create the conditions for displaced people to return to their communities. As military tensions and armed conflict have decreased, "reconciliation" has become a new buzzword in Chiapas. Some focus on reconciliation as the pursuit of justice while others criticize reconciliation as granting impunity for paramilitaries. Pablo Salazar established a Commission of Reconciliation for Communities in Conflict, which has paid monetary compensation to victims of violence and has encouraged refugees to return to their lands. A number of NGOs have expressed concern that this shallow model of reconciliation will only exacerbate tensions and forestall true peace or justice (Sipaz 2002).

At the same time, many groups in Chiapas—from religiously based movements to peasant organizations and NGOs—are engaged in activities to promote social and political reconciliation.[12] Community-based projects insist on

---

[12]Some of the most well-known projects involved in reconciliation include SIPAZ (International Service for Peace), CORECO (Committee for Unity and Community Reconciliation), Las Abejas, and the Ecumenical Bible School.

the co-existence of liberation—broadly defined as the eradication of oppression and domination—and reconciliation, the process of restoring dignity while rejecting violence, vengeance, and hatred (see Kovic 2003). Women play a central role in reconciliation through the potential they have shown to unite around their commonalities as women and to de-emphasize their political and religious differences.

Overview of Scholarship about Women in Chiapas

In the 1960s and 1970s, a number of women anthropologists attempted to correct male bias in social science research by focusing on women's experiences. Empirical research in Chiapas about women's experiences during this time took place primarily in indigenous communities where researchers expected to find alternative gender and household relations to those of Western cultures. They were not disappointed. Early ethnographic studies of social structure and relations in native communities described the gender specialization that characterized life in highland Chiapas. These studies noted that involvement in tradition was a daily aspect of life for women, complementing men's more formal roles defined by ritual events (Collier 1968, 1973; Linn 1976; Nash 1964, 1970; Cancian 1964, 1965; Greenfield 1972; Laughlin 1963; Modiano 1973; Price 1966; Siskel 1974; and Wali 1974). It became apparent from these studies that native women did important work for their societies—for example, as healers and household managers—and that their conceptions of gender incorporated notions of complementarity and interdependence. It was also clear that gender and age created interlocking hierarchies in indigenous communities.

In the 1980s and 1990s, anthropologists integrated data on women and gender into whole fields of study, including economics (Nash 1993; O'Brian 1997; Rus 1990); health and reproduction (Freyermuth Enciso 2001); sexuality and religion (Barrios and Pons 1995); tradition and myth (Rosenbaum 1993); and alcohol studies (Eber 2000 [1995]). By the 1990s, scholarship about women and gender took its place in a larger body of literature about Latin America and the global economy that analyzed the contribution of women in domestic production and the new international division of labor into which women were increasingly drawn (Nash and Fernández-Kelly 1983; Nash and Safa 1985).[13] In keeping with findings about women and development from earlier decades (Boserup 1970), research in Chiapas suggests that top-down economic development plans introduce or bolster already existing structures

---

[13]See Susan Kellogg's manuscript, *Weaving the Past: A History of Latin America's Indigenous Women* for similarities and differences in the history of indigenous women in Chiapas and in the rest of Latin America. See *Rereading Women in Latin America and the Caribbean: The Political Economy of Gender,* edited by Jennifer Abbassi and Sheryl Lutjen for comparative studies of indigenous and nonindigenous women.

and ideologies of male dominance and frequently degrade physical and social environments. (Eber and Tanski 2001; Nash 1993; O'Brian 1997). Graphic examples of this process in Chiapas are the Plan Puebla Panama discussed in the last section of this introduction and the government's use of the military to repress resistance to prevailing and proposed development models.

Contemporary scholarship on gender and women is notable for exploring the intersection of gender, class, race, and ethnicity, among other factors, rather than taking gender as an isolated concept (Davis 1981; Mullings 1997; Stephen 1997). Recent scholarship has also benefited from feminist critiques of European and middle-class bias in feminist research (Abu-Lughod 1993, 2002; Mohanty, Russo, and Torres 1991; Trinh 1989). Scholars writing from a variety of social positions address issues of difference experienced by men and women caught in the throes of colonial diasporas, labor migrations, and displacement by wars and global capitalism (Alexander and Mohanty 1997; Tsing 1993). Taken together these studies are useful to understand overlapping forms of oppression as well as differences among women.

This book contributes to recent efforts to explore difference and multiple layers of oppression. Although it is apparent that all women in Chiapas experience gender inequality by living in a male-dominated society, strong divisions exist between them based on their socio-economic status, whether they are mestiza or indigenous, and whether they live in cities or in the countryside, among other differences. Indigenous women throughout Chiapas share the experience of being oppressed by racism and male dominance, yet scholars have noted significant differences between indigenous townships, as well as within. For example, in Amatanengo del Valle, women can take their husbands to court for violence or even the threat of violence (Nash 2001), whereas women in San Juan Chamula have less protection from abusive men (Rosenbaum 1993).[14] The chapters in this book address the roots of differences between people by examining the broader historical, political, and economic contexts in which townships are situated. Differences between townships are an important reminder of the necessity of a place-centered, ethnographic approach to exploring gender relations and social change in Chiapas. The chapters in this book demonstrate variations in women's status and experiences from one township to the next, as well as the variety of ways that religious affiliation and economic conditions shape gender roles and relations within and between townships.

Since the Zapatista uprising in 1994, writings about women have tended to focus on their involvement in the political arena. Journalists, activists, and scholars in Spain and Mexico have produced several books in Spanish and in

---

[14]See Anna María Garza Caligaris 1999 for an exploration of gender and norms of dispute in San Pedro Chenalhó.

English.[15] Over the past decade, attention has broadened to include issues of representation and positionality, important themes in the social sciences and humanities.

Feminist scholars have been leaders in debates on the politics of writing about gender and culture (Abu Lughod 1993; Behar and Gordon 1995; Haraway 1991). Of critical importance to feminist scholars is recognizing that knowledge is situated. This awareness necessitates that scholars explicitly locate their position vis-à-vis those they represent. In Chiapas, a growing number of scholars are responding to this challenge by collaborating as colleagues with members of the communities where they conduct research. For example, in 1989 a team of writers collaborated with women of three communities to write a book in Tzotzil and Spanish about the experiences of leaving their highland homes due to lack of land to live in the Lacandon rain forest (Calvo et al. 1989). María Komes Peres collaborated with Diane Rus and Xalik Gusman to write a booklet about her work and life as a weaver from San Juan Chamula (Komes Peres 1990).[16] A number of indigenous women have recorded and published their own stories and histories, a reversal of "outsiders" (mestizo or foreign anthropologists) writing about indigenous people's lives. In the 1980s two indigenous women began to write plays about their own

---

[15]See Rosa Rojas's *Chiapas ¿Y Las mujeres, qué?* (*Chiapas, And What about the women?* Vols. 1 and 2); Guiomar Rovira's *Mujeres de maíz: La voz de las indígenas de Chiapas y la rebelión Zapatista* (*Women of Corn: The Voice of Indigenous Peoples of Chiapas and the Zapatista Rebellion*); and Hernández Castillo's *La otra palabra: mujeres y violencia en Chiapas antes y después de Acteal* (*The Other Word: Violence and Women Before and After Acteal*). In 2001 *The Other Word* was reprinted in its entirety in English. In addition to editing *The Other Word*, Hernández Castillo has published several articles on women organizing for social change in the years following the Zapatista uprising (1994a, 1994b, 1997). In 2001, Teresa Ortiz published *Never Again a World Without Us! Voices of Mayan Women in Chiapas*. Other scholars have written articles and books that incorporate material about women's participation in social change—e.g., Collier (1999 [1994]); Harvey (1998); Hernández Castillo (2001); Gossen (1999); Nash (2001); Ross (2000); Stephen (2002), and Weinberger (2000).

[16]Komes Peres's story is part of an oral history project that publishes the works of indigenous writers in Spanish and Tzotzil sponsored by INAREMAC. Diane Rus (1997) collaborated with several Coleta (nonindigenous) women in San Cristóbal de Las Casas to publish the life stories of these women in their own words. *Conjuros y ebriedades* (Past, ed. 1997) contains songs and poems by Tzotzil and Tzeltal women. Two notable collaborations from the Tojolabal region are *San Miguel Chiptik: Testimonios de una comunidad tojolabal* (Van der Haar and Lenkersdorf 1998) and *Rosa Caralampia: historia de una mujer tojolabal* (Aguilar Gómez 1998). *Voces de maíz: Relatos Tojolabales* (2001), published in Spanish and Tojolabal, contains stories by the indigenous writers Delfina Aguilar Gómez, Hermelindo Aguilar Méndez, and Juan Méndez Vázquez. Two women's organizations discussed in Yolanda Castro's chapter (18) in this book are involved in a project to record the testimonies and life stories of women weavers. Testimonials constitute an important collective picture of grassroots struggle in Latin America (Stephen 1994).

views of history and culture. Petroṇa de la Cruz Cruz from Zinacantán and Isabel Juárez Ch'ix from Aguacatenango began to write plays as members of Sna Jtzibajom, an indigenous writers collective. The women wrote plays depicting problems of contemporary life, such as drinking and domestic abuse (Cruz Cruz and Juárez Ch'ix 1993; Steele 1994). Eventually, the women formed FOMMA (Strength of the Maya Women). In 1992, Cruz Cruz became the first indigenous writer in Chiapas to receive the state prize for literature.[17]

Representation is a critical methodological concern in this book and the contributors address the issue in a variety of ways. The play, Indigenous children: We Are Not to Blame (Chapter 5), Prayer for Carly (Chapter 13), and the Song for International Women's Day (Chapter 21), are written by three indigenous women, Ruperta Bautista Vázquez, Margarita Pérez, and Flor de Margarita Pérez Pérez, respectively. Through the medium of theater, prayer, and song, the three women present their own views of social change and social suffering. (See part overviews and introductions to these pieces for additional commentary.) A number of chapters make use of life history or testimony to present women's perspectives (albeit mediated through an outside observer/editor) on issues of importance in their lives—childbirth, marriage, religion, and the struggle to make a living. Juana's Story (Chapter 2) is a narrative that Graciela Freyermuth Enciso compiled from testimonies of women about their own childbirth experiences and the deaths of female relatives and friends due to childbirth complications. Women's testimonies are also presented in the chapters by Kelly, Eber, and Gil. Life histories and testimonies are particularly suited to show the complexity of individual women's actions and the multidimensional nature of their identities (Eber 1999).

Several chapters address the complex relationship between urban-based (foreign or mestiza) women and indigenous women of rural communities. Foreign or mestiza researchers writing about indigenous communities stress the need to be respectful of the differences between women, particularly the need to understand indigenous women's selected paths of liberation, which differ considerably from those of Western-European feminists (see especially Forbis, Chapter 22). As Lila Abu-Lughod states (2002: 787–788): "We may want justice for women but can we accept that there might be different ideas about justice and that different women might want, or choose, different futures

---

[17]The plays of FOMMA are one of several projects in which indigenous peoples are writing and presenting their own stories. Indigenous women and men photographers have exhibited their work and published books under the auspices of the Chiapas Photography Project (chiapasphoto@wabash.edu). *Creencias de nuestros antepasados*, by Maruch Sántiz Gómez (1998), one of the book's produced in this project, combines Sántiz Gómez's photographs with sayings about daily life in Chamula. Since the Zapatista uprising, the Chiapas Media Project was founded to enable teams of indigenous people to produce their own videos (www.chiapasmediaproject.org).

from what we envision as best (see Ong 1988)? We must consider that they might be called to personhood, so to speak, in a different language."

In relation to politics and activism, a number of contributors write about the struggles to bridge the differences between rural/indigenous women and urban/mestiza women in the struggle for social justice in Chiapas. Yolanda Castro writes candidly about the complexity of her role as a mestiza adviser to two indigenous women's weaving cooperatives (Chapter 18). In a letter to family and friends, Heather Sinclair, a U.S. human-rights observer in a divided Tzeltal village, writes openly about the limits to her understanding of events in the community (Chapter 7). The letter is a poignant and powerful example of the barriers to understanding others' lives.

The Contributors: Points of Alliance

The contributors to this book reflect the diversity that has become integral to studies of women, gender, and culture. We are from Mexico, Spain, England, and the United States. We are academics, researchers, students, artists, healers, activists, and community organizers. Our different ways of working in the world are reflected in the variety of forms our writing takes—for example—a play, a prayer, songs, and scholarly essays. As editors, we decided to bring these diverse forms of writing together into one book to respond to a growing realization that people live in broad fields that encompass many ways of working and of expressing understandings of social change. Although we strive in this book for a factual accounting of women's lives, we also reach for deeper emotional and political truths that poetry, songs, and plays reveal. We hope that readers will find in the diversity of contributions some points of connection with women of Chiapas and windows into the larger field of history and contemporary life that we share.[18]

Although our views of feminism vary, overall, this volume emphasizes the concerns of "grassroots feminisms," which recognize that women's oppression is embedded in racism and post-colonialism, as well as in patriarchy. We examine women's concerns about basic survival as well as their related concerns about gender subordination. We explore the complex relationship between gender, race, ethnicity, and class.

Despite our differences, we first acknowledge some common concerns that create alliances between us. These concerns provide the intellectual, emotional, and political contexts for this book. Foremost, we share a commitment to pay attention to how issues of power affect our own and others' lives as well

---

[18]The creative works in this volume follow in a strong tradition of fictional works about life in Chiapas including writings by Rosario Castellanos (1952; 1962); Miriam Laughlin (1980, 1981, 1982, 1987, 1989); and Carter Wilson (1995 [1972], 1966).

as what political engagements across borders of ethnicity, class, gender, and nationality might be helpful to resolve conflicts in Chiapas and to assure human and women's rights. In our efforts to work across the boundaries between us, we struggle to perceive our limitations and biases and have found that we need each other to point these out. With time, collaborative projects, and different forms of communication, we strive to correct the limitations of both privilege and oppression, as well as points in between these extremes. Complementarity, a native concept used to conceptualize difference and hierarchy, is useful to recognize that even when equality may not exist between people, they may collaborate in mutually beneficial ways by exchanging complementary skills and resources. The chapters in this book illustrate the challenges and rewards of recognizing the larger fields that people share and of imagining relationships as ongoing. Writing as an anthropologist who has struggled with these issues, Lynn Stephen states, "If, however, we imagine ourselves in permanent, ongoing relationships with those people we study and work with, 'the field' disappears and becomes part of larger global relations that we do not create but simply live in, like everybody else" (2002:9).

Second, the contributors to this book share a concern to take seriously people's local and place-centered experiences and points of view, and to integrate these with global perspectives in our analyses. Although increasingly we see ourselves as living in a larger field of global relations, places remain important sources of strength and knowledge for women of diverse backgrounds in Chiapas (Nash 2001). Places often serve as moral locations and anchors for women and their families. Many rural women remain committed to semisubsistence farming on ancestral lands despite their nation's efforts to refocus their emotions and energies to commercial production. These women base their arguments against the homogenization of cultures and for the validity of their place-based life-ways on their consistent and continuous relationship to the land over hundreds of years. Land lies at the heart of existence in indigenous world views.

As we conclude this book, Mexican policymakers are launching the first phases of Plan Puebla Panama (PPP), a development project aimed at creating an export-processing zone along its southern border similar to the one along the U.S./Mexico border (Simonelli and Earle n.d.). The construction of railroads, highways, electric plants, and petroleum-processing plants are planned as part of this project. At regional, national, and international forums, numerous nongovernmental organizations and activists have protested the PPP, stating that it will benefit large corporations at the expense of rural producers and at a great environmental cost. In addition, there is concern that *maquiladoras* will push peasant farmers to sell their lands, only to become low-paid workers in factories producing goods for export. It is likely that as young women are drawn off into wage labor in factories in Chiapas, gender tensions will exacerbate and women may become victims of still more violence and repression.[19]

At the same time as economic changes bring concerns about women's futures, through artisan cooperatives, and political, and church organizations, women in Chiapas take advantage of global connections (see chapters in Part 3 of this book; Eber and Tanski 2001, in press; Stephen 2002). The contributions to this book show women's capacity to reach beyond their regions to link their concerns to those of national and international women's and social justice organizations. Together, these organizations form a "transnational advocacy network" uniting people of different social and geographic locations (Keck and Sikkink 1998). Since the Zapatista uprising, solidarity groups and sister communities in the U.S. and elsewhere have constructed spaces of "transnational resistance" through denouncing human rights abuses and offering economic and moral support (Sampaio 2002).

The contributors to this book emphasize the ways women make their own histories, but in circumstances not of their own choosing (to turn on a phrase from Karl Marx). Even in extraordinarily difficult circumstances, diverse groups of women have come together to improve their own lives and that of their communities. From forming weaving cooperatives, to leaving abusive husbands, to physically resisting the incursion of federal soldiers on their lands, women work to change relationships in their households and to promote structural change. Some of the contributors to this volume place greater emphasis on the constraints on women's lives, whereas others emphasize women's struggles for dignity and the advances made in recent years. In some ways, the images presented in this book are of the glass half empty and the glass half full. Yet, the chapters work together to avoid dichotomous conceptions. They illustrate the complex tensions between polarizations such as self and community, hope and despair, and personal and structural change. They show women as actors on the stage of history striving for their own and others' liberation.

---

[19]On the U.S.–Mexico border where *maquiladoras* have been in existence for over 30 years, women initially comprised the majority of workers, as they could be paid lower wages than men and were believed to have less experience in labor organizing (Fernández-Kelly 1983; Nash and Fernández-Kelly 1983). Plant owners commonly violate Mexican labor laws by requiring workers to take pregnancy tests in order to avoid granting mandatory maternity leave (Human Rights Watch 1998). In one Mexican border city, Ciudad Juárez, women face increasing social tensions and violence, and since 1993, more than 200 women have been murdered (Nathan 1999).

Box 1

The Revolutionary Women's Law

This law was disseminated by members of the EZLN on January 1, 1994.

In its just struggle for the liberation of our people, the EZLN incorporates women in the revolutionary struggle, regardless of their race, creed, color, or political affiliation, requiring only that they share the demands of exploited people and a commitment to the revolutionary laws and regulations. In addition, taking into account the situation of Mexican working women, the Revolutionary Women's Law incorporates their just demands for equality and justice.

First: Women, regardless of their race, creed, color, or political affiliation, have the right to participate in the revolutionary struggle in a way determined by their desire and capacity.

Second: Women have the right to work and receive a just salary.

Third: Women have the right to decide the number of children they can have and care for.

Fourth: Women have the right to participate in community affairs and to hold office if they are freely and democratically elected.

Fifth: Women and their children have the right to primary consideration in their health and nourishment.

Sixth: Women have the right to education.

Seventh: Women have the right to select their partner and not to be forced to marry.

Eighth: No woman shall be beaten or physically mistreated by her family members or strangers. The crimes of rape and attempted rape will be severely punished.

Ninth: Women can occupy leadership positions and hold military rank in the revolutionary armed forces.

Tenth: Women will have all the rights and duties stated in the Revolutionary Laws and Regulations.

Workshop for midwives in Chalchihuitán led by Sebastiana Vázquez. Photo by Graciela Freyermuth Enciso.

Women putting together pipes for potable water system in Tzeltal community of Las Cañadas.
Photo by Melissa M. Forbis, 1997.

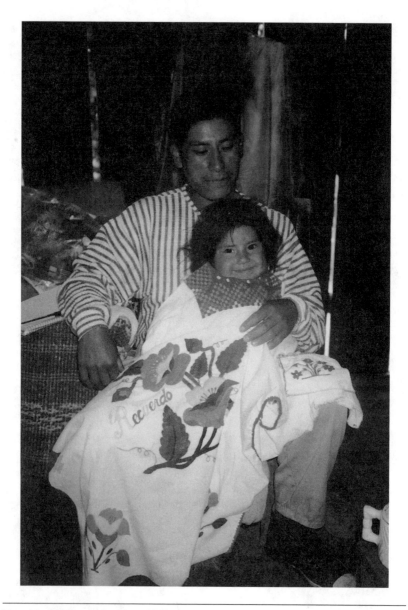

Manuel Porfirio (Paco) Arias Pérez with his daughter, Erica. In addition to working in the fields, Paco embroiders products to sell through Xojobal C'ac'al (Light of Day), a weaving cooperative in Tzabalhó, Chenalhó. Photo by Christine Eber, 2001.

Women's Regional Basketball Tournament in Las Cañadas. Photo by Melissa M. Forbis, 2000.

I
Poverty, Discrimination, and Violence: Women's Experiences and Responses

1
Overview

CHRISTINE KOVIC
CHRISTINE EBER

Part 1 presents the various forms of violence that women experience, including poverty, racism, exclusion, and political repression. Discussions of violence frequently focus on the physical and political violence of war, neglecting structural violence: the oppression rooted in social inequality including poverty, and race and gender hierarchies, "the social machinery of oppression" (Farmer 2002). Physical and structural violence are intertwined, at times indistinguishable. War and militarism are based on and reinforce inequalities (Lutz 2002).

In Part 1 we emphasize structural violence in order to explore the relationships between all forms of violence: domestic violence; violence related to poverty and racism; and violence perpetrated against women and men by the military and paramilitary as a means of controlling them and their communities. To assess women's experiences with and responses to various forms of violence, the chapters in Part 1 address two complementary but sometimes conflicting issues: the multiple forces that limit women's life opportunities and women's responses to these forces, which often take the form of open resistance. The chapters explore the many ways women resist violence, including making a living in the face of racism and discrimination; deciding to remain single to avoid further impoverishment and potential violence; and protesting military incursions into their communities.

Chiapas is one of the poorest states in Mexico, and within Chiapas, indigenous communities are the poorest. (Box 2, p. 36 gives an overview of the socioeconomic conditions in Chiapas.) Households lacking electricity, potable water, and sewage systems are common in rural communities of Chiapas; in many cases the majority of homes in indigenous communities lack these basic services. The high rate of infant mortality in indigenous communities of Chiapas—54.7 deaths per 1000 births, twice the overall rate for Mexico—illustrates the power of structural violence and its link to suffering.[1] The rate of maternal mortality in the indigenous township of Chenalhó is six times the national average (see Chapter 2).

---

[1]On infant mortality and other indicators of Chiapas marginality, see Howard and Homer-Dixon (1996).

No one can deny that women experience constraints at the local level. Domestic violence, being forced to marry, being denied inheritance, and not being allowed to attend school are a few of the complaints that mestizas and indigenous women have voiced. Indigenous women active in organizing for social change also complain of fathers, husbands, and brothers forbidding them to attend meetings outside their homes or communities. Yet, focusing exclusively on the ways women are limited *within* their communities obscures the broader forces that constrain women's lives and suggests that women's "liberation" could be achieved simply by changing local beliefs and practices. Racism, economic crisis, lack of social services, and militarization are a few of the factors that severely constrain women *and* men. In addition, these structural factors are often directly linked to the violence women experience within their families. For example, from a historical perspective, drinking and domestic violence in highland communities cannot be isolated from the harsh conditions of work on coffee and sugar cane plantations and the economic insecurity faced by men struggling to support their families.

The chapters in Part 1 address the different types of violence that impact women in Chiapas and how women experience violence differently from men. The women quoted in Shannon Speed's chapter (3) stress the gender differences in violence and social suffering. These women's statements reflect a long-standing reluctance among indigenous women to rank men and women's suffering. Rather, women tend to focus on the different ways that men and women suffer and the story of collective suffering in their communities. The pieces by Freyermuth, Speed, and Sinclair (Chapter 7) detail women's experiences of violence in rural areas; the pieces by Vázquez (Chapter 5) and Kelly (Chapter 6) focus on urban areas.

Graciela Freyermuth's chapter opens Part 1 with the story of Juana, a woman from San Pedro Chenalhó who dies in childbirth. The unnamed narrator is Juana's sister. Freyermuth constructed the narrative from interviews with women about their own and others' experiences during pregnancy and childbirth. Juana's story highlights the structural conditions of poverty and racism, which limit indigenous women's life expectancy and overall health. Midwives and *iloletik* (traditional healers) are important sources of support before, during, and after childbirth in Chiapas. However, when complications occur requiring surgery or other medical procedures, midwives are not equipped to handle these emergencies. Clinics and hospitals where women could seek help are few and far between in rural areas. Even when clinics exist and are within walking distance of communities or women can afford the bus fare to travel to one, they may hesitate to go to them because the doctors are not indigenous people and usually do not know the native language. In the wake of the Zapatista uprising, various Zapatista communities have built clinics staffed by health promoters, nurses, and doctors, many of whom are indigenous and are sympathetic to the Zapatista cause. Some women and their families travel long distances to these clinics where they trust the staff and know that the staff respect their struggle for justice, even if a government clinic is closer to their homes.

Juana's story also draws attention to changing marriage patterns in Chiapas. Until recently in indigenous communities, it was uncommon to marry someone outside of one's township. Still today, despite pan-indigenous solidarities nurtured by the Zapatista uprising, parents and elders frown upon marriages across community boundaries. By defying her parents' authority and marrying a man from another township, Juana removed herself from support networks through which kin typically assist women during childbirth complications. After seeing her mother being beaten and ordered around by her stepfather, Juana's sister decides to defy traditional marriage norms by rejecting marriage. Ironically, Juana's brother supports her in this decision; he provides her a place to live and rejects all suitors who come to ask for her hand in marriage.

In addition to poverty and abuse, women also experience violence from the militarization and paramilitarization of their communities. Most estimates of the number of Mexican troops in Chiapas from 1995 to the present hover around 60,000.[2] In response to these conditions, thousands of women have moved out of the confines of their households into the public squares and thoroughfares of their hamlets where they have used their bare hands to fend off the Mexican army and paramilitary groups. Women's open resistance to domination seems to be a significant change from previous decades when women did not lift their voices, much less their hands, against powerful men. However, women's activism did not begin after the Zapatista uprising. As discussed in the Introduction, women's courage and imagination to create alternatives to domination has precedents in colonial history and has been growing in recent decades. Chapter 3 by Shannon Speed in this part details the detrimental effects of militarization on men and women's lives. Speed notes that the violence of militarization and paramilitarization impacts women in specific ways. The presence of soldiers is often accompanied by an increase in prostitution, alcohol abuse, rape, and sexual harassment. Yet, Speed notes that gendered fear has generated gendered resistance. Women in rural communities are organizing themselves in multiple ways to defend their communities against violence. Their collective actions combine with everyday forms of resistance to contest the hegemony of patriarchal social norms.

Chapter 4, The Birth of Guadalupe, simultaneously narrates women's experiences of violence and their protest against it. The song tells the story of Guadalupe, a woman killed by state police during a January 1998 protest

---

[2]The Secretary of National Defense, SEDENA, estimates that there are a total of 17–25,000 troops in Chiapas, but numerous nongovernment organizations place the number closer to 60,000 (Castro 2000).

against the Acteal massacre and increased militarism in Chiapas. The words of the song state clearly that protests rather than silence will mark Guadalupe's death and that the struggle for "a true and just peace" continues.

Deepening poverty in Chiapas provides the context for Chapters 5 and 6 by Ruperta Bautista Vázquez and Patty Kelly, respectively. The women and children addressed in these chapters were forced to leave rural areas to search for work in cities due to economic conditions. In Chiapas, the process of urbanization began in the 1970s and has intensified over the past decade. It has been fueled by land scarcity, high population growth, the slow collapse of the plantation system, the lack of investment in the countryside, and the drop in the international price of coffee (see Rus, et al. 2001).[3] Many peasant farmers work in the city to help support their families, but retain ties to their land. The types of work available to these displaced peasants in the Chiapas cities of Tuxtla Gutiérrez, Tapachula, and San Cristóbal de Las Casas are concentrated in the informal sector. Jobs such as street vending, domestic work, day labor, construction work, and taxi driving provide low income and no access to health insurance and other benefits. In addition, indigenous workers commonly face discrimination and violence.

The contributions by Bautista Vázquez and Kelly provide powerful examples of women and children's experiences of structural violence. In a highly stratified society, their opportunities for work are limited by their gender and ethnicity. Chapter 5, Indigenous Children: We Are Not To Blame by Ruperta Bautista Vázquez, uses a dramatic form to evoke the difficulties that indigenous children, especially girls, face when selling gum and artisanry on the streets of the city of San Cristóbal de Las Casas. The play recounts the racism and poverty that mark the children's daily lives as they attempt to earn small amounts of money through sales. Kelly's chapter addresses women's involvement in the government-regulated sex industry of the Zona Galáctica in the state capital Tuxtla Gutiérrez. She notes that women's poor educational background and gender severely constrain their job opportunities in a diminished labor market. The pieces by Kelly and Bautista Vázquez examine the coexistence of oppression and resistance: even as society labels the sex workers of the Zona Galáctica as "whores" and the young street vendors of San Cristóbal as "dirty Indians," the women and girls insist that they be treated with respect and dignity.

This part concludes with Chapter 7, Letter from a Peace Camp, by Heather Sinclair. Sinclair reflects on the challenges of her experiences as a U.S. woman observer in a village divided between Zapatista supporters and nonsupporters.

---

[3]In other regions of Mexico and Latin America, the phenomenon of rural to urban migration began to intensify in midcentury as a result of economic development policies favoring import-substitution and industrialization, hence concentrating investment and infrastructure in urban rather than rural areas (Roberts 1978). The fact that these development projects were not implemented in Chiapas is evidence of the persistent exclusion of this state from the national project.

Her encounter with the villagers is made especially poignant and problematic by the suicide of Margarita, a 16-year-old girl living on the Zapatista side of the divided village. Margarita's suicide takes place within the context of increased militarism and village factionalism. Yet, her suicide shares much in common with others in Chiapas not directly related to militarization. As Sinclair notes, suicide by the ingestion of pesticides was a cause of death in rural communities well before the Zapatista uprising. Reports of suicide by pesticide ingestion in areas of conflict suggest that this practice may have increased in recent years.

Sinclair's experiences are part of a larger story of cooperation and solidarity that has evolved from the outpouring of concern in Mexico and throughout the world for protecting human rights and fostering a climate for peace with justice in Chiapas. This transnational civil society network brings women like Sinclair together with women of diverse backgrounds in Chiapas.

Box 2

Socio-economic Conditions in Chiapas[1]

*Chiapas and Natural Resources**

State generates 48 percent of Mexico's hydroelectricity
State generates 8 percent of Mexico's total energy production
State produces 47 percent of Mexico's natural gas
State produces 21 percent of Mexico's oil
*(Source: *Chiapas: Present and Future.* 1999. Publicaciones Garcia Lourdes.)

Poverty in Chiapas as Compared to Mexico**

	Mexico	Chiapas
Households without sewage system (1995)	25%	43%
Households without electricity (1995)	6.7%	21.4%
Households without access to running water (1995)	14.4%	33.2%
Women 6 years of age and older with no primary school education (1990)	15.3%	32.7%

**(Source: Instituto Nacional de Estadística, Geografía e Informática, INEGI, 1995 and 1990)

Indigenous Township of San Pedro Chenalhó†

97.8 percent of homes, women cook in open fires on dirt floors
56.5 percent of homes do not have access to running water
78.12 percent of homes do not have electricity
92.3 percent of homes do not have drainage for sewage
62.5 percent of women age 15 or older cannot read or write
51.38 percent of children under age 15 cannot read or write
†(Source: INEGI 1990)

---

[1]Christine Eber and Janet M. Tanski compiled these statistics as part of a project on women and economic change in Chiapas.

2
Juana's Story

GRACIELA FREYERMUTH ENCISO
Translated by Heather Sinclair

I'm Cold, I Want To Get Warm

Two young men came to propose to Juana, but she didn't want to marry someone from her own pueblo.[1] She wanted to marry someone different.

The first to ask for her hand was Augustín, Pablo's son. But he was not accepted and returned home. Later, another young man arrived. He was a Chamula Indian from the village of Natividad. The family didn't believe him to be good enough and so he, too, was turned away. Juana didn't want to live in her community or nearby. Even a Chamula wouldn't do because some Chamula Indians lived in the same township.

Later, when my mother found out that a young man from Santa Martha was talking to Juana, she told her, "Don't accept him. Don't trust him—we don't know his people. You could become ill or die there. Just wait. Others will come who are like us, from our own township, who speak as we do."

But Juana replied, "I'm very much in love with him and if I choose, I will accept him."

And so she did. She alone made the decision to go with him. It was thought that she chose him because he was a rich man with many *cafetales*.[2] He had deceived her about his wealth, however. He told her that he had a car, when in truth he was only its driver. But Juana believed all of it.

"He's rich. He has a car, many cafetales, and many possessions in his home," she said.

This is why the poor thing fell in love. They left together and soon she was expecting a child. When I saw her she was pregnant, well and strong, walking quickly. It was clear at that time that poor Juana was healthy.

---

[1] This story is about a woman from San Pedro Chenalhó. It is reconstructed from recollections of several people—Juana's sister, her mother, her mother's friend, a midwife, and a community health worker. The story is told, however, in the first-person voice of Juana's sister to preserve its flow and to show readers how the people of Chenalhó themselves tell this story. In some cases the translation has been modified to make it read more easily. In Tzotzil there are no masculine or feminine pronouns. The gender is known from the nouns.

[2] A *cafetal* is a small plot of land planted with coffee trees.

Later, when she was about three months pregnant, she began to push away her serving of tortillas, beans, vegetables, and *pozol*.[3] She didn't eat anymore. This upset me very much as we had been very close. After that, I ate alone. I was used to our eating together when she would come to visit. I would ask her, "Why don't you eat just a little something?"

And she would reply, "I don't feel like it; food doesn't taste like anything to me anymore."

And I would say, "But you have to have strength. If you don't eat, you'll lose weight."

They lived in Santa Martha. They came and went on foot. She never stayed overnight with us, always leaving with her husband.

"Why don't you stay? Do you feel well? Has your pregnancy been difficult for you?"

"No, I'm fine. It feels better to walk. I feel better in my husband's home," she'd tell me.

"Stay here awhile. It looks awful for you to be walking behind your husband like that. Watch out or it's going to affect you and your pregnancy will suffer. Just stay here and let him walk back by himself. It's a bad trail. It's too steep. Just stay here," I told her.

But she answered, "My husband doesn't want to leave me here. He wants me to be with him always and that's why I go. Besides, I don't want to stay here alone. I'm happy when I am with him . . ."

She never paid me any attention. That's how it was throughout her nine months of pregnancy—always hiking to and from my house.

Her labor began while she was at home with her husband. She came by foot to my house while in labor, arriving here at 2:00 or 3:00 in the afternoon. I don't remember exactly. I was working in the cornfield when her husband came up to me and said, "Older sister, I have come to take you to my wife. Her labor has begun." We went quickly to my house where she was sitting outside.

"How are you?" I asked. "Are you feeling all right?"

"No," she said.

"Are you in labor? Do you think that is what you feel?"

"I'm not sure, but I think so because I feel pain every so often," she answered.

"If your labor pains are strong now, we need to get the midwife so that nothing will go wrong," I said.

We went for the midwife, and she came right away. She touched Juana and said that she was certainly in labor and that the baby was down low. She said that Juana would give birth soon.

---

[3] *Pozol* is a drink made from boiled corn kernels that are later ground and mixed with water.

She stayed to care for Juana, watching her as she labored. The baby, however, wasn't born until the next day. Juana was in labor all night and at 4:00 in the morning I awoke.

"Older sister, wake up!"

"Are you all right?" I asked.

"I feel the same. The contractions haven't gotten stronger. They feel weaker now," she replied.

"If you can't birth, little sister, then get your clothing ready and I will take you to Vicente Comate to see if he can give you medicine or send you to the hospital. You're not going to be able to do it here. Let's see if you can make it to town. Let's hope nothing happens to you along the way. What if I kill you?"

The midwife stayed sitting there as she had been all along. When I first went to get her, I told her, "If you can't do it, I will take her to the doctor."

That was our plan when I went to sleep. If the baby wasn't born by morning, I was going to take her. For this reason, when the baby wasn't born by 4:00 or 5:00, we left.

On the way to Vicente's house we walked past our brother Augustin's home. Without warning, Juana began walking toward it.

I said, "What are you thinking, girl? What are you doing? This isn't the doctor's house! We're on our way to the doctor's, not to visit our brother! Come on!"

"Be quiet and leave me alone. I want to see my brother," she said and she went inside.

"Come on!" I called to her. "We're going to Don Vicente's house."

"Hush," she answered. "I'm freezing and I want to get warm here inside my brother's house."

"Do you really think, little sister, that you are going to get the help you need here? Let's go to the doctor's or to Jovel [San Cristóbal] so that they can examine you and the baby."

But she didn't listen and stayed inside. Her husband, my mother, the midwife, and I went inside to be with her. It was about 6:30 A.M. We explained to our brother that Juana was in labor and that we were on our way to the doctor's when she decided to stop here and come inside.

"That's fine. You are welcome here," he said and went to bed.

After Juana got warm inside, her contractions started up again. Unable to sit any longer, she would stand and walk around. Finally she grabbed me and said, "Let's leave!"

My brother got up and asked "Where are you going, little one? If you are ready to birth, just go over to the other house. No one will see you there."

We did this and there Juana squatted down on the ground. The labor pains were coming stronger and faster now.

"If the contraction is strong, push! Push! Let's see if you can have this baby at last!"

My sister-in-law brought some clean rags to create a nest for the baby to be birthed into. We held Juana as she squatted and told her to push.

"Ay, Juana! Stop all this standing, sitting, and squatting down so hard! Don't your knees hurt? Stop it or you're going to kill yourself! Just stay put and push when the contraction begins."

She looked strong and brave, as if she didn't really feel the pain. Her husband never left her side from the moment her labor first began, holding her from around the waist from behind to support her. The midwife was still there, too. She stayed with us because we told her it was her duty to do so to care for her patient. There Juana birthed with all of us, my mother included, with her.

The baby was born and was fine, and then the placenta came without any problem. We were very pleased, as many women die before the birth is completed. In Juana's case, everything went well.

Soon after the birth Juana said, "Sister, bring me some water."

My sister-in-law had Juana's pozol ready so we gave her just enough water to wet her mouth and then her pozol to drink. When she finished it, I asked, "How do you feel, little one? Do you feel all right? Do you feel strong?"

"I'm fine," she told me. "I only hurt a little bit and that's probably natural."

"That's true. There's always some pain because you tear. Do you want to lie down?"

"Yes," she told me.

She was still squatting on the ground where she had given birth, her husband still embracing her from behind. I left to get some planks of wood for her to lie on.

When I came back into the room, her husband was saying, "What is it? What's the matter with you? You're falling asleep!"

I grabbed her and felt her skin clammy. She was very pale. Her face looked as if she had died already.

"What's the matter?" I screamed.

We laid her down on the ground. I felt her belly to see if what was bothering her was coming up, and then we quickly carried her to a bed. She was still conscious as we held her. She told me, "Don't push down on my stomach! It hurts. Don't do it!"

But we didn't know what else to do. While I was pushing down on her belly, she died. She had been so strong and yet she died. I watched her as she left us, taking her last breath. Her husband and I held her in our arms, and I watched as her hands and feet twitched. That's how she died. We were there to care for her, but we didn't know what to do.

While Juana had still been squatting, becoming pale and clammy, we sent a group for Don Vicente. When he arrived, however, she was no longer breathing. She was already cold. She died without a fight. It was like the killing of a chicken. For a few moments it runs around; that's how it was when Juana died.

One moment she was alive, squatting there and talking to us, demanding her pozol, and the next she was dead. She died like a chicken dies.

I felt so bad. I began to cry, saying, "I told you not to get married! Why did you do this, little one? How I suffer for what you have done!"

She had been my companion. We always gathered firewood together, worked together, went to the market together . . . She was all that I had, so I suffered terribly.

"Juana died of a hemorrhage," Don Vicente said.

I wonder if that is true, however, because we saw very little blood. Juana must have known what was happening while she was squatting there because she said to me, "Older sister, care for my child. I love him very much."

And I replied, "How can I take care of this damn kid if he is the one who is killing you?" I was wrong to answer her like that. I did it only because I hurt so much. And it was all his fault.

How else would you feel when the mother dies and the baby survives? It's horrible and that's why I spoke about the poor thing that way. If he hadn't been born, my little sister would still be alive. I still feel that way. Poor thing, he doesn't know what happened. He doesn't know who it is who takes care of him now.

Lots of people tell me to be strong and brave so that I can care for the child well because he is a boy. They tell me to take care of him and to love him as if he were my own son. I am taking care of him. He is big already and still growing. I didn't give birth to him myself but he has been mine since he was born. I accepted him as my own son. I am like a mother to him and he will one day call me "Mama."

I have to accept him. Sometimes, though, I still think about my sister and how if she were still alive, I wouldn't be suffering. At first, when the baby would get sick, it was my skirt that would get soiled, ruined, with his diarrhea. And all I could think about was, *If my sister were still alive, I wouldn't have to deal with this*. But now when he gets sick, I decide what herbal remedy to give him or what medicine to buy. If my mother has money, I go to her. It's as if she is my husband. She gives me money, and I am the mother to the child.

For This Reason I Have Decided Not to Marry

I have lived on my own because my stepfather, Juana's father, is a violent and angry man. He is a bad person. He wanted to make me marry against my will. He accepted the offer of every man who asked him for my hand just because he wanted the alcohol.[4]

---

[4]In the traditional marriage petition process, the young man along with a few relatives makes a series of visits to the house of the woman he wishes to marry and presents gifts to his prospective in-laws. These gifts may include alcohol, soft drinks, or other items. See this book's introduction for more background on marriage.

I think this way because of the way my mother lived. She married very young and was left a widow with two children. My father died very suddenly, after a bout of vomiting and diarrhea.

My mother remained single after that until my stepfather came to ask for her. My grandparents decided that she was still young and could marry again and they insisted on receiving gifts, just as they had with her first marriage. We were still very young at the time. My brother had just begun to walk and I was still a baby. My stepfather had four children. His wife had died as well, leaving him a widow. My mother says they talked it over and both agreed to love the other's children.

My stepfather beat my mother a lot. When he did, we tried to defend her and for this reason we were beaten as well. Sometimes he'd even grab a knife or machete, in which case we'd hide in the mountain, not going back into the house until he slept. He only did this when he was drunk. When he was sober, he didn't beat us. We lived with him for at least 20 years.

He had another woman who was my aunt, my mother's sister. My mother was with him first. My aunt didn't put up with all the yelling and hitting and left. At one point we all lived together under the same roof, but that didn't last long as my mother and aunt couldn't handle living together.

When my stepfather first showed up at the house with my aunt, we thought that now our mother would be left alone. He got the two sisters together and told them, "Let's see if you two can live together; I want to have you both in my home."

And my mother asked, "Will you still beat me when you are with her?"

"No," he replied. "I'm not going to beat you anymore."

"Well, that's fine then!" she said.

We thought he would do as he promised, but the opposite happened.

While my aunt was here, he continued to beat my mother and when my aunt left the house, he blamed us. If my mother said anything to him, he would beat her. He would find anything to accuse her of to justify his beatings. It didn't even matter that she had accepted his having another woman; not even that saved her from his blows.

My mother and my aunt did everything together: gathered firewood, worked, and made tortillas. Mother said that if the other woman had been someone else, she wouldn't have accepted her; but because she was her own sister, she had.

One day I said to my brother, "I don't want to marry, brother. I want to go away."

"Where are you going? Whom will you stay with?" he asked.

"With my aunt and uncle," I replied.

My brother then said, "If you want to go live there, that's fine. But think it over well. You better not turn out to be a liar or betray me. You better not leave me later."

"Don't worry," I replied. "I don't want to get married ever."

"Are you sure you're not going to want to get married one day or run after some guy? If you start running after someone, I will hang you with a rope."

My brother went with my aunt and uncle to find a place to build our house. When my stepfather found out we had found one, he was furious and threw us out. He said, "Go have babies together, you damn animals."

He thought that I was sleeping with my brother but that wasn't true.

There were a lot of things I was thinking about at that time—like how my mother was ordered around and beaten. I knew that if I got married I would be beaten just as she had. That's simply how men are. So, if I can work and support myself, why in the world would I want a man?

There was a man who wanted me. I told my brother, "If someone ever invites you to drink a soda, don't even think about accepting. I do not want to marry."

"My sister, can what you say really be true? Are you certain about what you say?"

"Yes," I replied. "That's the truth. I've given it some thought and decided not ever to be with a man because I've realized how bad they are. Besides, I don't want to leave you all alone. If I get married, I'll have to leave you and I won't be able to visit my mother anymore. As long as I'm alone, I can visit her whenever I please, staying a night or two at her house, and then coming back here," I said.

Two or three men came to ask my brother for my hand. "She's not interested in getting married," my brother told them.

"Why?" the man would ask.

"Because she's afraid that a man would disrespect and beat her. She doesn't want to be ordered around. This woman is a lazy one—doesn't want to do anything. She doesn't want someone telling her, 'Wash my clothes, wash my pants, mend my shirt.'" That's what my brother would tell them.

"I apologize but I can't make my sister get married if she doesn't want to. I can't just hand her over to you. You'd have to drag her screaming and fighting."

The other day the man came to the house to leave soft drinks and alcohol. Early that morning my brother asked me, "Are you really sure, little sister? Are you absolutely certain you don't want to marry?"

"Yes, I honestly and truly don't want to get married. That's my decision."

"Marry him!" my brother said. "The man really likes you. They'll throw lots of parties for you in his village."

"You can't force me to live with someone. I can make it on my own," I told him. "I have the right to live alone, eat alone, and work alone. I don't need a man. What would I want a man for? It's not like I could eat him, so what purpose does he serve? I can support myself, brother! Tell me the truth. If you can't support me, tell me, and I will understand. If so, I can go rent a house somewhere. Tell me if you don't want me here. It's better for me to leave you on good terms than with a fight."

"It's just that the man has been very persistent. And you are a woman, after all; you should marry. But if that's what your heart is telling you, not to get married, then don't do it. I won't make you. But don't come to me later when I am dying and cry about how hard it will be for you to be left all alone."

"I know how to work and you know it. It's enough to keep food on the table."

Men demand to be fed and that is what I don't want. And I'd rather just have to mend my own skirt. Or maybe I won't do even that—after all, only I will know.

After my stepfather died, I returned home to live with my mother and little sister. My brother gave my mother a warning. "Don't even think about selling my sister. If I didn't get to sell her while she was living with me then you can't either. And besides, why would you sell her if she doesn't want that? She says she doesn't want to marry and she's not going to budge."

"Let her be left there to die alone. Let her stay here. She can take care of us and visit with us."

When anyone gets sick, I am called to take care of them, just as I care for my sister's son. So, that is why I decided not to get married. I didn't want to be mistreated. I see it with my brother. If my sister-in-law isn't rushing about to get his meal ready, my brother starts yelling at her. When our children are bugging us, we just say, "Wait a moment, all right?" But if we were to say that to a man, he'd get so mad he'd start slapping us around. All this because we felt we had to have a husband. Obviously I am a woman, but I don't want to live like that. I'm lazy. You can see that by just looking at me. It's better that I be left alone to take care of myself. Nobody needs to worry if I eat or not. If I don't eat, I will die of hunger, but I prefer that to having a husband. Men only want to put us down. That's what I told my sister before she died, "Think about it really well before you decide to get married. You have to get up early, at 1:00 or 2:00 in the morning, to get the tortillas and breakfast ready. You try to see if you can do it. I can't—I'm too lazy. I wake up lying on the ground, not wanting to get up and no one is there to yell at me. A husband would be waking you up all the time. And if you don't obey him, he'll start yelling and hitting you."

My little sister would say, "Ok, ok. I'm getting up." I can't do that. Sometimes I stay in bed until the sun comes up. If I were to marry, I would be beaten just as my mother was.

Commentary

Juana's marriage to José was founded on a mutual agreement between husband and wife and was based on respect and support. Family and community support strengthened the marriage. Juana died because of the urgent medical condition associated with the birth of her first child.

Juana's family of origin was headed by women, an atypical family form in Chenalhó. The past history of her mother's alcoholism and the physical and emotional abuse inflicted on the family by her father and stepfather played important roles in the family's history.

As the eldest daughter, Juana became responsible for making key decisions for her family. While she was still single she was in a position of power in relation to her parents and older brother, traditional authority figures. This power allowed her to choose her own spouse and to establish a marital union different from that of most women in Chenalhó. Despite living in Santa Martha Magdalenas, her husband's village, Juana frequently visited her sister in Chenalhó. She decided where her son would be born, in Chenalhó, not in Santa Martha.

Santa Martha is a considerable walking distance from Chenalhó. Maternal death is frequent in the village. By marrying an outsider and living in his village, Juana could not count on the daily support of her kin. The couple's awareness of this fact and of the high incidence of maternal death in Santa Martha may have influenced their decision to go to Chenalhó to have their child. In Santa Martha the couple had the support of Juana's mother-in-law and sister-in-law who are midwives. Nevertheless, they placed more faith in the decision-making and support of Juana's family. The family chose Juana's aunt to be the midwife. In this decision, Juana, José, and Juana's family privileged Juana's kin networks over José's and over the perceived skills of the midwives. Together, Juana's family watched over her labor, which lasted more than fifteen hours. It was intensified by Juana's having walked on foot to her home to be with her family.

Traditionalist families in both Santa Martha and Chenalhó have limited experience with the national health system. When Juana had trouble giving birth, the family decided to take her to Vicente Comate, an indigenous health promoter rather than to a doctor at the Health Center in Chenalhó or to a first-aid center in Santa Martha. The family preferred the aid of a health agent closer to their culture, the jloktor ja' jchi'iltak (Tzotzil for one who is a doctor and a friend). Their choice suggests that they do not trust the public health system.

In highland Chiapas, pregnancy-related complications remain one of the principle causes of death among women. The maternal mortality rate in Chenalhó is six times the national average. Preventing pregnancy-related death is one of the greatest challenges that public health authorities face. Juana's story came out of the Maternal Death Study, a project begun in 1995 in San Pedro Chenalhó, in the highlands of Chiapas.[5] We have published a pamphlet of the stories of eight women who have died during their pregnancy or birth (Freyermuth Enciso and Torres 2001). Most women were under 30 years of age with small children. Several of these children did not survive the first

[5]This project was sponsored by the Program of Reproductive Health of the Colegio de México and was carried out with the support of CIESAS-Sureste and IEI-UNACH. The project was coordinated by Graciela Freyermuth Enciso and Ana María Garza Caligaris. Sebastiana Vásquez and Delmi Marcela Pinto of the Grupo de Mujeres de San Cristóbal and Juana Ruiz and Angelino López Calvo of IEI-UNACH also participated in the project.

year following their mothers' deaths. Women's testimonies and testimonies of their relatives have been very useful in identifying factors involved in maternal death and in developing proposals to reduce the maternal death rate in a manner that respects specific cultural contexts.

The study's objective has been to analyze the circumstances, contexts, and background of indigenous women's deaths during pregnancy, labor, and the postpartum period. The researchers are primarily interested in aspects that epidemiologists refer to as "cultural factors." These elements are often disregarded in planning health services. One of the study's most important findings is that 45 percent of maternal deaths are not reported. This statistic was calculated from the 40 cases of women's deaths tracked from 1989 to 1993. The study also reveals that only 10 percent of the 40 women sought help from health entities practicing Western medicine. The remaining women went only to local health centers in their communities (Freyermuth Enciso 1996).

Women who are severely ill due to complications from birth or the postpartum period do not normally seek help from Western health entities. This is due in part to lack of knowledge about access to services, the great distance that many women live from these services, and the poorly equipped clinics and hospitals where women still die of these complications.

Another factor affecting the reluctance of indigenous people to use nonindigenous health entities is the historical relationship between Ladinos and indigenous people. This relationship has been marked by asymmetry, inequality, and abuse. Based on this history, indigenous people have constructed collective social representations not necessarily related to personal experiences or medical interventions. Frequently, indigenous people perceive as traumatic interventions that medical practitioners deem successful.

Family and social structures, though constantly changing, still limit indigenous women's participation in personal, family, and community decision-making. For example, most women do not have freedom to choose their partners, to exchange ideas with men, and to leave their communities to study beyond sixth grade. Researchers in the Maternal Death Study have analyzed women's distrust of nonindigenous health entities in the context of what is known about gender relations in their communities. They have identified several factors that limit indigenous women's participation in decision-making. They have also identified ways in which women express their nonconformity with social norms that they find constraining and ways in which they are increasing their participation in family and community decision-making.

Progress is being made in the area of women's health in Chiapas. Self-help and popular medical resources can help solve indigenous women's health problems, particularly in the highland region. Women themselves are increasing their participation in family decision-making, as Juana's story illustrates. Despite progress, many obstacles still remain for women to make decisions regarding their own bodies, sexual practices, birth control, and personal health in general.

3

Actions Speak Louder than Words
Indigenous Women and Gendered Resistance in the Wake of Acteal

SHANNON SPEED

Introduction: Images of Resistance

The images are dramatic: In X'oyep, a Tzotzil woman pushes back a heavily armed soldier. She is small; the top of her head barely reaches his chest. But her arms reach up, one hand on the strap of his backpack, one on his neck, her gesture one of pent-up anger being released at last. His expression, of surprise and something like helplessness, is counterbalanced by the huge weapon at his side. In Yalchiptic, 400 Tojolobal women wearing ski masks and bandanas and holding wooden sticks confront the army and close the road with their bodies, forming a solid human blockade against the military's incursion. In Morelia, 60 Tzeltal women, many barefoot and carrying babies on their backs, run after more than 100 hastily retreating soldiers, chasing them several kilometers down the road to make sure they do not return.

Dramatic images of dramatic actions, in dramatic times. All of these events took place in the two weeks following the massacre at Acteal, in which 21 indigenous women (5 of whom were pregnant), 15 children, and 9 men were brutally slain by a pro-government paramilitary group. In the wake of the massacre, the Mexican government redoubled the Federal Army presence in the communities of the Zapatista base areas, which were already suffering high levels of military occupation. In this context of escalatory violence and militarization, the mobilizations by women to block the military incursion into their communities—blocking the soldiers with their bodies, chasing them out with sticks and stones—represent bold collective actions. These acts, the images of them, and the public discourse about them, have much to tell us about women's political participation and gendered resistance since the Zapatista movement began.

In this chapter, I analyze the testimonies of women who participated in such actions, and the images and official discourse that circulated nationally and internationally.[1] I explore the gendered nature of these women's acts of resistance, how they were understood and treated in the context of gendered assumptions of how the world is ordered, and their significance for women's rights in Chiapas, in Mexico, and beyond. Drawing on debates in New Social Movement theory, feminist theory, and resistance theory, I will argue that: (*a*) these actions were a gendered response to gendered violence and the female experience of war; (*b*) they constitute a form of participatory citizenship, which emerged along with other forms in the political space opened by the Zapatista uprising; (*c*) they blur theoretical lines that divide human actions into dichotomies such as feminine/feminist or everyday versus transformative resistance; and, finally, (*d*) the public discourse about the actions silenced indigenous women's voices, and contained hidden transcripts regarding women's inferiority and subordination, which, in fact, reflect the real challenge the actions presented to patriarchal social norms, and the reflexive attempt to reinscribe those norms.

"Our Suffering Is Different . . .": Gendered Experiences of (Para)Militarization

> The majority of us had never seen soldiers before. Since we've had to live with the military so close to our community we have had so many problems. . . . For the women, it has been hard . . . *our suffering is different.*[2]

To understand the specific kind of women's resistance discussed in this chapter, it is important to recognize the context of tremendous militarization and how it is experienced in distinct ways by men and women. Since the Zapatista uprising began in January of 1994, and particularly since the first major military invasion by the Mexican Federal Army into Zapatista-held territory in February of 1995, the base communities have suffered an onerous level of military occupation. At the time that the events took place (between December 1997 and July 1998), one-third of the Mexican Federal Army—approximately 65,000 troops—was stationed in the conflict zone of Chiapas (Global Exchange 1998; Global Exchange, et al. 2000). In some areas, the ratio of troops to community members could be as high as three to one, meaning concretely

---

[1]The testimonies included in this paper were collected by Robin Flinchum, Hilary Klein, and the author. Robin Flinchum and Hilary Klein conducted interviews immediately following women's actions to block the army in the first few months of 1998, Klein for human rights documentation and Flinchum for journalistic purposes. (Some of Flinchum's interviews were published in her 1998 article "Women of Chiapas.") I conducted interviews in August and September of 1998, several months after the incidents, and thus these interviews reflect more the "historical memory" of the participants, after they had had time to reflect on and interpret the events and their participation in them.

[2]All translations of testimonies and textual citations are the author's. I have given the women I quote pseudonyms out of respect for their privacy and their safety.

that a community of 400 people could be living with 1200 soldiers camped permanently on its edges.

The direct occupation or close proximity of military bases has taken a heavy toll on the social and economic fabric of the communities, creating a situation of constant fear and tension among the populace, complicating or impeding normal sowing and harvesting cycles, as well as introducing or exacerbating a gamut of social problems including alcoholism, drug abuse, prostitution, and sexually transmitted diseases. Maricela, a woman from the Cañadas region, notes a number of these problems:

> Since the soldiers came, it has been very hard. They set up their camp where we have to pass through to get to our coffee fields. Of course, it is impossible to go by their camp every day because they harass us and accuse the men of being Za-patistas, so our crops have failed. They cut the wires that fence in our cattle, so they escape. Also, the women are afraid to go down to the river where they always washed, because the soldiers are nearby. And, they have brought prostitution with them, and this is very bad for us.

These problems, among others, have plagued communities in heavily milita-rized zones.

As the quote that opened this section (*"our suffering is different"*) indicates, the social problems arising from the presence of federal troops affect women in specific ways. One example of this, mentioned by Maricela in the foregoing, is the introduction by soldiers of prostitution into indigenous communities. Local women are lured into prostitution through economic necessity, or at times through fear and intimidation. Prostitution has contributed directly to marital breakdown, social discord, and to the spread of sexually transmitted diseases. Women become victims of diseases they did not know existed and have no defense against, and their recovery is impeded by their lack of access to information and health care, which, never optimal, is made even more difficult by the military presence (see Physicians for Human Rights 1997).

Another example of the way that women are differentially affected by mili-tarization is related to the reintroduction of alcohol in some communities that had previously respected the EZLN prohibition of alcohol use. Whereas a de-crease in domestic violence with the decrease in alcohol use had been docu-mented (Garza Caligaris 1999), health providers have noted an increase in domestic violence against women in militarily occupied communities where alcohol use returned (Global Exchange 1998). The relationship between alco-hol and domestic abuse is not lost on the women. Maricela commented,

> My husband has hit me, yes. But only when he comes home drunk. For a while, he wasn't drinking because the community has prohibited alcohol, but now some are drinking again. . . . The soldiers sell it to them, that's what they say.

Clearly, alcohol abuse and domestic violence did not begin with militarization, and the men in these communities are responsible for their actions. Nevertheless, the presence of Federal Army troops has contributed significantly to reversing a process in which both were declining.

It is also worth noting that the increase in domestic violence may be tied to more than just an increase in alcohol abuse in militarily occupied communities. Though it would require further research to conclude as much in Chiapas, analyses of other militarized states have demonstrated that concepts of "honor," "masculine strength," and "courage" are made vulnerable by the presence of "enemy" male occupiers. This vulnerability results in a perceived loss of control and a concomitant increase in desire to exercise control over women, and in some cases an increase in domestic violence (Denich 1995). It seems possible that similar dynamics might be at work in the heavily militarized areas of Chiapas.

Another aspect of women's experience of militarization is that they suffer sexual harassment and violence by soldiers. This ranges from lewd comments made in passing to rape.[3] Direct harassment and the potential for violence against them provokes fear and anxiety. Adelina, also of the Cañadas region, commented,

> The women are afraid to go to the river where we used to bathe because the soldiers would come and watch us and make ugly comments. Also, they make comments when they walk through [the community] and pass by us. We are afraid to go out walking, because we know that they could attack us.

Thus, women in these communities must deal with fear on a daily basis, and it alters the routine and normality of their daily lives.

The effects of militarization have been amplified by the growth of paramilitary groups throughout the conflict zone. Beginning in the Northern Zone of the state with the groups called the Chinchulines and Desarrollo, Paz y Justicia, paramilitarization spread to the highlands and later to the jungle with groups like Mascara Roja and MIRA. Often shadowy, it is difficult to document their relationship with the government and the military. However, their pro-ruling party stance and a few high-profile connections—like a local congressperson who openly formed and directed Desarrollo, Paz y Justice, and an ex-governor who, while still in office, formed the Coordination for State Security through which money and training were channeled, have led a number of analysts to believe that they are state-sponsored (Centro de Derechos Humanos Fray Bartolomé de Las Casas 1996; Olivera 1998; Hidalgo and Castro 1999: see also footnote 5). The government's own human rights commission made some pretty damning conclusions about collusion between state security forces, state

---

[3]The rape of three Tzeltal women at a military checkpoint in Altamirano in 1994 became one well-known case. However, many women have declined to report rape because of fear of reprisal.

government officials, and the paramilitary violence in the Acteal case (Comisión Nacional de Derechos Humanos, CNDH 1998).[4] These paramilitary groups form part of a campaign of low-intensity warfare, a divide-and-conquer strategy designed to exhaust and terrify the rebellious population into submission (Global Exchange 1998; Olivera 1998; Ramírez 1997).[5] This approach has the benefit of making it appear that the conflict is not with the state, but rather within or between indigenous communities, and justifying further military presence as necessary to maintain control. In addition to some of the same problems provoked by militarization, the paramilitary presence increases even further the levels of tension and fear, since they are less visible and far less accountable for their actions than the Federal Army or State Security Police.

As we have seen with militarization, the experience of paramilitarization and paramilitary violence is lived differently by women than by men. The exacerbation of intra-community conflict through paramilitarization has caused the displacement of tens of thousands of people since 1995 (Centro de Derechos Humanos Fray Bartolomé de Las Casas 1996; Hidalgo and Castro 1999). Testimonies of displaced women tell us that the experience is devastating. Beyond the fear of fleeing for their lives and leaving everything behind, there is the pain of family separations, of seeing their children go hungry, and losing their homes, the principal space of their daily existence and the formation of their identities as women (Olivera 1998). Physical effects of these stresses manifest themselves—women lose their milk because of stress and can no longer breastfeed their babies, they have headaches, fail to menstruate, and suffer a variety of other malaises. Candelaria, a displaced woman from a highlands community, said, "My chest hurts all the time—I feel that I can't breath.

---

[4]In Recommendation 1/98, directed to Attorney General Jorge Madrazo Cuellar and Governor Roberto Albores Guillen, the CNDH attributed "legal or administrative responsibility," to, among others, the Secretary of the Interior in the administration of Julio Cesar Ruiz Ferro (governor at the time of the massacre); and to the Undersecretary of the Interior, the State Attorney General, the Assistant State Attorney General for Indigenous Justice, the General Coordinator of State Police, and the Director of State Police (Seguridad Pública), as well as other police commanders and officials.
[5]The Federal Army's counter-insurgency plan, "Chiapas Campaign Plan 94," was drawn up in October 1994 by Defense Minister Antonio Bazan and Chiapas army commander Miguel Angel Godinez. It was leaked to the weekly investigative magazine, *Proceso*, and published in January 1998 (*Proceso*, January 4, 1998). The document called for "the creation of government-supported armed 'self-defense' groups, the displacement of rebel supporters to isolate Zapatista insurgents, the 'disintegration or control of mass organizations,' and the use of psychological operations 'to destroy the rebels' will to fight and win the support of the civilian population" (Global Exchange 1998:6). The paramilitary groups discussed in this chapter are part of a counterinsurgency campaign against the EZLN. They should not be confused with the "Guardias Blancas," groups of armed guards hired by the ranchers and landholders of the region beginning in the 1930s to prevent the occupation of lands by landless campesinos and to eradicate labor organizing and worker dissent. These groups were also formed with the encouragement of the state government (see Benjamin 1996 [1989]).

Sometimes I think I will die. It is because my heart is in pain since we left (our home) community."

As for the gendered experience of paramilitarization, the terrible events at Acteal stand out for the dramatics of the violence toward women. Testimonies of women survivors tell of a particular cruelty toward women and a perverse use of the symbolics of maternity in the massacre. Many of the women who had been praying in the church in the refugee camp when the attack began, rather than fleeing and saving their own lives, tried instead to protect their children by covering them with their own bodies. They were shot in the backs. Testimonies of survivors tell of the paramilitaries macheteing the bodies of the dead women, cutting off their breasts and hacking the fetuses out of their bellies (Hernández Castillo 1998). Other testimonies tell of the paramilitaries tossing the fetuses from machete to machete, laughing and saying, "Let's do away with the seed" (Hernández Castillo 1998). Many of these facts are documented in the public records of the case.

Thus, the violence at Acteal was gendered violence, the symbolics of which reflected the context of patriarchality in which it took place. Reflecting on this, Olivera writes,

> By viscously massacring unarmed women as they did in Acteal they sent a message to all rebels in the symbolic announcement of generalized death. Destroying the mother, the children, and the lives still gestating was an announcement of the total elimination of the people, the ideas, the future of indigenous people who support the Zapatistas, but above all, the indigenous women who increased the forces of the insurgents by exercising their citizenship rights (1998:119).

The paramilitary violence waged against women in Acteal was not incidental—its motivation was the silencing of political opposition, and its logic and symbology was gendered in a way that rendered women most vulnerable to attack.

Militarization and paramilitarization of the indigenous communities have had detrimental effects on community cohesion and livelihood, and on individual psychological and physical well-being. This clearly affects all community members. However, the particular negative impact on women reflects the gendered nature of the experience of military occupation and war. Also worth noting here is the relationship of political violence to violence against women, a product of women's location in a patriarchal system that makes them more vulnerable to all types of violence. In the following section, I consider how the gendered experience of militarization and paramilitarization can result in gendered forms of resistance.

"We Won't Let That Happen Here": Women Resisting Militarization

> You know, they massacred women and little children. They say that all you could hear were the cries and screams of women and little children as they died. *We won't let that happen here.* Now we are angry.
>
> —Gabriela

Following the Acteal massacre, the Mexican government dramatically increased militarization, arguing that all armed groups in the state—not just the pro-government paramilitary groups of the kind that carried out the massacre—were to be eliminated.[6] The Mexican Federal Army began a systematic process of incursions into Zapatista–support areas, despite the fact that the events at Acteal did not directly involve Zapatistas or their supporters. Those killed at Acteal were members of the organization, *Las Abejas*, who, while at times have been supportive of Zapatista goals, reject armed struggle and violence. At the time that the massacre took place, relations between the Zapatistas and *Las Abejas* in the area were tense and strained. Nevertheless, within 10 days of the massacre, 6000 new troops were introduced into the highlands, military patrols in the eastern Lacandon region tripled, and random house-to-house searches began in numerous pro-Zapatista communities.[7]

As military incursion escalated, women in numerous communities organized themselves to mount a strategic defense against army incursion. The following are some well-documented examples from Zapatista base and other communities.

On January 1, 1998, the army entered the community of Nueva Esperanza, destroying personal and communal property while residents fled to the nearby mountains. There, the women organized, and, leaving the men in hiding, returned to their community to demand that the soldiers leave. Women from several neighboring communities joined them to support their resistance to the military's intrusion (Global Exchange 1998).

The following day, soldiers twice attempted to enter the community of X'oyep in the township of Chenalhó, considered a "second place of refuge" (after Acteal) for those fleeing paramilitary violence. Women of the community angrily impeded the army's entrance, forcing the soldiers to retreat several kilometers down the road to Yalchiptic.[8] The following day, a four-hour standoff between soldiers and women residents of the community (with the men standing behind them) resulted in pushing and shoving and hurled insults on both sides. Soldiers, who wielded batons and electric shock devices against the women, not to mention the huge weapons they carried, insisted that they had come to do "social work." The women shouted back, "Army, get out, you are of no use to us here!" and "Rapists of women, get out!" Witnessed and recorded

---

[6]It is worth noting that the Dialogue and Reconciliation Laws established in March 1995 to facilitate the peace process between the federal government and the EZLN recognized the EZLN as a legitimate insurgent force made up of "nonconformists" struggling for "just demands," which gave Zapatista's immunity from arrest. This distinguished them from paramilitary organizations whose legitimacy is not recognized and whose armed nature is illegal from any standpoint.

[7]*La Jornada*, Juan Balboa, January 3, 1998 and February 2, 1998.

[8]*La Jornada*, Juan Balboa, January 2, 1998.

by journalists, this incident produced some of the most eloquent images of women's resistance to a dramatically stronger adversary.[9]

On January 3, the army entered Morelia, taking the community by surprise. The women quickly organized, and, as the men fled into the mountains, 60 women drove out close to 200 federal soldiers who were conducting house-to-house searches and interrogating residents. The women then set up a round-the-clock roadblock, to make sure the soldiers didn't return. When they did return, on January 8, the women not only impeded their entrance to the community, but chased them several kilometers down the road for good measure.[10]

The following day, in the small community of Diez de Mayo, a lookout alerted the community that soldiers were approaching. Forty-five women, many carrying children on their backs, attempted to block soldiers and state police from entering their community. When they asked the army to turn back, the soldiers first verbally attacked the women, calling them "dirty Indian whores," then physically attacked them, beating them with rifle butts, shovels, and stones. Sixteen women and nine children were injured, including a seven-month-old girl and a one-year-old boy, both of whom lost consciousness from blows to the head. Several of the injured women were pregnant. Despite the violence leveled against them, the women did succeed in keeping the soldiers from entering their community (Global Exchange 1998).

All of these incidents took place in the weeks following the massacre at Acteal. But over the following months, as the Mexican government broadened its interventions to joint military-police raids designed to dismantle the autonomous municipalities in Zapatista zones of support, women's role in resisting also expanded. A notable case is that of the community of Nicolas Ruíz, invaded on June 3, 1998 by over 1000 federal and state police and soldiers. Women again put themselves on the front lines, attempting to physically block the entrance of security forces into the community. They were eventually overwhelmed by tear gas fired by the agents. One of the women who participated told me:

> We knew the state police were going to come. There had been rumors for days, and we were all tense and waiting. We women gathered and agreed to block their entrance, as the women had in other communities. We had seen videos and photos of the women who kept the soldiers out of their communities, and we agreed we would do the same here, that we would not let them enter.

As this comment indicates, the women's actions in Nicolas Ruíz five months later were openly inspired by images of the earlier women's actions. Thus the acts had a demonstration effect, engendering further women's resistance in other communities.

---

[9]*La Jornada*, Juan Balboa, January 3 and 4, 1998.
[10]*La Jornada*, Hermann Bellinghausen, January 5, 1998.

Taking these events at face value, it seems reasonable that these women, faced with the threat of ever-increasing militarization, acted to defy the army and challenge the right of the government to further invade their communities and their lives. But I would like to suggest that the fact that these actions took place immediately following the massacre at Acteal is due to more than just the accelerated rate of militarization that took place in that period. I began to consider this possibility after talking to a woman in Nicolas Ruíz about the events in her community. Her comment, which opened this section, bears repeating,

> You know, they massacred women and little children. They say that all you could hear were the cries and screams of women and little children as they died. We won't let that happen here. Now we are angry.

At the time, what I noted was that she so easily connected the State Security Police and the paramilitaries who had committed these crimes in Acteal. But on later reflection, I realized that her comment perhaps indicated something more important—that sometimes strategies of terror, which the Acteal massacre clearly was a part of, can have an effect contrary to their purpose. Such strategies, designed to generate fear that is paralyzing to rebellious populations, might, in fact, have engendered resistance. I later reviewed the comments and testimonies of women from other communities, and found repeated references to the events at Acteal linked to their anger and their resistance to army incursion, such as this one, from a woman in Morelia,

> We have seen what they did to our three compañeros [killed by the Federal Army in January 1994], we know what they did in Acteal. First they want to kill the men, next they attack women and children. We say, enough![11]

As this quote indicates, the women in militarily occupied areas have many reasons to oppose military incursion, not the least of which is the still-fresh memory of the men tortured or killed by the army following the uprising in 1994. But the "gendered violence" of Acteal, in which the majority of those killed were women, their bodies mutilated and babies torn from their wombs, deepened the anger and antimilitary sentiment of many women, who, in turn, responded with "gendered resistance."

"Fuimos Tomando Consciencia": Women's Participation and the EZLN

> After 1994, *fuimos tomando consciencia* (we began to develop our consciousness) . . . We began to see that we shared a lot of suffering with women in other places . . .
>
> —Gabriela

---

[11]The author is in possession of this testimony in written form. The information regarding the identity of the woman who spoke, as well as the interviewer, have been lost. It is likely that the testimony was taken by either Hilary Klein or Robin Flinchum, both of whom generously provided me with data for use in this chapter.

It is difficult to talk about the women's resistance to militarization without including a discussion of the EZLN itself in some way, not only because most of the communities that carried out this kind of resistance are Zapatista base support communities and all suffer militarization and/or paramilitarization related to the Zapatista uprising, but also because the Zapatistas have made women's rights and women's participation central to their political program. In this section, I consider the relationship between the EZLN, women's political participation, and the resistance to military occupation that took place following Acteal.

Since the first days of the Zapatista uprising, close attention has been paid to the significance of the Zapatista movement for issues of women's rights. The appearance of the EZLN, with a rank and file made up of 30 percent women, the issuance of the Revolutionary Women's Law (see Box 1, p. 23) and the generally high visibility of women within the movement, generated hopes that the Zapatista movement might give new impetus to the struggle for women's rights in Mexico. In the Revolutionary Women's Law, the Zapatistas put forward their demands for women's "equality and justice," among them the rights to control their fertility, choose their partners, be free from rape and physical aggression by strangers and family members, and participate in positions of authority in both the EZLN and in their communities. These were direct demands, which held the promise of dramatic change for indigenous women in Zapatista areas, and raised hopes of a movement committed to feminist struggle for participants in the women's movement—indigenous and mestiza, in Chiapas and beyond.

However, not long after the uprising began, criticisms of the Zapatistas' gender discourse and practice surged. Some pointed out that the Revolutionary Laws and other public statements by Zapatista leaders lacked a critical feminist consciousness, because they did not call for the elimination of the patriarchal system of oppression and simply inserted women into hierarchical structures of violence contrary, in their view, to feminist sensibilities (Bedregal 1994; Hernández et al. 1994). Others pointed to the notable disjuncture between the Zapatistas' discourse of women's rights, and their practice "on the ground" (Rojas 1995b).

In many of the base communities, women's subordinate position remained unchanged, and women continued to be excluded from community meetings and decision-making processes. Women in the base communities who do organize and become active have faced both state-sponsored violence from the army and paramilitary groups, and domestic violence from their own partners who are jealous or resent their loss of control over their women (see Hernández Castillo 1998). The lack of organizational response from the EZLN to incidents of violence against women, and the apparent tolerance of exclusionary practices, squelched the initial optimism of many women activists about the possibilities for change (Bonilla 1994).

The reality is, without a doubt, complex. Women's ability to organize has varied from region to region, and the outcomes of women's political participation have been mixed. Critical but sympathetic observers have argued that "changes in the subordinate position of women, although significant, have been few, and processes of transformation slow and difficult, but ... never, until now, has the inclusion of specific demands of indigenous women in a revolutionary movement been achieved" (Olivera 1995:176). This inclusion, it is argued, has real symbolic power. Further, the Revolutionary Women's Law, "like all laws, is an ideal to achieve, rather than a lived reality," and the Zapatistas' expressions of gender sensitivity represent only "the seed of a new culture which has yet to be constructed" (Hernández Castillo 1997:140). From this perspective, precisely what is important about the Zapatista movement is that it is not a finished product that is set to be imposed, but rather a social process that opens the possibility for many to incorporate their struggles and contribute to the on-going construction of a more pluralistic and just society.

Certainly, the discourse of women's rights did not spring spontaneously from the Zapatista uprising. It was built on a history of women's organizing that allowed the Zapatistas to articulate this discourse, which includes work by the Diocese of San Cristóbal, NGOs, campesino organizations, artisan's cooperatives, and women's health projects that opened spaces of reflection about inequalities and rights that had begun to be reappropriated by women in questioning gender inequalities and their individual rights (Garza Caligaris 1999).[12]

However, the Zapatista rearticulation of the discourse of women's rights at the center of their political project did impact women—even women not involved in (or even aware of) previous organizational efforts. Most important, the Zapatista uprising broadened the parameters of the democratization movement to the indigenous communities. Its high-profile discourse of women's rights brought the discussion of indigenous women's political participation to a broader national and international public—and resignified it as positive, necessary, and natural. Although in many areas the women in indigenous communities are not familiar with the details of the Revolutionary Women's Law, its existence has for many women become a symbol of the possibility of a better life. Garza Caligaris (1999) suggests that the Zapatistas' discourse regarding women's rights, and concretely the Women's Law, have

---

[12]It is also important to note that while I am addressing specifically the emergence of a discourse of women's rights and modern political action, there is a long history of women's participation in resistance in Chiapas, much of which has been ignored by historians and ethnographers (Hernández Castillo and Gall n.d.). Notably, the women's actions to impede the military were apparently not without precedent. Oral histories are told in Zinacantán of women in neighboring Chamula lifting up their skirts and mooning Ladino soldiers to "cool their weapons" during the caste War of 1869 (Laughlin and Karasik 1996), and of a woman who led the soldiers to a cave and made them disappear (unpublished manuscript by Witek Witold in possession of author).

contributed to creating what Karl Werner-Brand (1992:2) calls a "cultural climate," that "generates a specific sensibility for certain problems, narrowing or broadening the horizon of what seems socially or politically possible." She notes that "the EZLN with its Women's Law had known how to harness a climate firmly embedded in the daily lives of the indigenous communities and the breaking of previous consensus about the manner in which masculine authority was exercised in those communities" (Garza Caligaris 1999).

Thus in the Zapatistas redeployment of the discourse of women's rights, the resignification of indigenous communities as the space of democratization and indigenous women as political actors, created a "cultural climate," or in New Social Movement theory terms, an opening of political spaces of expression. Escobar and Alvarez (1992) argue that the "opening of political spaces" by new social movements represents one aspect of their "transformative potential." That is, although they are not pursuing immediate and revolutionary transformation of society, new social movements do contribute to social transformations through the opening of spaces of political participation. Within these spaces, new types of participatory citizenship can be recognized, which, not restricted to efforts to redefine the political system, instead encompass struggles to redefine social and cultural practices (Alvarez, et al. 1998).

This theory of the opening of political space in which new forms of participatory citizenship emerge is helpful in understanding the relationship between the Zapatista movement and women's collective actions such as the mobilizations to resist militarization, which I interpret as a form of participatory citizenship in the broad definition given by Alvarez.

In at least one community where women carried out actions to block the army, women tied their actions directly to the EZLN uprising and an evolution of their consciousness. For example, in the comment from which the opening quote of this section was drawn:

> After 1994, we began to develop our consciousness (*fuimos tomando consciencia*). In 1994, we were all priistas. But we saw what the Zapatistas were doing and saying, and we began to say, "they are right," and we entered the struggle. That was when people from what we call civil society started to come, and they wanted to work with us, with the women. We started several projects . . . and we began to see that we shared a lot of suffering with women in other places . . . And they showed us the videos (of women in other communities resisting military incursion) and we said, we will do this, too, if we have to.

In this comment, Gabriela clearly links the community becoming Zapatista, the arrival of outsiders interested in organizing women, becoming more conscious of a shared oppression as women, their viewing of images of women resisting, and their eventual participation in blocking the army and police incursion into their community.

Whether the EZLN as an organization has achieved dramatic change in women's roles and levels of political participation within the base communities, their rhetorical advocacy of such change created the cultural climate and opened that political space in which these women undertook this form of political action. In the following section, I argue that the women's actions, although not directed to redefining social norms or the political system, did deploy alternative conceptions of social relations that challenge dominant cultural meanings and practices.

To Defend Our Community . . . to Protect the Men: Practical Goals/Strategic Outcomes or Everyday Transformative Resistance?

> We held a meeting and decided that we were going to chase the army out if they came. . . . We thought, well, if they want to shoot us, then they'll shoot us. We're ready *to defend our community, and to protect the men* . . .[13]

As discussed in the preceding section, some feminists, in analyzing events in Chiapas, have argued that the EZLN itself—both in its discourse and its practice—retains fundamentally patriarchal forms of organization and social interaction (Lagarde 1994; Rojas 1995b). From this perspective, the women's struggles associated with the EZLN are not "feminist," in that they "only put forward a few claims for women, and not a proposal from a critical and conscious female experience . . ." (Bedregal 1994).

While these specific critiques were not made in relation to the women's mobilizations against army incursion, which had not yet taken place, the authors would not be likely to revise their statements in light of these actions, given that they were directed to one specific and limited goal, and certainly were not tied to an analysis of patriarchy and the pursuit of new forms of social relations.

The distinctions these analysts draw are consistent with a long-standing differentiation in Latin American women's movements between "feminist" and "feminine" movements, in which struggles for specific goals related to women's lives (e.g. access to health care, direct investment for women's cooperatives, etc.) are understood as "feminine" projects, and "feminist" projects that question women's position in the current configuration of social relations (Sternbach, et al. 1992). There is thus a perceived dichotomy between "practical," feminine goals, and "strategic," feminist goals (see Molyneux 1986).

In her study of women and social movements in Latin America, Stephen (1997) concludes that such dichotomies are difficult to apply to movements "on the ground," arguing instead that many movements are simultaneously seeking practical goals, and challenging accepted norms about women's roles

---

[13]Woman from Morelia, cited in Global Exchange 1998. Italics are mine.

in society. This insight is crucial to understanding the significance of the recent women's mobilizations against militarization in Chiapas. Their resistance was directed to a practical goal: keeping the army and state security forces out of their communities. It was rather clearly not directed at a strategic goal of challenging systemic gender inequality. Nevertheless, by mobilizing as women to protect home, family, and their right to continue to work and live their lives (however oppressive these may be), they are simultaneously reversing the male role of protector of partner and community, as well as inserting themselves into the traditionally male role of physically opposing an armed invader. The quote that opened this section—"We're ready to defend our community, and to protect the men . . ."—was echoed in other testimonies, and in the actions of the women who stood face-to-face with soldiers while their men hid in the mountains. Some have suggested that the women took these actions because women would be understood by the soldiers to be less threatening, and their blocking the army's entrance less of a challenge (Global Exchange 1998). But I think that perhaps the opposite is true. Within the patriarchal logic that places emphasis on men's ability to protect "their" women, and subjects women to physical attack as symbols in male struggles against male enemies (see Denich 1994, cited in Hernández Castillo 1998), the mobilization of women greatly challenged culturally inscribed norms about male and female roles of dominance and subordination. The women's collective acts of resistance thus blur the line between "practical/feminine" undertakings and "strategic/feminist" ones, challenging not just the army's incursion, but the whole set of underlying gender dynamics and social norms.

The practical-strategic dichotomy has parallels in the literature on resistance more generally. Scott (1987), in theorizing "everyday forms of resistance," has argued that there are "quieter," more routine forms of resistance that do not directly challenge the structure of power and domination. A debate generated by Scott's work has revolved around the question of whether actions must be consciously directed at transforming the status quo in order to qualify as resistance.

Prior to the Zapatista uprising, research exploring issues of women's resistance in Chiapas focused largely on everyday forms of resistance (Eber 2000 [1995]; Eber and Rosenbaum 1993; Rosenbaum 1993). Performing the important task of bringing women's voices and experiences to the fore, these works emphasized women's central role in cultural resistance as the bearers and reproducers of indigenous tradition. However, they gave less attention to women's engagement in overt political actions that directly challenged structures of domination, whether political or social. Before 1994, this approach to women's resistance made sense, since in most cases indigenous women themselves did not talk about or frame their actions in this way. After 1994, as the "cultural climate" changed, women began to frame their collective actions in explicitly political terms, often tying them to political affiliations such as "Zapatista" that rendered almost any action a challenging act of resistance. Some recent works on the history of women's political participation and resistance argue that the previous lack of political framing served to diminish recognition of women's political agency—making them resisters by default as the bearers of tradition, rather that active participants who consciously seek to transform their world (Hernández Castillo and Gall n.d.). Others have presented histories of women's organizing and political participation that preceded the uprising, demonstrating that there was more going on than everyday forms of resistance in this earlier period (Eber 2000 [1995]; Garza Caligaris and Toledo 2002).

What all of this discussion makes clear, in my view, is not which category of resistance women's collective actions fall into, but rather that theoretical dichotomies—practical-strategic or everyday-transformative—can obscure more than they enlighten. That is, many women's collective actions fall into either category depending on the perspective of the analyst describing them; that is, most are, in fact, both. The women's actions to resist military incursions are a good example of the porosity of theoretical dividing lines. As I have noted, these acts were not consciously aimed at transforming structures of domination—patriarchal or any other. Nevertheless, as I have just argued, their actions *did* symbolically challenge structures of gendered domination and subordination. Further, the women's resistance to militarization is precisely an assertion of their political agency. Although it was tied to the defense of a way of life and the reproduction of tradition, it was also a struggle that openly challenged power relations and, consciously or not, contested gendered forms of power.

In the following section, I argue that this challenge was clear to the Mexican State, and that that recognition was reflected in the official discourse about the women's actions.

Let the Leaders Show Their Faces: Hidden Transcripts of a Gendered World

> [The Zapatistas] are cowards, they put their women and children first. Let *the leaders* to show their faces.
>
> —Military police commander

> We women got together and said, "We've" got to get [the soldiers] out of here. *Que se vayan.*"
>
> —Adelina

A notable aspect of these mobilizations was the public discourse about them. The official discourse of the Mexican government portrayed this as a Zapatista strategy of putting forward "their" women to ward off the army, while making retaliation politically difficult. The president himself claimed that "exemplary soldiers are being insulted and hit by women and children *who are sent to do this*" and chastised "those who shamelessly do not hesitate to *use indigenous women and children for their own provocations,* and would not stop short of using them as cannon-fodder."[14] In a similar vein was the comment of the military police commander: "[the Zapatistas] are cowards, the*y* put their women and children first. Let *the leaders* show their faces."[15] The "clever Zapatista strategy" interpretation got broad play in the press, even in some articles highly celebratory of the women's courage and determination. In this reading of events, it is understood that "the Zapatistas" (or at least those who make the strategies) are by definition men, and that women are little more than pawns to be moved by the Zapatistas when politically expedient. Once again, indigenous women's agency as political actors is negated, erased.

Significantly, the testimonies of the women involved in these mobilizations contradict such interpretations. The following are a few examples:

MARICELA We women decided among ourselves that the army would not enter our community. We told them, go ahead and kill us, but we don't want you here.

DOLORES It's the men the soldiers come to take. We said, "we don't want them to take our husbands. We don't want our husbands to die . . . We won't let [the soldiers] return."

MARIA The army destroyed all of our crops, everything in the milpa . . . We think it is more dangerous for the men, but we also know that the soldiers could attack us or rape us. We were frightened, but then anger got a hold of us. . . .

JUANA We had heard the word that women in communities were organizing to defend their homes. And we decided we would do this, too. The army only comes to steal and to frighten our children. So we said, we won't let them in.

Many more testimonies illustrate these women's anger, strength, courage, and resolve. What one hears in these statements are why and how women decided *among themselves* to defend their communities, their children, and their men. What one doesn't hear in any of the testimonies, is any indication that they were given orders or were in any way persuaded by others to take part in such actions. In fact, when asked explicitly about this issue, women in one community said that not only were they *not* ordered by the Zapatistas to do so, but rather that they had requested that the EZLN support their actions (see Flinchum 1998).

Although the implication that women are not capable of acting on their own without the direction of their male "leaders" is overt in the rhetoric of the government and implicit to differing degrees in that of others, the fact that these women's actions were so often conceived of in this manner makes evi-

---

[14]President Ernesto Zedillo, quoted in *La Jornada,* February 13, 1998, p. 12, and February 20, 1998, p. 6. Italics mine.
[15]Quoted in *La Jornada,* January 4, 1998, p. 5. Italics mine.

dent a "hidden transcript" that reads all women as subordinate to men. I refer here to Scott's (1990) concept of hidden transcripts, or covert ideas contained in popular culture as signs of resistance. Stephen (1997) applies this concept to social science paradigms and resistance to change within them. In this same sense, I use the term here to refer to signs of resistance to change by both Mexican government representatives, as well as journalists and others involved in the production of public discourse. The hidden transcripts that read through in official and unofficial discourse about the women's mobilizations to resist army invasion are universal, unstated assumptions about how the world is gendered. I intend this not just as a fancy way of saying the Mexican government makes sexist statements about Indian women's mobilizations, but to refer to a process in which the Mexican government, in attempting to discredit and undermine movements that challenge its power (i.e., the Zapatistas), utilizes discourses that contain other messages—specifically that of women's inferiority and subordination to men.

It is worth noting that this gendered hidden transcript has its race and class corollaries. Official statements abound that imply or state openly that the indigenous Zapatistas are controlled and manipulated by nonindigenous outsiders—most often Sub-Commandante Marcos, a middle-class, educated Ladino from Mexico City. The hidden transcript read, of course, that a bunch of Indians would certainly not be capable of organizing or leading themselves, or doing much of anything other than following the orders of a non-Indian man. The infantilization of innocent indigenous males controlled by Marcos bears a similar message to that of the discourse that portrays women Zapatistas as controlled by men—that is—their inferiority and subordination.

Thus the hidden transcripts contained in official discourse responded to a double challenge: the explicit challenge of an insurgent group to existing forms of rule, and the implicit challenge to existing social norms of domination. Thus, the official discourse served a double purpose: undermining the credibility of its political adversaries, and reproducing cultural meanings of race, class, and gender.

Fortunately, the images of the women's actions also make up part of the public discourse. These images were widely circulated, and though women's versions of what happened were often silenced in favor of the official story of their manipulation, the images spoke loudly, impacting the collective imaginary about indigenous women. Consider for a moment the few images of indigenous women that are most often seen in Mexico or abroad: La India María, tourist ads showing women as bearers of a cultural past, or, worse yet, the foolish and illiterate servants on the popular television soap operas. In this context, the images of indigenous women confronting the army also confront hidden transcripts of a gendered world, reinscribing indigenous women in the collective imaginary as strong and courageous, as the defenders of home and hearth, and even as the protectors of their men before a powerful enemy.

Conclusions

The dramatic acts of resistance to military occupation in the weeks and months following the massacre at Acteal leave no doubt about the political agency of indigenous women in Chiapas. Gendered responses to a gendered experience of militarization and paramilitary violence, these acts reflect the context of patriarchal social relations within which both the real social dynamics of gender and the symbolic meanings attached to womanhood make women vulnerable to violence in particular ways.

Like the larger struggles of the Zapatistas and *Las Abejas* that they are related to, the women's actions are part of complex social processes that are not easily characterized in abstract categories such as "feminist," "nonfeminist," and so forth. Although a radical rethinking of gendered social relations has not been part of Zapatista discourse or practice, the Zapatistas' rearticulation of a discourse of women's rights—particularly their discursive resignification of the indigenous woman as a political actor and a subject of rights—has contributed to opening political space within which these women act, and within which their actions have a particular meaning. The acts are a form of collective action that, though not directed at redefining the systems of domination, does challenge social and cultural practices of inequality.

Understood in this way, the actions blur the lines of theoretical debates about women's resistance. Although not aimed at strategic goals of dismantling patriarchy, they nevertheless represent a significant subversion of gender norms. The strategic/feminist-practical/feminine theoretical distinction is thus challenged by collective actions that are directed to practical goals yet ultimately do contest women's subordination to men.

The official discourse regarding the women's mobilizations is evidence of the fact that these actions *are* understood as a significant threat. Such discourses reflect a reaction, not only to the overt issue of the Zapatistas' direct contestation of the relations of power within the Mexican state, but to this not-so-subtle redefinition of gendered, raced, and classed social relations. They thus entail more than just sexism, but a covert response, a hidden transcript that reflects official resistance to the evident challenge of the women's mobilizations.

The indigenous women's acts of resistance to military occupation give voice to their experience of the triple oppression of racism, classism, and gender inequality, and of the violence and fear of counterinsurgency that is part of their daily lives. Most important, they also tell us of the women's agency as political actors in a context where their agency has so often been erased. Despite the many words that were used against them, these women's acts of resistance speak louder than the official discourses intended to silence them.

Note:

The research for this chapter was conducted with funding from the SSRC-MacArthur Fellowship on International Peace and Security in a Changing

World, while I was an affiliated researcher at the Centro de Investigaciones y Estudios Superiores en Antropología Social (CIESAS-Sureste) in San Cristóbal de Las Casas. Writing was also conducted with support from the Ford Foundation and the American Anthropological Association. I gratefully acknowledge comments made on earlier versions of this chapter by Jane Collier, Kathleen Dill, Christine Eber, Melissa Forbis, Charles Hale, Aída Hernández Castillo, Christine Kovic, Mercedes Olivera, Carol Smith, and the participants of the internal seminar at CIESAS-Sureste.

4

The Birth
of Guadalupe

Translated by Melissa M. Forbis

On January 12, 1998, in the town of Ocosingo, a number of peasant and civil society groups held a public demonstration against the Acteal massacre and militarism in Chiapas. During the march, the *seguridad publica* (state police) fired randomly into the crowd. Their bullets killed Guadalupe Méndez López, a 38-year-old woman demonstrator, and injured her infant child. The state police were in Ocosingo as a result of Roberto Albores Guillén, substitute state governor at the time, ordering police and military incursions into the communities of autonomous townships.

Members of Zapatista base communities and other groups of women sing this *corrido* or ballad in memory of Guadalupe and her struggle. The corrido is a form of storytelling that has been popular in Mexico for well over 100 years and was especially important during the Mexican Revolution (1910–1920) as a way of keeping the deeds of heroes and villains in the popular memory.

The corrido format has been used for decades throughout rural Chiapas to record and remember stories of community struggles, achievements, and tragedies. For example, members of *Las Abejas* (The Bees), a group dedicated to nonviolent resistance in Chenalhó, have written numerous corridos that document their history. "The Voice of the Displaced," a Las Abejas choir based in X'oyep, Chenalhó, has produced several cassettes of these corridos.[1]

> My friends, I'm going to tell you
> what happened in Ocosingo.
> The hands of the cowards,
> they killed Guadalupe
> on the 12th of January
> of the year 1998.

---

[1]Cassette tapes by the choir feature corridos in Tzotzil and Spanish about the formation of The Bees, the massacre at Acteal, and the rights of women. One cassette is entitled, "In Memory of the Martyrs of Acteal." Songs on the various cassettes include "*Las Abejas*," "Ave María of the Oppressed," and "Injustice."

She was 38 years old,
a saint, Guadalupe,
mother of a wounded girl,
injured by the assassin bullets
for defending her people
and all of the oppressed.

For demanding justice
the response was violent,
opening fire with weapons.
The infant Isabel
in her mother's arms
was injured, too.

In her face and her gaze,
her tears spilled,
she saw her daughter fall,
and her blood being spilled
from the gunshots
of the cruel policemen.

With black ribbons,
the people mourn.
We didn't stay silent.
Protests are everywhere
against the bad government,
of Roberto Albores Guillén.

In the San Carlos church
blessings they gave to her
to take her to her burial
in the community of La Garrucha,
township of Ocosingo
where Guadalupe was born.

I didn't want to remember.
There was weeping and rage.
All together we shouted:
"¡Viva! ¡Viva, Guadalupe!
Death to the supreme government
and its assassin forces."

Guadalupe's name remains
engraved in history
like those who have died
fighters for peace,
and true justice
for the oppressed people.

Fly, fly little dove,
all over the world.
Take this message to them:
That the people have risen up
in order to reach the victory
of a true and just peace.

5

Indigenous Children
We Are Not to Blame

RUPERTA BAUTISTA VÁZQUEZ
Translated by Beth Pollack

In the streets of the colonial city of San Cristóbal de Las Casas, indigenous girls and boys of all ages attempt to earn a few pesos shining shoes; cleaning car windshields; and selling handicrafts, gum, cigarettes, newspapers, and other items. These children spend hours in the streets each day, yet they are not street children in the traditional sense because they do not sleep in the street. Each evening they return to their homes and families in the *colonias,* unregulated urban settlements that surround the city.

The following play by Ruperta Bautista Vázquez is about the lives of these children. Bautista Vázquez is an indigenous woman who grew up in San Cristóbal and for several years has been working with street children under the auspices of Nich K'ok', an NGO.[1] The main characters are Tzotzil Mayan children originally from Chamula and Zinacantán, who now live in a colonia. They are unable to attend school as they must help support their families by shining shoes and selling gum and bracelets. The play illustrates the racism and paternalism that mark the relationships between the children and mestizos and foreigners, including tourists, government officials, and wealthy residents of the city.

Dozens of colonias surround the city of San Cristóbal.[2] For the most part, residents are indigenous people who left their communities of origin for economic and political reasons. Displaced from land that once was their home

---

[1]Nich K'ok' is a Tzotzil term meaning "flower of the fire" or "spark." It forms part of Melel Xojobal (The True Light) a nongovernmental organization whose mission is "to accompany urban and rural indigenous communities in order to strengthen their own processes of growth and development from their own identity and autonomy in the areas of culture, communication, and alternative education" (www.laneta.apc.org/melel). The NGO was founded with the support of the Dominican Fathers of the Catholic Diocese of San Cristóbal de Las Casas. Nich K'ok' is the area of Melel Xojobal that carries out educational projects for indigenous children.

[2]*Rumbo a la calle: El trabajo infantil, una estrategia de sobrevivencia* (2000), a booklet researched and written by Melel Xojobal, describes the growth of colonias surrounding the city of San Cristóbal.

and that provided a means of subsistence, these uprooted campesinos commonly work in the informal sector and as a reserve labor force for mestizo merchants. They struggle to make a living as street vendors, domestics, taxicab drivers, street sweepers, and unskilled day laborers. Each household group depends on the income of a number of its members. In the context of extreme poverty, the money children earn, even if it is only a few pesos a day, can make a significant difference to a family's survival.

The racism that permeates the mestizo-dominated city of San Cristóbal adds to the difficulty of surviving. For example, many hotel and restaurant owners do not allow indigenous people to enter their establishments to sell handicrafts to tourists. Until recently, mestizo merchants, whose shops line the colonial streets, held a monopoly on purchasing and selling handicraft items. This monopoly has weakened over the past decade as a result of sales to mestizo "middlemen," the proliferation of indigenous artisan cooperatives, and the establishment of an open-air indigenous market in front of the Church of Santo Domingo. In addition to fearing the loss of their monopoly, Coletos (mestizo residents of San Cristóbal) fear that as more and more indigenous people come to live in and around San Cristóbal they may one day take over the city.[3]

Various conflicts have arisen as the Coletos and indigenous peoples compete for space in the city. One conflict in January of 2001 followed the decision of the mestizo PRI-affiliated municipal president to "clean up" the city by sending the police to violently evict all indigenous vendors from the Plaza of Santo Domingo. For years indigenous people (primarily Chamulas and Zinacatecos) have sold handicrafts in this plaza. The outdoor market is mentioned in tourist guidebooks as one of city's main attractions. Yet, on this cold January morning, without warning, the police told the vendors to gather their wares and leave the plaza. The vendors began to pack their goods, but before they could finish the police began to violently evict them. A number of people were beaten and the police fired tear gas. Later the same week, police patrolled the city's central plaza to prevent the ambulatory vendors, women and children from Chamula, from selling their "friendship bracelets." In the end, the vendors prevailed. They had been organized in unions and were back in their original positions within a week.

The indigenous vendors were forced to abandon the plaza, albeit temporarily, because Coletos saw them as both competitors and blemishes on the city's beauty. The incident in the Plaza of Santo Domingo highlights both racism

---

[3]The Catholic Diocese has played a prominent role in supporting indigenous artisans. In the 1980s, the Diocese developed artisan projects in Guatemalan refugee camps in Chiapas. It was also instrumental in the establishment of the indigenous market in front of the Church of Santo Domingo. See Chapter 9 for more background on Coletos' anger toward the diocese for its economic support of indigenous people.

and the precariousness of selling in the streets. In addition to facing threats of eviction, sales vary dramatically, depending on weather conditions, the volume of tourists in the city, and many other factors over which vendors have no control.

Indigenous Children: We Are Not to Blame is one of many theatrical works by indigenous playwrights exploring the history and experiences of indigenous people in Chiapas.[4] The play was first performed in 2000 at the anniversary of the Casa del Pan, a vegetarian restaurant and bakery, just a block from the indigenous market in the Plaza of Santo Domingo.[5]

—Christine Kovic

Characters

LOXA: A 9-year-old indigenous girl from San Juan Chamula. As a little girl, her father, a drunk, abandoned her and her mother, leaving with another woman. Loxa's mother sold potatoes in the San Cristóbal market. One day on her way from Chamula to the market, she was in an accident and instantly died. Left alone, Loxa was sent by people in Chamula to live with her uncle Mach in San Cristóbal.

CHILD 1: A 10-year-old shoeshine boy who does not attend school.

CHILD 2: An 8-year-old shoeshine boy who does not attend school.

CHILD 3: A 4-year-old boy who accompanies his mother selling crafts.

CRISTINA: A 34-year-old woman who temporarily works in the Plaza Santo Domingo selling crafts because there is no permanent space available for her.

XUN KA': An 8-year-old Tzotzil Indian girl from Zinacantán living on the streets. Her mother does not have work, and Xun Ka' earns enough money to buy food for the day selling crafts in the streets and plazas of San Cristóbal.

MACH: The 35-year-old husband of Cristina. He works selling tacos from a cart, his only means of income. Sometimes he is not able to sell as much as he wants in order to provide for his children and his orphaned niece.

ROMIN: A 27-year-old merchant who sells potatoes in the San Cristóbal market. He is the father of five children.

TUMIN: She is 25 years old and sells handicrafts on the main streets of San Cristóbal.

KAJ K'ANAL: A shoddily dressed 10-year-old indigenous girl who wants to change the difficult conditions, but has little prospect of being able to do so.

---

[4]Of particular interest are the plays written and performed by Isabel Juárez Ch'ix y Petrona de la Cruz Cruz of *Fortaleza de la Mujer Maya* (Strength of the Mayan Woman-FOMMA). See Cruz Cruz and Chi'x 1993.

[5]For several years, Bautista Vázquez has written an annual play to commemorate the restaurant's anniversaries. Kippy Nigh, the owner of Casa del Pan, has been engaged in a number of projects with indigenous people in San Cristóbal.

Scene 1

(In the center of the room is a small table, two benches, a clay pot, and an old straw mat and old clothing hung on the walls. It is still dark as it is early morning. Loxa lights a candle to see and gets up to start her day. She lights the fire to make tortillas and breakfast.)

CHILD 1: *(asking Loxa for food)* Loxa, it's 6:00 in the morning. Give me something to eat.

CHILD 2: *(crying)* I'm very hungry.

LOXA: Wait a bit. The water still isn't hot for your *pozol*.

(Just then, the baby wakes up crying to the shouts of the 4-year-old. Loxa goes to calm the baby down. Cristina enters and begins serving breakfast).

CRISTINA: Mach, come get your pozol and your tortilla. Hurry up! It's almost time!

MACH: *(offstage)* Wait a minute. *(Mach enters. He sits down on the floor without anything to drink while Cristina brings tortillas).*

CRISTINA: Here's some tortilla I put aside from yesterday. *(Loxa has been able to quiet the baby and carries him with her. She sits on the floor near the other children who wait for everyone to gather so they can begin breakfast. Cristina is the last one to sit down.)*

CRISTINA: Go ahead and eat. *(The first to begin eating is Mach, then the others after Cristina hands each one a tortilla. After a bit Mach gets up.)*

MACH: *(speaking to Cristina.)* I'm going to get going. Hurry up and you can catch up with me there, at our place.

CRISTINA: Okay, get going. I'll be along in a little while.

(Mach exits the scene.)

CHILD 2: *(gets up and speaks to Child 1)* Hurry up already. Let's go!

CHILD 1: All right.

(They pick up their shoeshine boxes and prepare to leave.)

CHILD 1: We're going, Momma.

CHILD 2: And, I'm going to go, too, Momma.

(They exit the scene.)

CRISTINA: Okay, you kids be careful with the cars there today. When you are paid, count your money carefully and, please, don't lose it.

(Loxa helps Cristina pick up the breakfast things.)

CRISTINA: *(speaking to Loxa)* I'm going to go put my stuff together.

LOXA: Yeah, I'm going to do that in a little bit.

(Cristina leaves. Loxa goes to one side of the bedroom and takes down two bags hanging from the wall. She puts them within Cristina's reach. Cristina reenters in a hurry and speaks to Loxa.)

CRISTINA: Hurry up, Loxa. *(She exits with the children.)*

LOXA: Okay, I'll hurry.

(In the background, sad music plays. Alone Loxa carries the breakfast things outside. She returns to the table, picks up the straw mat. She brings a portable stove

and places a large ceramic pot on it. Afterward she begins to wash clothes. Upon finishing, she puts everything in a basket and takes it offstage. She returns to pick up a big bag of merchandise and exits.)

Scene II

(It's 10:00 in the morning. Mach enters with his taco cart. He hasn't sold anything all morning.)

MACH: *(in a loud voice)* Taquitos to appease your hunger! Sir! Look how good my tacos are! Take some to work.
(Just then, Cristina arrives with the two boys. She also carries her merchandise.)
CRISTINA: I'm leaving immediately to go sell. I'll leave my bag here with you to buy three handfuls of greens.
MACH: *(desperate)* Woman, there aren't any sales! People don't want to buy anything, and the day after tomorrow Don Juan is coming to collect his money; I haven't paid him for the cart in an entire year. He told me if we didn't pay him, he would take the cart away from us. *(First, he looks at Cristina and, then the cart.)*
CRISTINA: It's only 10:00. Maybe you'll sell something in a little while.
MACH: *(worried)* I don't know, from your mouth to God's ear, if he wants it that way. If not, we'll lose the cart.
CRISTINA: Hey, hold on a minute man; we'll see what God has to say. Well, I'm going to start selling. *(She takes the little boy's hand and exits while Mach remains behind reflective.)*
MACH: *(he begins hawking again)* Buy a taquito to get rid of your hunger, mister. Buy very fresh taquitos of brain, tripe, or tongue. *(He stays quiet for a bit and then, begins again.)* Pick up great taquitos! Cheap! I'll throw in an extra one free! *(There is no answer. He puts his hand on his head scratching it and remains silent. He begins again.)* Pick up some taquitos! Taquitos! An order of cheap taquitos! *(He looks at his watch and exits the scene with his cart.)*

Scene III

(The area around the central park of San Cristóbal. Xun Ka' is walking around looking to sell her handicrafts.)

XUN KA': Buy an ankle bracelet from me! *(She shows her bracelets to the public.)* Buy a little bag from me for your money! Look, only two pesos, buy from me . . . Buy it so I can pay for my tortilla!
(Just then, two American women tourists wander by with their backpacks. Xun Ka' runs toward them pulling out a belt. She puts it around the waist of one of the tourists.)
XUN KA': Buy this belt, it's beautiful. Look how pretty it looks on your belly.
(The tourists refuse, answering in a friendly way.)

TOURIST 2: No thanks, I bought one this morning. I don't need another one. Thanks *(with an American accent).*

XUN KA': Then buy this bracelet, you can have three for five pesos, they're cheap. *(The tourist finally agrees, buying three bracelets from her.)*

TOURIST 2: *(Taking off the belt from around her waist, she hands it to Xun Ka'. She also hands back the bracelets. The tourist takes money out of her bag and pays her.)* Okay, I'll buy the bracelets from you.

(At that moment, Loxa arrives and runs toward the tourist, carrying belts, bracelets, bags and other things on her back.)

LOXA: Buy this bracelet! Look how pretty it is! It's a bracelet for your ankle and for your hand. *(She places a bracelet in the tourist's hand. The latter is upset.)*

TOURIST 2: We've already bought many things this morning. We don't want anything else, understand?

LOXA: *(insists with a pitiful voice)* Buy from me, too. Is cheap, three for five . . . just for my tortilla. My stomach is hungry. Look, it's only five for my tortilla. *(The upset tourists refuse to buy from Loxa. Tourist 2 pushes her away and she falls to the ground.)*

TOURIST 1: Stupid girl, understand I don't want to buy anything else.

(The two tourists leave the scene; meanwhile Loxa's crafts are strewn on the ground. She cries because she was shoved. Xun Ka' runs over to pick up Loxa's things and brings them to her.)

XUN KA': *(sadly to Loxa)* Mu xa xa 'ok.' Likantalel mu xavaak'ta vonton. Ilbaj xilotik li mu jk'ulejike. (Don't cry anymore. Get up, don't worry. The great wealthy lords discriminate against us.) *(She helps Loxa get up, they walk a bit and the two of them sit down. Awhile later, they exit the scene.)*

Scene IV

(The plaza in front of the Cathedral. Loxa's brother is there.)

BOY 1: Shoeshine, shoeshine! Two pesos for a shoeshine! *(Nobody answers him so he paces from side to side. He addresses the audience.)* Can we shine your shoes? Two pesos for a shine.

(He sits down on his shoeshine box; Boy 2 arrives with his box.)

BOY 2: How much have you earned today, brother?

BOY 1: *(sadly)* Not a thing, and you?

BOY 2: The same. I don't know what we're going to do. *(Boy 2 takes Boy 1 by the shoulder and they exit.)*

Scene V

(At the Plaza de Santo Domingo, Tumín walks around selling her handicrafts.)

TUMÍN: Buy a shawl to cover yourself when it's cold! Look, it's pretty for your head! *(Cristina enters carrying her sack full of crafts. She puts the sack down in order to set out her merchandise for sale that day, and all the while, her baby and small boy are next to her. The jewelry artists also arrive to set up their stands. The collector arrives at that moment and moves toward the artists. He pulls out a payment stub and hands it to the craftspeople. They pay and the collector moves toward Cristina. She pays and he hands her a payment stub.)*

COLLECTOR: Filthy Indians, I hope they all die. I can't stand seeing their disgusting clothes, and their stupid lice-infected kids.

(Cristina remains in her place. The PRI candidate arrives to campaign.)

CANDIDATE: Good day artisans. I come today to bring you new words, constructed by the new PRI. Today, more so than ever, we are going to win with change because we are new. I've come to ask you to vote. If you give me your vote, I promise to bring progress to all of you. There will be new schools for your children. They will learn to use computers and many other things that the new party offers. This is the new PRI! Because we are new, like the new lemon Fab. I await your votes.

Scene VI

(Loxa enters with her merchandise. She sits down in her place. At that moment, someone walks by eating potato chips and throws the bag on the ground. Loxa runs to pick it up and sits down to eat the crumbs. Just then Xun Ka' arrives, sits down beside Loxa and puts out her merchandise. Two teachers walk by them.)

TEACHER 1 (MESTIZA): Oh my God! How I pity those girls, to see them sitting there, waiting to sell their little things.

TEACHER 2 (MESTIZA): Ay, Miss Lupita, you pay too much attention. Can't you see? They are lazy, lice-ridden local girls. All they like to do is be in the street getting dirty and playing. They don't think. They don't even go to school and they don't speak Spanish. They're stupid indigenous girls.

TEACHER 1: Don't treat them so harshly. It's not their fault. Don't you think you are also to blame for these girls and boys and the way they are? *(Teacher 2 doesn't respond. Upon walking in front of the girls, she looks disdainfully down her nose at them, throwing her garbage on their merchandise. They exit the scene. The girls collect their wares and exit.)*

Scene VII

(Cristina accompanied by her two children arrives to put out her merchandise. Tumín enters afterward to sell her bracelets. Later Loxa and Xun Ka' enter to accompany their mother. Just then, a Patronizing Do-Gooder couple enters.)

PATRONIZING DO-GOODER MAN: *(talking to his wife)* Give these to those children over there.

PATRONIZING DO-GOODER WOMAN: *(Without answering, she takes out shabby toys and ragged clothes and shows them to the girls.)* Look girls, we've brought you some things. *(Loxa extends her hand to accept, but her mother interrupts.)*

TUMÍN: You've brought unusable things. You've used them up and don't know where to leave them. They're trash. That's why you've brought them to us, the poor. Maybe you think we don't know what things are useful and what's useless, huh?

(The couple put their bags down beside the girls. They exit. Upset, Cristina and Tumín pick up their merchandise.)

TUMÍN: Xun Ka', let's go.

CRISTINA: Loxa, bring along your younger siblings. Hurry up! *(They exit.)*

(Kaj K'anal enters looking at the sky. Then she addresses the audience.)

Stupid Indians! Idiots! *Chamulitas!*[6] Snot noses!
These names are thrown in our humble faces
To vent their anger built up over time with no reason.

Why do you put us down? Why do you hate us?
Is it my fault my hair is dark and not blonde?
That my eyes are dark and not green?
That I speak Mayan and not English?

Our ancestors used to live on this land.
The winds used to sing.
Their voices were silenced
When evil spirits took their land.

Ever since, I ask, what is my crime?
Why do they attack us?

You can laugh at our tears,
Stare at us without seeing.
You're young, but your flesh weighs of ages.
You're happy dancing in our poverty.

Ay, chulti' ants![7]

You say you heal and pray,
but throw fiery barbs that torment us
You say you love but send hate.
You construct ideas only to destroy them.

Ay, chulti' ants!

You claim to understand us,
but carry only burdens of ignorance.
Say you listen, but are deaf.
Say you are good, but are evil.
Cry liberty, but enslave us with your greed.

---

[6]*Chamulitas* ("little Chamulas") is a derogatory and patronizing term for indigenous people from the township of Chamula.
[7]In Tzotzil *chulti'* means "lie" and *ants* means "woman."

Ay, chulti' ants!

You say you seek justice but curse humanity,
Say you want equality, yet climb over the poor,
Like to fly, but clip our wings.
Want peace, but sow hatred and war.

Chulti' ants,
Why won't you stop your lies?

6

"I Made Myself from Nothing"

Women and Sex Work in Urban Chiapas

PATTY KELLY

I grew up in a very humble house. We ate sitting on a mat on the floor, tortillita
with salt and lime. And since I have been a woman who has suffered, today I am
the happiest woman in the world. . . . I have what I have from nothing. I made
myself from nothing. Never did I think I would have a cassette player, or an air
conditioner of two horsepower, or three pieces of property, thanks to God.
I never imagined this, and three, four electric fans.
—Magda

Introduction

These are the words that Magda offers as we sit drinking tea in her small room
in the Zona Galáctica, a legal, municipally administered brothel in Tuxtla
Gutiérrez, the capital of Chiapas. At age 50, Magda has worked as a prostitute
for over 22 years.

In this chapter I tell the stories of four women who work alongside Magda
in the Zona Galáctica, examining their diverse experiences of sex work and
their common struggle to defend their dignity as they perform highly stigmatized labor within a society that devalues them for doing so while simultaneously defining their work as a *malnecesario*, a necessary evil. Regulated and
controlled prostitution is regarded by many Tuxtlecos (residents of Tuxtla) as
necessary to an orderly society—in a culture where male sexual desire is constructed as "need" and prostitution is sometimes viewed as a preventative to
rape.[1] Women who do sex work occupy an uneasy position: though they may
earn more money than many Tuxtlecos, their clients included, this economic
power buys them neither gender equality nor social parity. Though considered
by many an essential element of a well-ordered society, they are stigmatized
and made invisible: the Zona Galáctica, like many zones, is located in an isolated area on the periphery of the city. It is precisely the intersection of the
structural violence of gender inequality and class oppression that creates the

---

[1]City officials claimed having a regulated tolerance zone decreased crime and rape in
the city center; some sex workers themselves felt they were providing a public service by
assisting with rape prevention. But, rape, which is more about power than sex, is not
prevented by access to a consenting partner.

circumstances under which many women enter prostitution. The following pages will make visible the struggles of women who labor in sex work, one of the few lucrative job opportunities available to unskilled and often uneducated women in a diminished labor market offering little more than other forms of less-profitable service sector employment.

Tuxtla Gutiérrez: Modernity, Migration, and Work in Urban Chiapas

Anthropologists and other social scientists have been at work in Chiapas for over half a century; most research has centered upon the indigenous peoples of the Highlands region—the 1994 Zapatista uprising extended the researchers' field of vision both thematically and geographically. The rich work produced by scholars over the decades has generated a particular image of Chiapas—a Chiapas that is agricultural, indigenous, impoverished, and deeply conflicted over issues of ethnicity, land, class, and politics. Chiapas is indeed all of these things, but it is also urban, Ladino, and for some, a place to seek economic prosperity. This aspect of Chiapas has received little attention from anthropologists.

Located in the hot Lowlands of Chiapas, Tuxtla Gutiérrez, state capital and home to the Zona Galáctica, is a city of nearly half a million people. It is perhaps not what one thinks Chiapas should be. Writing of Tuxtla in 1939, Graham Greene referred to Tuxtla as "the new ugly capital,"[2] suggesting that Chiapas "should be all wild mountain and old churches and swallowed ruins and the Indians plodding by" (1984 [1939]:194). Tuxtla has no ruins, many of its churches, aside from the Cathedral San Marcos in the city center, are modern in design,[3] and despite the area's Zoque origins, less than 2 percent of Tuxtlecos over the age of 5 speak an indigenous language (INEGI 1993:22).

Throughout Mexico, rural and traditional patterns of consumption and subsistence are being sacrificed to the neoliberal agenda of economic "modernity"—rural life is increasingly threatened by agribusiness, economic hardship, political violence, and migration to urban centers. Although migration to cities is hardly new, increasing rural poverty under neoliberalism and the militarization of vast regions of the state following the Zapatista uprising have forced people out of the countryside in growing numbers. Women, increasingly responsible for financially supporting the domestic unit, comprise a large number of these migrants. They often find poorly paid work in domestic

---

[2]Tuxtla Gutiérrez became capital of Chiapas in 1892, when it was moved from San Cristóbal de las Casas by Governor Emilio Rabasa, who hoped the transfer would rid the state government of provincialism and politically modernize Chiapas (Benjamin 1996 [1989]:45).

[3]The majority of Tuxtla's colonial-style buildings were razed in the 1940s during a period of state-led development.

service, street vending, prostitution, and other sectors of the burgeoning informal economy.

Recent government studies indicate that population growth in Chiapas is twice the national average; data suggest that existing cities will experience unprecedented growth and that new cities will emerge (Gobierno de Estado de Chiapas 1995:63). Tuxtla stands as an example of such trends: annual population growth rate in the city is 7.3 percent, a figure that worries public officials as shanties sprout up along the hills surrounding the city and immigrants from throughout southern Mexico and Central America converge upon Tuxtla. Two-thirds of Tuxtla's population increase is due to the migration of economic refugees from both rural and urban Mexico and Central America. Tuxtla also demonstrates the vast inequalities that exist between city and country in Chiapas: as the capital of one of Mexico's most impoverished states, the city is one of the nation's least marginalized municipalities.[4]

The Zona Galáctica, Tuxtla's only legal brothel, is not separate from these political economic trends, but rather was borne of them. The 1991 construction of the Galáctica was the realization of the Proyecto Zona Rosa, a pet project of Governor Patrocinio González Garrido (1988–1993).[5] Despite neoliberal doctrine about downsizing the public sector, the Proyecto Zona Rosa sought to give the state greater control over sexual commerce in Chiapas, even as it was withdrawing from other sectors of the economy. Among the goals of the project were the modernization and regulation of the sex industry throughout the state. And so, the Zona Galáctica was born, and women from cities and rural areas throughout southern Mexico and Central America came to work. These are their stories.

Ramona

Ramona is a 25-year-old Chiapaneca who has worked in the *ambiente* (the life of sex work) for two years. Of her work, she says, " I have never liked it, never— more than anything because of the infections, because one of these days, one of these men . . ." She trails off, then continues, "I could end up with a *sidoso*

---

[4]Nationally, nearly 13 percent of Mexican homes lack electricity. In Chiapas this figure is a staggering 33 percent whereas in Tuxtla it is just 3.2 percent. Tuxtla also boasts higher rates of literacy and access to potable water than the rest of Chiapas (Centro de Información y Análisis de Chiapas, et al. 1997:40).

[5]Governor González Garrido played an unusually large role in the creation of the municipal Zona Galáctica, provoking a great deal of gossip. During a visit to the State Department of Public Health, an official whom I questioned about the governor remarked, "That guy was *really* interested in prostitution," which is ordinarily a matter of municipal, not state, concern. A former general, González was also well known for the use of repressive tactics against the peasant populations of Chiapas during his term in office, often promoting military solutions to social problems (See Collier 1994; Ejército Zapatista de Liberacíon Nacional, EZLN, 1994).

(person infected with HIV). Sometimes I say to myself, "He is going to infect me . . . I am in danger."[6]

Ramona grew up in rural Chiapas, where her family had a small farm. She left school in the third grade in order to help her father and sisters tend plots of corn and beans they grew both for sale and subsistence. Reflecting on her childhood, she feels little nostalgia: "I worked hard." She attributes her dark skin to the many years spent working under the hot sun: "This is why I am so sunburnt, because I spent so much time in the fields." It is more likely that Ramona's skin coloring comes from indigenous descent than from a childhood spent toiling under the hot sun. But in a society and a market that privileges those with lighter skin, her attitude is not surprising.

At 15, Ramona left home for Tuxtla. This decision was precipitated in part by a desire to escape the difficult life of the fields. She got a job as an employee in a small shop, where she worked for eight years earning "good money," until she met and fell in love with Damian. Soon afterward the two moved to Puebla, where Ramona says they lived "like man and wife," until the day they came to live as pimp and prostitute. She expected to work in Puebla, yet she never could have guessed that the man she loved would demand that she prostitute herself. But soon after their arrival in Puebla, Damian insisted that Ramona engage in sex work to support them. "I began to understand then that what he wanted was money; before, I didn't know what his intentions were." Ramona refused, thinking of her family, "What would they say?" and of the physical dangers, "That cannot be, that kind of work is horrible, a person runs the risk of infection." Damian did not accept her refusal:

> And he told me I couldn't say no and that was when he came at me and started to hit me. "You have to work, you have to do it," he said. And that's how he did it, hitting me until I said yes.

Ramona began to work the hotels of Puebla, earning money selling sex and giving her earnings to Damian, who would threaten, hit, and occasionally buy her clothing and new shoes. In those days, Ramona worked without a condom and received no medical care. Following an outreach to sex workers by a local social-services organization, Ramona told Damian she wanted to see a doctor. His response was, "Ay, what for? Here's your doctor right here, I can examine you whenever you want." On one occasion, when she became infected with a

---

[6]In 1999 there were less than 500 registered cases of HIV in the state—a figure that is surely greatly underreported. In the Zone, doctors claimed there had never been a case of HIV, but after the municipal government switched laboratories that were performing the workers' medical tests, four women tested positive. It is suspected that the original laboratory was not actually testing the blood or simply not reporting the results. This event, which occurred after my time in the field, received little attention in the Zone and to date no investigation of the matter has been undertaken.

sore on her genitals, Damian applied to it a liquid, which burned terribly and "like that he sent me out to work." Since that time, Ramona says, she has tried to always use a condom; "I said to myself, 'It's my life.' It's not his life, he does nothing more than ask for the cash, but it is my life that is at risk."

Frequent physical abuse by Damian spurred Ramona to demand that he take her back to Chiapas, where she could be closer to the emotional (though not economic) support of her family, who did not know that she had become a sex worker. Reluctant to lose a source of income, Damian brought Ramona to Tuxtla to work in the Galáctica. During this period the pair did not live together and Ramona began to suspect that he was seeing another woman. What she would soon find out was that Damian had four other women working for him in the Zona.

The majority of 140 Zona workers are independent, but nearly a dozen women are *obligadas*, women obligated, or coerced into prostitution by one of two pimps active in the Galáctica. Women generally become obligadas through physical and verbal abuse by men they presume to be their boyfriends. The *padrote* (pimp) may take the woman away from her home and familiar surroundings to a place where she has no social relationships or support, as Damian did with Ramona, thereby increasing her vulnerability and his control. The obligadas generally arrive at the Zona by way of Puebla, and for this reason are sometimes referred to as *Poblanas* (residents of Puebla), a word that in the Zona has become synonymous with "pimped." Obligadas often have less control over their work: they may work cheaply, without a condom, or perform special services (anal or oral sex) to attract more clients to meet the economic demands of their pimp.

Obligadas also tend to engage in less social interaction with independent Zona workers and may go to great lengths to protect both their padrote and his business. They are often seen in one another's company, which allows the women to effectively police one another for the benefit of their padrote; when independent workers Leticia and Flor advised a certain woman to leave her pimp, they were threatened by the other women working for him.

Ramona recalls the "very painful day" that her relationship with Damian ended. On this day he arrived at Ramona's apartment and accused her of infidelity, an act that would threaten his physical, emotional, and financial control over Ramona. He beat her and tried to strangle her.

> He would have preferred I were dead before I left him, he told me. "Oh God," I was saying, "Oh God protect me," because before I had believed in God. *Bueno*, I still do believe, but one quickly forgets when one begins to do this kind of work.

Ramona escaped with her life, though Damian retained control of her apartment and her belongings. Following this event, she moved to the southeastern city of Comitán and worked the Zona there for a few months, waiting for the air to clear, serving mostly soldiers brought from northern Mexico by the government due to the ongoing Zapatista conflict.[7]

Ramona eventually returned to the Galáctica, but to work for herself, selling sexual services to clients for 30 pesos, 50 if they would like a position other than missionary style. Other services, such as oral or anal sex, she does not do; she works "normal." Of Damian, she says she has little contact with him and has told him she will go to the police if he bothers her. For the moment, the four other women who continue to work for Damian leave her alone but their anger is clear:

> You can see it in their faces. Before, I would come and they would greet me, "*Hola*. How are you? How good that you have come." Very happy. But now they just turn their faces away and that's it. They see that I'm no longer giving [money to Damian] and that's what really gets to them—that I am working and earning my own money. My own money that is mine. That's what bothers them.

Although sex work is not Ramona's optimal choice of work, it is, in her view, the best way for her to earn money. She speaks of other unskilled workers who earn as little as 300 pesos a week and of the lack of opportunity in her home community and says, "As I see it, in part, what attracts us most is more money." Like many other sex workers, Ramona hopes to be able to earn enough money to leave the ambiente and to open her own small business selling shoes, perfumes, and, she adds with a laugh, "all those little trinkets they sell downtown." Until that time comes, she says, "For now, I am at peace here in my room, I work and at 10:00, I go home."

Ramona's family wishes she would return home: "My papa has told me, 'Come home, *hija*. Come to the house, don't stay there. What are you going to do in Tuxtla?'" But Ramona does not like the rural life. Like many new urbanites, she has become accustomed to the comforts of city living and she speaks of the hardships of rural life: "One has to haul water with buckets, taking it out of the well. One washes clothing by hand in the river—going to the river carrying big bundles of clothing—it's tough. Making the food over firewood—because of lack of resources—there is no stove. And another thing, making the tortillas! (She laughs). That I don't like."

---

[7]Immediately following the Zapatista uprising, soldiers flooded into the Galáctica. One worker remembers how the Galáctica was like a "green zone," filled with uniformed men. Today, though there is a large military installation in Tuxtla, soldiers do not constitute a great presence in the zone. Most clients are employees, blue-collar workers, students, retirees, and underpaid white-collar workers such as teachers, engineers, and low-level government workers. Wealthy men and men of public importance who buy sexual services do not frequent the Zona, preferring the privacy of hotels or "hostess" agencies.

Leticia

It is nearing 9:00 in the morning, and a group has gathered on a downtown corner waiting for the pirate taxi that will take sex workers and clients to the Zona. Leticia soon arrives, carrying one bag of bread, another of sweet rolls, accompanied by her daughter who is on her way to school. We greet one another and she asks, "Are you going *allá*?" There. By "there" she means the Zona, though sex workers rarely refer to the Zona by name when not in the Zona. Rather, it is euphemized as *allá*. The stigma associated with being a sex worker causes most women to keep their work a secret from family and neighbors. Friends, if they exist, are often others in the ambiente and such friendships are fragile and prone to rupture due to the competitive environment of the Zona.

Of her work, Leticia says,

> I could earn more than an accountant. It's possible if I were to try. That's an advantage [of the work], that I can provide for my family. In this work the disadvantage is that my dignity goes right through the floor. It's not that it [the work] is bad. It is bad because we are not understood by society and it is bad because one feels bad, morally. And you cannot say, "I work as a prostitute or sex worker." You cannot say it. No, you have to hide it . . . because you feel bad. For example, I am your friend and I met you in the street and you made friends with me and after awhile you say to me, "*Oye*, Leticia, where do you work?" "Mmmmmm, I work in a store." I won't tell you, because if I tell you I work in the Zona, you won't talk to me anymore.

Leticia's four years in the industry have given her insights into the constructed nature of gender and sexuality. Regarding sexual relations between partners, she says,

> In the moment you are going to have relations, it's nothing more than normal [missionary position]. Then what does the husband do? He goes and looks to the prostitutes to pay them so they give him oral sex, so they give him services they don't do for him in his house. It's logical that he has to find a way to realize the fantasies he has in his head, because his woman doesn't let him [at home]. It happened to me one time, my husband said to me, "Put yourself in that position" and I was going to agree but then he said, "No, better you lie down and put yourself normal again." And I was left thinking, "Why?" Now, I am not thinking "Why?" because I know why. Because the woman of the house is the woman of the house and he doesn't want to disrespect her. I have talked with men. I say to them, "And why do you come here? Your woman doesn't let you ask that you do it de perrito [dog-style] or some other position?" And they say "No, because when I ask she tells me, 'Get out of here, I am not a whore for you to treat like that!'" So it is logical that the man comes here.

Leticia is critical of the ways in which the prevailing moral order separates and categorizes women, demonizing some while sanctifying others. "Society should think that this is a job; for example, that if one person won't do it, another will, as long as they are paid." She adds, "The decent women, they say decent, but decent between parenthesis because they aren't decent. Sometimes they cheat on their husbands, without charging. And we, yes, we charge."

Thirty-four years old, Leticia is from the state of Puebla. Unlike Ramona, who was forced into prostitution by an abusive partner, Leticia saw sex work as a path toward freedom from her physically and verbally abusive husband. Without education (Leticia left school at age 9 and left home to work as a servant at age 12), a new partner to support her, or resources, and with children to support, it seemed the only way she could escape a decade-long financially sound, but unhappy marriage to a man who beat and humiliated her.

> Who is going to accept you into his house with children? Nobody is going to say to you, "Come, I accept you with the kids and everything." So, I knew about this, that this work existed. It exists every place. If I was going to go, I would put myself to work, even if it was in this, in being a prostitute.

And so Leticia left her husband, moved to Tuxtla, and became a sex worker. She could have worked as a servant, she says, but the earnings from such work would not allow her to pay the rent, send her children to school, and feed them properly. In the Zona, the majority of women, approximately 70 percent, are single mothers. Yet as Leticia notes, the jobs available to women with few skills or little education (servant, cook, factory worker) are poorly paid.[8] As Leticia sees it, it is her job as a sex worker that enables her to fulfill her role as a mother:

> I couldn't allow that my children ate nothing more than beans or some simple little thing, or that they didn't have their milk. I have to see how I am going to provide for them.

Although the work allows Leticia to care for her daughters in the way she wants to, and though she says she has become accustomed to the work, which she sees "like any other job," she acknowledges that the stigma associated with sex work has had a powerful impact on her, and for some time, her relationship with her children. Zona workers are demonized for stepping beyond the boundaries of acceptable female behavior; the stigma disciplines not only sex workers but as McClintock notes, "the whore stigma is used to discipline women in general" (1993:3). The stigma associated with working as full-time prostitute circumscribes one's social relations, causes fear and shame, and creates situations of inauthenticity in daily life. In short, it is a stressful existence. Leticia, like most workers, attempts to keep her employment a secret, even

---

[8]As Maria Patricia Fernández-Kelly notes in her study of maquiladoras in Ciudad Juárez, "factory work offers wages and benefits that keep women only a step removed from the circumstances that can lead to prostitution" (1983:143).

from those closest to her. This requires a great deal of effort and can generate an enormous amount of anxiety and alienation.

Lying to family members who live in another city, state, or even country can be difficult for sex workers, but even more difficult is lying to the children who live with them. Many women find that as children grow older they become more curious, and sometimes, even suspicious. As Leticia's children grew older they often asked her what she did for work and even requested that she take them with her, as she used to when she held a job as a seamstress back in Puebla. Initially, she told them she worked as a waitress, a cook, and sometimes as a maid. But Leticia chose to tell her children when she felt they were old enough to understand. As she explains it, "I could not bear any longer what I carried inside from lying to them and so when I saw that she [Xímena, her eldest daughter] was getting older and was already in her second year of secondary school, I told her I wanted to talk with her." Leticia knew that her daughter already probably had some idea of what prostitution was from watching movies, *telenovelas*, and dramatic television programs such as *Casos de la Vida Real*, a show that reenacts real life stories of emotional drama.

Though fearful she would be rejected by her children, Leticia felt the need to tell. She recounts the event:

> So, I said to her, "Listen, Xímena, I want to talk with you. What would you do if you were told that your mama is a woman of the street or that your mama works in a place that is not decent—that is indecent?" She just sat there looking at me and said to me, "Look, Mami, if it is in order to raise us, I will defend you. Even if they were to say you are the worst of women, to me you are the best of mamas because for me and my sister you are Papa and Mama at the same time." I told her "Thank you" and I felt like she didn't disappoint me because I thought there are many children that reject their mamas when they find out they work in this. And I feel they shouldn't reject them but, on the contrary, they should support them and love them more because even though here we are filled with sex with men, we don't do it with pleasure. It's because they are paying you a certain sum that you endure it.

Leticia's story illustrates the complex interactions between stigma, morality, familial love and responsibility. Many Zona women work as prostitutes in order to support children and extended families, but do so at the risk of losing the emotional support and respect of those very people they support financially.

Since my time in the field, Leticia has left the ambiente. She also has a new partner, a man she began dating while she was still working in the Zona. Even though her partner had wished that Leticia could stay home rather than work in the ambiente, his meager salary did not allow him to support Leticia and her children. Once she had saved enough money she was able to leave the Zona and open a small stand selling chicken in downtown Tuxtla, where she is often accompanied by her daughters when they are not in school. The earnings are far less than in the Zona (and indeed some Zona women call her foolish and mock her for leaving the Zona to become a street vendor—a decidedly glamourless and far less lucrative job), but Leticia is happy with her decision.

Of her work in the ambiente, she says, "If I had the opportunity to speak to people I would ask them not to devalue us, because we are people too and we have dignity and feelings and if we do it [sex work], we do this work because of necessity, to raise our families."

Lorena

> Oh, I have had a thousand uses—I worked in fishing, I worked sowing melon in the *campo*, I worked harvesting, cutting melon, lime, mango. I worked packing, carrying, shipping, picking, and [was a] personnel manager. My strength has always been brute force; before, I had a good job in a PEMEX (Mexico's national oil company) store in Mexico City—I was a security guard. I was a bodyguard. My value was in carrying heavy things, before I had my son. The moment they gave me the caesarean, I lost half my life. I couldn't lift the same way, keep up the same rhythm that I had previously. I was practically left, as they say here, an invalid.

Lorena is a 31-year-old woman born and raised in Chiapas, though at times she may say she is Guatemalan:

> You know why I am Guatemalan? Because if many people were to know our real history they would know why I say I am Guatemalan. I am Guatemalan because of the simple fact that before, the state of Chiapas was part of Guatemala. Mexico bought it. And for some piece of paper that says we are Mexicans, because of this we are Mexicans. But these details aren't known by many people, only by a person who in reality is prepared—that has been to school, has studied history.

Unlike the majority of Zona workers, Lorena *has* been to school and *has* studied history, along with secretarial studies and three years of university, where she studied psychology. Lorena finds the field of psychology interesting and useful in daily life. She says her studies were not about earning money but rather a way for her to understand both herself and others, to "give respect to others and see your own value too."

But for work, Lorena, a large and imposing woman, has always used her body. She became a sex worker over three years ago, following the complicated birth of her son, which left her weakened, and during a difficult period with her girlfriend, who had been working in the sex industry for over a decade.[9] Before entering the ambiente, Lorena had remained at home, caring for her own child and the two children of her partner. But relying upon her lover for financial support was difficult for the independent Lorena, and it made her feel, she says, like a *padrotito* (a little pimp). Furthermore, rumors had reached Lorena that her lover was romantically involved with another Zona woman;

---

[9]A number of lesbian women currently work the zone. Though their work involves intercourse with men, it is linked neither to sexual desire nor sexual orientation.

her partner would often arrive home drunk and belligerent. Lorena decided to take control of her crumbling home life by becoming a sex worker herself:

> So, I said to her, "Know what? From here on in, I'm no longer going to be the fool. You stay home and I'll go to work. I'll show you what it is to work." And so, she returned to the house and I began to work in this.

There are elements of the work that Lorena does not like, such as having sex with clients. Unlike some women, who say they become used to the work, Lorena says that she has not become accustomed to it, and that when she works "I do it thinking of the money. I close my eyes and I don't give a damn if he is nice, if he is handsome. I close my eyes and I am mentally blocking it out so that my eyes don't record the image in my brain."

Politically savvy and well-spoken, Lorena often speaks out on the behalf of other workers, though she rejects any leadership role at work, saying "I don't want to be the representative of the Zona." Despite this claim, Lorena is often one of the first workers to be involved in discussions of work issues with landlords or administrators, who describe her as "difficult." Lorena decries the high rents paid by workers to private landlords who own the *modulos* (barracks-style buildings in which the women work).[10] "The price of gas goes up, our rent goes up five pesos." She also decries the ways in which they try to quell dissent by "running out" women who protest, particularly Central American workers whose precarious immigrant status makes them more vulnerable to exploitation.

She is concerned about the elements of control and exploitation present in the Zona: domineering police, exploitative landlords, an administrative and medical staff that judges and disciplines workers: "They call this place a tolerance zone? What do you think tolerance means? For me tolerance means to put up with a lot and to permit a lot. But here they permit nothing."

Greatly disturbed by working conditions and the lack of organization among Zona workers, Lorena says:

> One could say that the tolerance zone is one of the cheapest places there could be in the Mexican Republic. Yes, Tuxtla Gutiérrez and its tolerance zone is one of the cheapest places there is. Not Oaxaca. Not Mexico City. Minimum, minimum, minimum. A woman works a normal service for 50, 80 pesos minimum. And here 20, 15 sometimes. A woman who is elderly will charge you 10. That is a lack of organization, a lack of communication. I would like to organize, but that is to complicate matters for no reason. A group came here to speak to us, talked to us

---

[10]Zona workers pay up to 1000 pesos a month in rent to the private landlords. The rooms are dark and small (they fit a twin bed and perhaps a dresser or small nightstand). There are no cooking facilities, though they do have a private bathroom. Many workers must live in the Zona as they cannot afford to pay additional rent for an apartment or room in the city center. For 1000 pesos a month one could rent a two-bedroom house in a middle-class neighborhood with its own private security guard.

about SEMEPO, the union of, one could say, "*chicas elegantes*" throughout the republic in the federal district. They already have a syndicate, everything. They are better organized. So they tried to organize us too, but it was like I wanted to cross the river swimming without a life jacket or anything. Just me alone. Nobody got involved to support it.

Of the Poblanas, she said, "All that interests them is money. They aren't interested in well-being, that one day they are going to be old women." And though there were some Central American workers interested in organizing and taking a trip to Mexico City for a conference, their immigrant status prevented them from doing so. Furthermore she says,

> The landlord will squash you, the city will squash you, half the world will squash you in order to put out the blaze you want to ignite. This is why I say it is like complicating matters for no reason.

Despite the difficulties of the work, Lorena says she is for the moment at peace: she feels physically secure at work due to the presence of the police and the medical service; she is financially secure, able to support not only herself, but her children, her sister's children, and her mother. Furthermore, she appreciates the independence of sex work: ". . . you don't have a yoke around your neck, nobody telling you get up, get to work, do this, do that. It is up to you if you work or not and how you are going to pay your debts."

As for the stigma, she works to respect herself and demands that same respect from others:

> I have said to my clients, from this door to there [the rear wall of her room] you can take down my pants as you wish, because that is what I do. But outside, respect me. I ask that they respect me so that I can respect them. If I am out with my daughter, my sister, my people, respect me. That I will always guard—that I ask for respect. Anything can be in this life, with knowing and having a bit of respect for oneself in order to have respect for others.

Liliana

Liliana and I were slowly climbing the stairs inside the Statue of Liberty, crowded in along with hundreds of other tourists. As we climbed higher, the steps narrowed to a small, single-file staircase that spiraled up and up and up, seemingly endless though we knew we would eventually reach the crown and the tiny windows that would offer us a complete view of lower Manhattan. Though we were all there by choice, the other pilgrims surrounding us moaned and complained about the trek. One woman huffed about the physical effort required of her. Others cast anxious looks at their watches, worrying aloud about missing the Broadway show for which they had tickets. A few gave up shortly after beginning, and squeezed their way back down the steps, against the throngs pushing upward. One guide book to New York City describes the journey of 154 steps as "excruciating."

Amidst the complaining crowds, Liliana, a former prostitute from El Salvador who worked in the Galáctica, recounted the story of how she came to the United States to find work. She, along with nearly 30 others, had paid a *pollero* to help them cross Mexico's northern border into the United States. Of the journey, Liliana, who has experienced a great deal of suffering in her 31 years, said, "Never, Patty, never have I suffered like that." The group walked without pause for two and a half days. On the first day Liliana consumed all the water she had brought. By the second day, her dry lips began to crack open, spilling blood down her chin. Days were unbearably hot and nights painfully cold. Liliana's shoes were not made for such a journey and one by one her toenails began to fall off. She wanted to stop, but she was encouraged to continue by other Salvadorans who were traveling alongside her. She was the only woman among them. She wished that the *migra* would come along and send her back. A few elderly people unable to continue were left behind, alone. Liliana eventually made it to Los Angeles, but decided to travel to New Jersey to settle in a Latino immigrant community where she had an acquaintance—a woman who was the niece of her former landlady in the Galáctica.

Liliana came to the United States from El Salvador by way of Chiapas. In urban El Salvador she lived in a small room with her son and the father of her child, whom she eventually left after a violent argument about his infidelity. She also left, she says "because of the poverty I was living in. I wanted to have my own things, so that I would be able to say, 'This is mine.' But when I left my house, I thought there were jobs that paid well here [in Mexico]."

As Galáctica workers are a floating population, it is impossible to cite fixed statistics, but at any given time, anywhere from 30 to 60 percent of the worker population may be foreign-born—specifically, Central American. The Reglamento de la Zona de Tolerancia (Regulations of the Tolerance Zone), as well as Mexican law, states that registered prostitutes working in regulated zones must be Mexican citizens. However, this law is only sporadically enforced, depending on location, practices of corruption, and current public opinion regarding undocumented immigrants.

Although Chiapas is one of Mexico's poorest states, for many Central Americans, its urban centers are places of hope where they can settle and achieve a relative degree of economic stability, or a place to stop and earn money for their trip to the United States. Foreign Zona workers come primarily from Guatemala, El Salvador, and Honduras, countries with histories of warfare, extreme poverty, or in the case of Honduras, disasters like Hurricane Mitch, which devastated the country. Throughout much of Mexico, and in particular Chiapas, which shares a border with Guatemala, there is a great emphasis on detention and deportation of undocumented migrants. Under pressure from the United States, the Mexican National Migration Institute (INM) works to decrease the migration of Central Americans, stopping many hopeful migrants long before they ever reach the northern border.[11]

In Chiapas, authorities have initiated programs such as Operation Seal the Southern Border to quell this migration and have increased the presence of INM officials and operations in border towns and cities. Undocumented Central Americans are seen as both a source of and victims of delinquency in the state, particularly in the south. Newspapers are replete with stories of detainees carrying drugs, robbing citizenry, and contributing to vice, in particular prostitution and the spread of AIDS.[12] So synonymous have delinquency and illegal migration become that the two are often paired together in newspaper articles, though the described incidents may be completely unrelated. Yet this population is also vulnerable to abuses by delinquents, suffering rapes, robberies, and abuses at the hands of both polleros and corrupt migration officials.

Liliana first came to Chiapas with her infant son at the invitation of a woman she had met in El Salvador. The woman told Liliana that she had many businesses in Mexico—stores, clothing boutiques, a restaurant. Liliana packed a bit of clothing, some milk and sugar, and found herself crossing borders with five other girls, some as young as 14. When they arrived at Mexico's southern border they came upon a manned migration checkpoint. She was told by those transporting her to get out of the vehicle and to run. Unable to move quickly with her baby in her arms, she hid herself in bushes, covering the child's mouth with her hand so that his cries would not give them away. After some time, she began to walk, crossing the border into Chiapas.

Liliana settled in southeastern Chiapas where she found work as a servant. During this time, she encountered the woman who had transported her to the Chiapas border. The woman charged that Liliana still owed her for the transportation and forced her to work in a club in Tapachula by separating her from her son. Of this time, Liliana said, "I had only had one man in my entire life, how was I going to go with others? But that señora said to me, 'If you don't want to come out of your room, girl, you'll lose your son—I'll give him away to who knows who because you don't want to work for him.' And so I went to work. They put makeup on me. Never before had I worn makeup."

While in the bar Liliana met a man who saw she was upset. She told him her story and the man, an INM official, demanded that the woman let Liliana and her son go or he would call the police and put a *demanda* (legal action) against the woman. Liliana left the bar with her son and returned to work as a servant.

Soon after, while in the market, Liliana happened upon another girl with whom she had made the journey from El Salvador and who had also escaped

---

[11]According to one newspaper account, each month nearly 10,000 undocumented Central Americans cross Mexico's southern border, fleeing extreme poverty.

[12]The state attorney general also targets undocumented migrants as part of their "Zero Tolerance Against Delinquency Program."

from the señora. The girl said to her, "Listen Liliana, why are you working here as a servant? The 50 pesos you earn here in a month you can earn in a day." And so Liliana took her son and went to Tuxtla to work in El Cocal, the city's first (unofficial) Zona, and later in the Galáctica. When her son became old enough to "understand things," Liliana brought him back to El Salvador to live with her mother and brother. She did not want him to be in the ambiente. Furthermore, she had begun to drink heavily and did not wish for her son to see her in such a state. She told her family that she worked selling clothing—the job she initially thought she would get when leaving El Salvador.

Liliana worked in the Galáctica for five years; she says that despite the lowering of her self-esteem, troublesome and perverse clients, physical risk, increased materialism, and gossip, hypocrisy, and a lack of solidarity among workers, she got used to the work.

> You get used to it, but in the end, you always know that it is bad. That this, this isn't good. It's badly seen by society and all that. It is difficult, because, well, one time, I saw an interview with Gloria Treví [a controversial singer] and Verónica Castro [a television personality] where Verónica Castro said to Gloria Treví, "What do you think of prostitution?" and Gloria Treví says to her, "Well, I tell you that I understand they are mothers, they are admirable because they will even sell their bodies to take care of their children." And Verónica says, "I would never do it, how would I plant myself on some street corner? Even if I were offered a gold mine, I wouldn't do it, go to bed." And she [Gloria Treví] says to her, "Because you were born with silk diapers and you had everything and it was easy. But it is not easy to put yourself in another person's place."

Liliana used her earnings from the Galáctica to support her mother, brother, and her son in El Salvador. She funded an expensive operation for her mother and even took her son to Cancún for a recent trip. She smiled as she showed off the photos of herself and a teenage boy with their arms around each other standing in front of Planet Hollywood–Cancún smiling. "He told me it was the best present I ever gave him." Liliana hopes that her son will go to school and one day be a professional.

Of her time in the ambiente, she says, "People who have everything cannot imagine what I have to do to earn money. Sometimes I don't understand it either . . ."

Today Liliana lives in a community of Latin American immigrants in New Jersey, where she works in a fast-food restaurant.[13] Unlike many Galáctica

---

[13]In his wonderful study of the fast food industry in the United States, Eric Schlosser examines the ways in which recent immigrants, along with the elderly and disabled, have replaced teenagers as the bulk of the fast-food restaurant workforce. He asserts that more than one-third of all fast-food workers do not speak English and that many "know only the names of the items on the menu; they speak 'McDonald's English'" (2001:70–71).

workers who hope to leave the ambiente, but cannot find a way out, Liliana was fiercely determined to make her way to the United States in order to find better work and a better life for herself and her family. She is enrolled in English classes and hopes to one day bring her son and mother to live with her.

Afterword

Writing of poor tenant farmers in the American South in the 1930s, James Agee suggests that they "are cheated of their potentials," such things being "the gifts or thefts of economic privilege" (1939:279). He writes:

> I believe that every human being is potentially capable, within his "limits," of fully "realizing" his potentialities; that this, his being cheated and choked of it, is infinitely the ghastliest, commonest, and most inclusive of all the crimes of which the human world can accuse itself. . . .

The stories of Ramona, Leticia, Lorena, and Liliana provide a look into the lives of women workers made invisible as they are "cheated and choked" of their potentials by an economic system that exploits, a construction of gender that oppresses, and a moral order that demonizes. Yet their stories also offer insights into the faith, defiance, and dignity that endure in the midst of such extraordinarily constraining circumstances.

The lives of women in the ambiente are filled with deep contradictions: sex work offers them good money but is accompanied by great emotional and physical risk. Through sex work they gain some degree of personal and financial independence, but they still live within a larger framework of dependency and inequality. Defined as both essential and expendable by society, they struggle not to internalize the stigma associated with prostitution while demanding respect and asserting their value as human beings.

Ultimately, their stories show that sex work can neither be condemned as wholly oppressive nor liberating, as feminist theorists on either side of a highly polarized debate would assert. Rather, the work, performed within a broader system of unequal power relations, and enveloped by the terrible burden of stigma, contains within it a complex blend of both exploitation and freedom. Entering sex work, women cross both geographic and moral borders, doing work that is, in Liliana's words, beyond the imaginations of most people. This work sometimes allows women a small degree of economic stability that by virtue of their class, education, and gender would normally be unavailable to them. Magda, Ramona, Leticia, Lorena, Liliana, and the scores of other women laboring in the Zona Galáctica, do work that is beyond the imagination in an effort to live lives that should not be, but for many women, often are, beyond the imagination. As Magda said:

I have what I have from nothing. I made myself from nothing. Never did I think I would have a cassette player, or an air conditioner of two horsepower, or three pieces of property, thanks to God. I never imagined this . . .

Note:

This paper was written with the support of the American Association of University Women.

7

Letter from
a Peace Camp

HEATHER SINCLAIR

In the fall of 1996, I left for Chiapas to spend six months there as a human-rights observer. Like many others in the United States and elsewhere, I had been inspired by news of the Zapatistas' struggle and vision. The list of demands coming out of indigenous communities in Chiapas in the face of NAFTA mirrored those we were calling for in our own local struggle for justice for sweatshop workers in El Paso, Texas. Therefore, when the call came from Bishop Ruíz and the communities for volunteer human-rights observers, I responded.

Volunteer observers were to provide a presence in the Zapatista communities that had been attacked by the Mexican Army in February 1995. During this military offensive, the army permanently occupied some communities while destroying others, home by home. Leaders were arrested and some were tortured. Zapatista communities requested peace camps, the name given to this presence of outside observers, to serve as both a witness and deterrent to military abuses. Thousands of people from throughout the world have responded to the call. In Mexico, the peace camps were coordinated through the Catholic Diocese's Center for Human Rights Fray Bartolomé de Las Casas and other nongovernmental organizations (NGOs). Several international NGOs channeled volunteers into the camps. I went through Global Exchange, a U.S.–based human-rights organization that works to build international partnerships and promote global awareness of social justice.

During the time of my stay, tensions in the region were growing. Despite the signing of the San Andres Accords in February 1996, military and police persecution of indigenous communities was increasing. In the Northern Zone of Chiapas, PRI-affiliated paramilitary groups acted with impunity, burning homes and killing opposition members. In November, violence toward NGOs working for peace in Chiapas erupted. Offices in San Cristóbal were vandalized and firebombed, a worker and his family were abducted, and leaders of various NGOs received death threats. Low-intensity warfare has clearly been the Mexican government's strategy of choice.

While living in a peace camp, I wrote letters home to share some of my impressions of life in the communities where I lived. The following letter describes the death of Margarita, a young woman I had come to know while living in *La Alianza,* the pseudonym of a Tzeltal community.

It is important to note, as I have recently learned, that suicide by the ingestion of pesticides in Chiapas is not a new development but rather had been an all too common occurrence in the region since before the conflict began (Tinoco, et al. 1993). It is not clear whether the problem is growing as a result of militarization—a topic worthy of study.

I also want to mention that the rumors about why Margarita chose to take her life grew in the months following her death. Though some said conflicts arose because she had a boyfriend from the priista (PRI supporters) side of the community, close friends of hers believed she was upset by a male relative's sexual advances.

I don't believe I will ever know what was going on in Margarita's head that morning and, looking back now, I don't believe I was meant to. What I can state is that the work of international solidarity took on a very human and horrifying face for me that day. It became a much greater responsibility than I had envisioned it to be before. I returned home feeling overwhelmed and much humbled. I enrolled in a midwifery program and now work as a health educator and midwife with Mexican women living in the US–Mexico border region. And many of the questions remain . . .

January 17, 1997
Dear Family and Friends,
    More than a month has passed since I last wrote and I have a lot to share with you . . .
    I was sent by Fray Bartolomé Human Rights Center to La Alianza, a Tzeltal community in Las Cañadas [or canyons of the Lacandon rain forest]. The community is divided: one-third Zapatistas and two-thirds priistas (government supporters). Peace campers live among and have contact only with the Zapatistas. The Zapatista side of La Alianza lives on the slope leading down to the river; across the river live the priistas.
    The peace camp—a kitchen and a small bedroom—stands at the top of the slope next to the community school. They are simple one-room structures with dirt floors, but it is a happy place. People stop by throughout the day to say hello, and if they aren't too busy, or it is Sunday, to chat awhile. During the afternoon I occasionally visit with some of the women, helping them grind corn for tortillas or washing clothes in the river. Although most women speak little Spanish, we have some good talks. Once I went out into the fields to pick beans.
    When it gets dark around 6 P.M., and if there is no community meeting of which there are many, some people come by to play cards (I taught them Spoons which is their current favorite), backgammon, or chess. As we play, they teach me Tzeltal and I have learned a good bit. Everyday I look forward to this time—there's little better in life than sitting around a crowded kitchen table in candlelight talking, joking, laughing, playing. Most nights it is the young people of the community who come, but occasionally the men stop by and tell us about their history, what

the community suffered in 1995 when the Mexican Army arrived in the Cañadas and occupied the region. They told us how the soldiers beat the men, severely torturing one, ransacked their homes, stole livestock, and harassed those who chose to stay in the village. In La Alianza, as in many other villages, the men fled into the mountains where they lived for months while the women and children stayed. Elsewhere, whole communities fled, children and the elderly included.

Weekday mornings I am with the children in the school. On average, eight come. They haven't had a teacher since 1994, which makes for a difficult situation. They need a teacher from among their own who can teach them in their own language and in a way that works within their culture. But they do not have this person and so the community asks that the peace camp volunteers work with the children. This is hard on them because we volunteers are only there for two to four weeks, each of us having ideas and teaching methods different from the one before. And of course there are the language and cultural differences, the lack of resources, etc. And yet some good is done—most of the children now know basic addition and subtraction, the alphabet, and they participate in group activities.

Nevertheless, the children's future, which is the future of the communities and their struggle, is worrisome. Living under the specter of war affects people in many ways that are not so obvious. You cannot plan well for the long term because tomorrow you may be attacked. You have to dedicate all your energies and resources to that possibility and meanwhile all else must be put to the side.

Living with such tension, uncertainty, and fear, as well as with a community division that before 1994 was not so marked, has terrible psychological and emotional consequences as well. The morning of December 28th, two weeks into my stay in the community, Margarita, a 16-year-old girl, drank poison and died, less than an hour after her family found her sick.

When the family found Margarita, they came and took me to her. The nearest clinic was hours away. She was already very sick. At first no one knew why—she hadn't said anything to anyone. Together with her father, a small, older man, I held her up, talking to her. Her mother, sisters, and others who had gathered stood outside her bedroom door, scared and crying, some screaming. One of her brothers had smelled the poison on her earlier. It was an organophosphate pesticide called Asuntol—a liquid applied to horses to keep bugs away. When I saw the opened bottle, I realized there wasn't much hope. By this time all her family was there, her older brothers having rushed in from the fields. Some now had gone into the room to be with her.

Her sisters took me to her mother who had collapsed in the kitchen. I was with her when Margarita died and stayed by her side throughout the day and night. She had a heart condition, and her children feared she would die as well.

Margarita was the youngest of nine children, and like the youngest sister in my family, the most outgoing, impulsive, and bubbly of the bunch. Her brother Manuel is the community's leader, so she was often at the center of the community's activities.

The evening before her death, she visited me in the peace camp. We stood outside quietly together as the sun was going down. At one point she sighed and I asked her jokingly, "Aya lekol?" (Do you have a sweetheart?) Relationships are the foremost topic of lighthearted conversations here. It is one of the first questions asked when you arrive, after what are the names of your mother and father.

Margarita giggled, covering her mouth with her shawl, at first denying having one. Then she whispered, "I'll tell you the night before you leave."

As we walked up to the camp's kitchen where other young people had begun to gather, she asked me, "Why do you get sad sometimes?"

I asked her why she thought I was sad.

"Sometimes I see you sitting alone at the kitchen table like this," and she crossed her arms in front of her and set her chin down on top of them.

I denied to her that I was sad sometimes, which of course was not true, and turned the conversation in another direction. Looking back now with regrets, I wonder if she asked that because she wanted to talk about what she was feeling.

When we got to the kitchen, she and I sat outside on a bench as the others played games inside. I had asked Margarita to show me the community's Bible to read the lesson from that Sunday, which was from St. Luke. (I went to the mass but it was in Tzeltal, of course.) With a flashlight we read it together, first in Spanish, then in Tzeltal with Margarita correcting my pronunciation. She said that she liked to read the Bible in Tzeltal and had, in fact, read it up to the first chapters of St. Luke. (It is with the Bible that most learn how to read in their native language.) When we were done she said good night to everyone, saying she had work to do, and headed down the hill to her home.

From what I was told later, Margarita had an argument later that night with her mother. Her mother had gotten angry with her for having danced at the Christmas Eve party with a young man who had come over from the priista side. Relationships that crossed the community division, permitted until recently, are now strongly prohibited. The next morning Margarita took the poison and died.

Apparently this is at least the third suicide of a young person in the region within the last year. One of the others is similar—a young Zapatista man who was not given permission to marry a woman from the priista side. He drank the same poison Margarita drank.

After Margarita's death, her family and community, as well as we volunteers, have been struggling to understand why this happened. To find some sense in it. How do you see it? Sadly, some people in the community blame the mother for coming down too hard on her children.

Here in San Cristóbal I have been talking about this with some organizations and the church, asking that they respond in some way to the series of suicides in the region. Chi'iltak, a women's organization and member of CONPAZ, has given me letters of sympathy and support to take to the family, especially the mother. Bishop Ruíz will give me a letter and gift of a rosary today as well: this, I know, will bring the family great comfort.

In the end though, what I can do is little. The fact is I don't come from their world, don't know how in their culture they deal with such grief, pain, and mystery. I can only be present with them.

For me, Margarita's death had been a very painful and challenging experience. It has been good to be able to give some comfort to her family, something that I know can mean a lot in a time of pain. It has brought up new questions for me, for which I was not lacking in the first place, but for which I could be grateful. Ha.

Well that's that. Today I will be buying things to take back to the community—books for the recently born community library, school supplies, and a typewriter. I miss you all. . . .

II
Religious Change
and Women's Empowerment

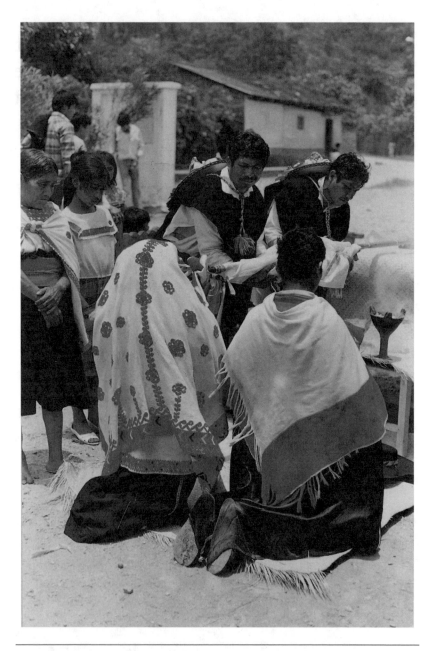

Fiesta leaders, María Arias Pérez and Manuel Pérez Cura, being blessed at the Feast of Saint Peter, San Pedro Chenalhó. Photo by Christine Eber, 1987.

Funeral Procession after massacre at Acteal, San Pedro Chenalhó. Photo by Luis Reyna, December 25, 1997.

8
Overview

CHRISTINE KOVIC
CHRISTINE EBER

A spiritual thread weaves throughout the story of the struggle for autonomy, human rights, and women's rights in Chiapas. Beginning in the 1700s, indigenous people initiated several revitalization movements that were religious in character. Women played important roles in these movements, some of which incorporated armed uprisings. Along with their kinsmen, women challenged the hypocrisy of the colonists who were not acting according to the Christian faith that they were preaching. For example, in 1712 in the Tzeltal community of Cancuc, 13-year-old María de Candelaria reported that the Virgin Mary appeared to her. When Ladino priests refused to recognize the appearance of the Virgin, a revolt ensued with indigenous leaders pronouncing that Saint Peter, the Virgin Mary, and Jesus had called them to liberate themselves from Ladino control (Rosenbaum 1993). In this and other rebellions and in daily life, indigenous people creatively link their beliefs about Mayan deities with their understandings of Catholicism. In contemporary prayer and dream accounts, they often speak of female spiritual beings interchangeably as Moon (an ancient Maya deity) and the Virgin Mary, the mother of Jesus Christ (Eber 2000 [1995]: 115). The prayer by Margarita Pérez in this part (Chapter 13) illustrates the eloquent ritual language that iloletik (traditional healers) use to seek the aid of God and the saints to restore people to health. Throughout her prayer, Pérez refers to God, Father, Lord, and Ladino as "nichimal/ flowery." Nichimal reflects the belief that people are responsible to keep the universe in flower. They do so by decorating caves, crosses, and other sacred places with flowers. Women weavers fulfill their obligation through the many designs depicting fecundity and beauty that they weave into garments and cloths to wrap tortillas (Morris 1987). Weaving and prayer remain powerful forms of communication between people and spiritual beings in highland Chiapas. They draw attention to the life of the spirit. To Mayan peoples—including those who have converted to various Protestant churches—changes of the spirit go hand in hand with material changes.

There is no word in the Mayan languages of Chiapas for a separate sphere of experience called "religion." "Having a religion" did not become a popular conception until the mid-1900s when Protestant missionaries began to live in indigenous communities and convert people to their faiths. Prior to this period, most people in Chiapas practiced a folk Catholicism (often referred to as traditionalism) focused around prayer, communal cargos, saints' fiestas, and pilgrimages to places of sacred significance to both the Catholic and Mayan foremothers and fathers.

By the 1970s and '80s, thousands of people, mestizo and indigenous, had become active participants in Protestant churches, as well as in the Word of God, the new project of the Catholic Church. In the 1970s, the Catholic Diocese of San Cristóbal de Las Casas under the leadership of then Bishop Samuel Ruíz Garcia, committed itself to construct a church that worked with and for the poor. Bishop Ruíz and pastoral agents were profoundly influenced by liberation theology and the historic meetings of the Second Vatican Council (1962–65) and the Conference of Latin American Bishops in Medellín, Columbia (1968). As they witnessed the poverty and oppression of daily life in rural communities, the bishop, priests, and nuns changed their approach to evangelization. They moved from a top-down model of disseminating information on salvation and prayer to a participatory model that placed the concerns of the poor at the center of their work. Training indigenous catechists to take on important social roles in their communities that extend beyond preparing people to receive sacraments was an important move in respecting the ability of communities to create their own path to liberation.[1] Indigenous participants in this diocesan project use the term the Word of God to refer not only to their reading the Bible, but also to their participation in different activities of pastoral work. Adherents to the Word of God participate directly in the pastoral projects of the diocese, read the Bible, and partake in the formal sacraments of the Catholic Church, at the same time as they continue many of the practices associated with their ancestors (Kovic 2003).

Today in Chiapas indigenous and mestiza women are active participants in the diocese as catechists, prayer leaders, and coordinators of small reflection groups, even though men occupy the majority of leadership roles in the church. For indigenous women, conversion to Word of God Catholicism embodies a number of changes in their daily lives. Male and female converts reject the use of alcohol, linking it to domestic violence, illness, and the "waste" of money as men spend precious cash on alcohol rather than on food or other necessities (Eber 2000 [1995]; Kovic 2001). In addition, Catholic men and women have developed a discourse that strongly criticizes domestic violence and men's abandonment of wives and children.

The chapters in this part address the diverse ways that religion shapes women's lives. The authors address Catholics (Eber, Kovic, and Gil) and Protestants (Robledo and Rostas). The traditional prayer by Margarita Pérez reflects

---

[1]See Ruth Chojnacki 1999 for a discussion of indigenous catechists in highland Chiapas.

influences of both traditionalism and Catholicism. In fact, all the chapters show how women incorporate aspects of new religious beliefs and practices into the ones they previously followed. For the most part, the chapters focus on the experiences of indigenous women in rural communities, yet Eber and Kovic also describe the experiences of woman in urban areas. Several chapters present the words of Protestant and Catholic women struggling on the basis of Christian values for a better life for themselves and future generations.

The part opens with a chapter by Christine Eber comparing the experiences of two Catholic women, one an indigenous woman from San Pedro Chenalhó and the other a Coleta (the term for descendents of the colonists in San Cristóbal de Las Casas). Her portrait of Antonia, a Zapatista supporter, illustrates how participating in the Word of God in the 1980s enhanced Antonia's critical thinking skills and deepened her faith in God. Eber's sympathetic portrait of Gabriela, the Coleta, helps explain the widespread antagonism among Ladinos in Chiapas to the diocesan project. Eber explores the capacity of Antonia and Gabriela to understand people of different social positions and suggests that this capacity facilitates alliances that could help bridge the conflicts and contradictions in Chiapas.

Christine Kovic's and Pilar Gil's chapters (10 and 12, respectively) treat women's participation in the Catholic Church demonstrating the ways that women have been empowered by their participation. In light of the Catholic Church's patriarchal character and historic role in repressing indigenous peoples (particularly in the colonial period), it may appear contradictory to link women's empowerment to Catholicism. Yet, the Catholic Church, like other institutions, has been a site for resistance as well as repression. In many ways, indigenous peoples participate in the church on their own terms, appropriating elements that are relevant to their lives. In the Catholic Diocese of San Cristóbal, thousands of women participate in local women's groups where they critique the unequal relationships between men and women at the household level. In these groups, women also examine the ways their oppression stems from structural forces of racism, the legal and political system, and the implementation of neoliberal economic reforms. As Gil argues, these groups blend elements of a survival movement (in which members work to improve the economic well-being of their families and communities) and a women's rights movement (in which members discuss gender oppression). Since 1992 these local Catholic women's groups have been formally linked through the Coordinación Diocesana de Mujeres (Diocesan Coordination of Women, commonly referred to as CODIMUJ).

Today the Women, the song depicted in Chapter 11, exemplifies songs written and sung by Catholic women in meetings of CODIMUJ. The song uses passages from the Bible to assert the rightful equality between men and women. At the same time, the words of the song reaffirm the many ways that women struggle to change their situation—"to bring down the powerful and lift up the lowly."

Perez's prayer in Chapter 13 exemplifies the power of sacred language in the form of prayer to heal and empower a woman. In this case Pérez prays to help a woman with an alcohol and drug problem. At the same time as she assists other women and men in and outside of her community to become healed and empowered, Pérez receives status and respect for the important service she provides to her community.

The chapters in this part on women converts to Protestantism correct a misconception that the religion represents a conservative force supporting traditional gender roles. The authors show how Protestant women participate in dramatic shifts in their households and communities as a result of becoming involved in a church community. For example, Protestant women share with Catholic women a strong critique of alcohol abuse, domestic violence, and abandonment.

According to government census data, the percentage of Protestants has increased dramatically in Chiapas, from less than 5 percent of the population in 1970 to over 21 percent in 2000, as compared to well under 10 percent for Mexico as a whole. The most important churches include Adventists, Baptists, Evangelicals, Pentecostals, and Presbyterians. The latter denomination has the largest membership. Although Protestant churches can be found throughout Chiapas, indigenous townships in the Lacandon rain forest, the Northern Zone, and the Highlands show the highest conversion rates.

Scholars studying Protestant conversion in Chiapas and other parts of Latin America note how women find in Protestantism ways to meet their needs and resolve pressing problems. For example, in their study of religion and sexuality, Walda Barrios and Leticia Pons (1995) found that Tzotzil women living in San Cristóbal emphasize that their relationships with their spouses improve after conversion to Protestantism. Gabriela Robledo's chapter (14) examines changes in household dynamics following conversion to Pentecostalism in the township of Teopisca. She finds that female-headed households are more common among Protestants than Catholics, and that Protestant women find a supportive network in their local congregations. In addition, she notes that Pentecostal women place great importance on rejecting alcohol that commonly accompanies conversion. Overall, Protestant women speak of the value of their new religion in helping them to resist alcoholism, illness, violence, and extreme poverty. In Chapter 15 on Tzeltales of Tenejapa, Susanna Rostas argues that Protestantism empowers women by giving them a new arena to express themselves and to share their experiences with other women. Rostas points to economic development and modernity as pivotal factors influencing indigenous people to explore alternatives to traditional spiritual practices.[2] Rostas argues that changing one's religion is especially meaningful for young women because it provides new social contexts in which to develop themselves

---

[2]A number of scholars have linked religious conversion, particularly the conversion to Christianity, to political and economic changes of modernity (see for example, Hefner 1993 and Van der Veer 1995).

and to challenge gender subordination at the same time that they continue to value many traditional practices. Notwithstanding, women seldom occupy leadership roles in Protestant churches, even at the community level and economic development in Chiapas has led to far fewer opportunities for women than for men. Rostas concludes that belonging to Protestant churches in Tenejapa does not provide women a place in the male world.

The period from 1970 to the present has been characterized by dramatic social and economic changes in indigenous communities as well as by high numbers of people converting from traditional folk Catholicism to Protestantism and to the Catholicism of the Diocese of San Cristóbal. Although economic and religious changes intersect in significant ways, one need not view modernity as the cause of conversion in order to recognize that women interpret changes in their lives through the lens of new religious experiences. Through religious participation people both initiate social changes and find ways to explain changes already happening.

The chapters in Part 2 report striking commonalities in women's experiences of religious change. Most notable is the critique of alcohol. Every chapter including Today the Women (Chapter 11) refers to women's struggle to curb alcohol abuse. In addition, women in all the religions discussed in this part share a critique of domestic violence and abandonment. Overall, Catholic and Protestant churches are opening new spaces in which women can listen to each other's experiences and share moral and economic support. Both within communities and in regional associations, such as in meetings of CODIMUJ, religious affiliation enables women to discover new solidarities and bases of community that are especially meaningful to them.

While both Catholic and Protestant religions provide a framework through which women justify their rejection of alcohol, organizing around this issue is also a focal point in secular arenas. Zapatistas and their supporters reject all alcohol use, and in some cases have set up checkpoints to assure that no alcohol enters their communities (Eber 2001b). Although both Catholic and Protestant converts attribute their changing perspectives on gender relations to their newfound religion, other groups in Chiapas have rallied around gender issues. Women in Zapatista support bases are especially vocal speaking out against male dominance. The commonalities between the social agendas of Zapatistas and Protestants and Catholics draw attention to how spiritual beliefs and religious affiliation shape activities in Zapatista civilian support bases. In her Letter from a Peace Camp (Chapter 7) Heather Sinclair describes reading the Bible with a Tzeltal woman who is a Zapatista supporter. The image of members of Zapatista base communities attending religious celebrations and reading the Bible challenges the assumption that religion, particularly Christianity, is an antirevolutionary force. Indeed, for many Catholic women, participating in local Catholic groups in the 1980s was an important step on their path to more overt political activity in Zapatista support bases or in other types of political movements.

9

Living Their Faith in Troubled Times

Two Catholic Women

CHRISTINE EBER

For years only the Catholics went to San Cristóbal or Tuxtla to march. And the government didn't pay attention to us. . . . It treated us like animals, like monkeys, like flies, like flies that fill up the streets. . . .
—Antonia

Before the uprising we all had a normal relationship. I feel we had this until the church started dragging up things from 500 years ago. We all saw Indians as our brothers, as each in his half. And I think that we lived in peace.
—Gabriela

Introduction

Antonia and Gabriela stand out among the women who befriended me when I began fieldwork in highland Chiapas in 1987. In 1987 I lived in Antonia's household in San Pedro Chenalhó.[1] At that time Antonia was 28 years old, living in a rural community with her husband and three children. That year I also rented a room in the urban center of highland Chiapas, San Cristóbal de Las Casas, from Gabriela, at that time 41 years old and living alone. Although I tried to stay in Chenalhó as much as I could and eventually felt at home there, I appreciated coming to the city to talk with Gabriela about my experiences in *el campo* (the country) and to enjoy the comforts of her home.

Moving back and forth between Chenalhó and San Cristóbal in the late 1980s reminded me of images I had seen of places in the world shaped by racism. Only a few decades before I came to Chiapas, if a native person dared to walk on the high sidewalks in San Cristóbal it was acceptable for a Ladino (a

---

[1]The majority of the inhabitants of Chenalhó are indigenous people who speak Tzotzil, a Mayan language. Although Antonia speaks and writes Spanish well, most women are monolingual in Tzotzil. In 1994 Chenalhó's population was 30,680. The 1990 Mexican census gives the latest figures for conditions of life in Chenalhó in INEGI (Instituto Nacional de Estadística, Geografía e Informática). Socio-economic indicators provide a picture of a severely marginalized township. For background on the cultural traditions and history of Chenalhó see Arias 1985; Guiteras-Holmes 1961; Eber 2000 [1995] and 2001a; Moksnes 2003; and Garza Caligaris 1999.

nonindigenous person) to swat the person off into the street. Still today, indigenous people often complain of Ladinos treating them like animals, as in
Antonia's statement that opened this chapter. Before migration to San
Cristóbal began to intensify in the 1980s, the city was the land of the Ladinos
with their language and traditions. Indigenous townships, in contrast, were
lands of the ancestors where cornfields formed part of a sacred geography.

Despite divisions between Indian and Ladino societies, native men and
women have consistently worked for periods of time outside of their communities. In the first half of the twentieth century indigenous men, and sometimes
whole families, worked in debt peonage on plantations of hardwoods, coffee,
sugar, or cotton. Even now indigenous people work on plantations when work is
available. Antonia's husband, Domingo, and most of her relatives have worked
on sugar cane plantations or cattle ranches at points in their lives. Many Ladinos
have also had to leave their families to work for plantation owners, as Gabriela's
father did. For many years, he traveled back and forth between the Highlands
where his family lived and the Lowlands where he worked for a German plantation owner. Non-native women as well as men travel throughout native communities selling bread, sugar, rum, cattle, dried beef, coffee, cocoa, corn, beans, skirt
material, and other cloth and yarns (See Rus 1997). Native women also travel to
sell agricultural products, firewood, pottery, and weavings.

Except for young women from the wealthiest of San Cristóbal families,
most Ladinas have had to work very hard since childhood. The effects of economic policies on women in urban areas of Mexico since the crisis began in
the 1980s have forced them to work even harder than before to make ends
meet. Increasing numbers of women have become involved in making food,
crafts, or raising agricultural products and then selling these products on city
streets or from their doorways. Intensifying household production during periods when this becomes necessary, is a common experience for both Ladinas
and indigenous women.

Despite the influence of racism, Ladinos and native people have been involved in mutually beneficial relationships. In the process of exchanging goods
and services, many indigenous and nonindigenous people have built reciprocal,
albeit unequal, relationships as friends, trading partners, and *comadres* and *compadres*.[2] Labels like Ladino and indigenous or Indian tend to reify differences
that in certain contexts are not as important to people as other identities. When
asked to identify themselves, Ladinos often give their neighborhoods, indigenous people their townships. Antonia and her fellow townspeople identify
themselves as Pedranos, sons and daughters of St. Peter, the patron saint of San
Pedro Chenalhó.

---

[2]Women and men who serve as sponsors for children during rites-of-passage, such as
baptism, become *comadres* (co-mothers) and *compadres* (co-fathers) to the parents of
these children.

While hosting me in their different cultural worlds, Antonia and Gabriela took on similar roles in their relationship with me—sister, mother, friend, teacher, spiritual counselor. But in my mind the two women's lives were so different that I did not often think about the many ways they are alike. Exploring similarities, as well as differences, is necessary for a deeper understanding of social change in highland Chiapas and of women's lives cross-culturally. In this chapter I focus on the common bond that Antonia and Gabriela share as Catholics and the similarities and differences in their experiences of Catholicism. I also explore the continuum of feminist consciousness within the women's different expressions of their faith.

Focusing on common bonds between people in the various groups in conflict in Chiapas is also helpful to the peace process. Although peace in Chiapas requires broad, structural changes, particularly in relation to indigenous peoples' economic and political marginality, it also means changing relationships between the various groups in conflict. Antonia's and Gabriela's daily struggles to live at peace and their visions of equality and unity suggest possibilities for reconciliation.

To Love Is to Defend

In 1987 when I lived with Antonia and her family, not a day passed without my witnessing long and complex discussions about religion between family members and neighbors. Religious diversification began in the 1950s when Protestant missionaries came to highland Chiapas. Pastoral agents of the Catholic Church began to extend their work into indigenous communities in the 1960s. Before the arrival of these groups, Pedranos considered themselves Christians, but did not recognize religion as a separate institution in life.[3] Today Pedranos divide themselves into three religious groups: Traditionalists who weave the worship of Mayan and Catholic dieties into the fabric of community life; Protestants who belong to a range of denominations, the largest being Presbyterian; and followers of the Word of God, the term Pedranos give for the Preferential Option for the Poor of the Catholic Church.[4]

The spread of Protestantism concerned Traditionalists because Protestants were reluctant to serve community cargos (roles in township governance and spiritual guidance) and to contribute a small amount of money for ceremonies

---

[3]Kirisyanoetike (Christians) is Tzotzil for "people." No word exists in Tzotzil for "religion."

[4]Today Protestants make up 19.69 percent of the population over 5 years of age in Chenalhó, almost five times the national average (see Viqueira 1995). For background on the Catholic Church in Chiapas see Fazio 1994 and MacEoin 1996. For a discussion of Catholicism in Chenalhó see Moksnes 2003, Michel Chanteau 1999, and "El Sampedrano," a bulletin on Catholics in Chenalhó found on the Web page of the Diocese of San Cristóbal de Las Casas, Chiapas, http://www.laneta.apc.org/curiasc

held several times a year at sacred places in the hills to ensure good harvests and collective well-being. Traditionalists and some Word of God members argued that Protestants should donate, that masses for the hills and saints' feasts were focal points of unity and important for the survival of the township. Protestants argued that their new relationship with Jesus promised them personal salvation and released them from any reason to be involved in communal rituals to obtain salvation. The idea of personal salvation through Jesus Christ threatened Traditionalists' beliefs in nurturing a collective soul that would outlast those of individuals and be able to defend them when the day of judgment came. Rather than force the issue of Protestants' cooperating, Traditionalists left it pending. Protestants have tended to cooperate at a minimal level and Pedranos have avoided the mass expulsions that took place in San Juan Chamula (see Chapter 10).

As news spread of changes in the Catholic Church, many young indigenous men and a few women became catechists.[5] Through participating in workshops and services, these young people grew in their understanding of structural inequalities and began to confront oppression by fellow Pedranos and Ladinos. For example, in the late 1980s Catholics criticized Traditionalists who became wealthy through selling rum and or affiliating with the PRI (The Institutional Revolutionary Party, the ruling party in Mexico and Chiapas at that time). Women were particularly active in organizing to control alcohol sales (Eber 2000 [1995]: 229–231).

In the early 1980s Antonia and her husband, Domingo, were attracted to the Word of God. A few years before, Domingo had become a *predicador* (prayer leader) through a dream in which St. Peter came to him to tell him to stop drinking (Eber 2000 [1995]: 55–58). Subsequently, Antonia and Domingo attended retreats where *madres* (nuns) led them in reflecting on scriptural passages and helped them join theory with practice. The couple often sang songs with their children around the fire at night that symbolized this connection. One song used both words and gestures to convey the process of moving from ideas to action:

Ver, ver, ver (See, see see)
Pensar, pensar, pensar (Think, think, think)
Actuar, actuar, actuar (Act, act, act)
Todo en comunidad (All of this in community)
Todo en comunidad (All of this in community)

---

[5]See Ruth Chojnacki 1995, 1999; Kovic in press; and Moksnes 2003 for the experiences of young catechists. Under the direction of Bishop Samuel Ruíz (1960–2000) pastoral workers sought to learn about the cultural and social strengths of indigenous people. Important changes in the Catholic Church in Chiapas resulted from this commitment, including decentralized decision-making, broadened roles for laypeople, and women's increased participation in lay roles.

Antonia and Domingo were passionate about social change. Domingo joined a coffee cooperative, Union Majomut, through which he worked with other members to obtain fair-trade outlets for their coffee. Antonia intensified her efforts to organize women in a three-hamlet area into a weaving co-op in order to take advantage of tourism and fair-trade networks (see Eber 1999). Together the couple worked with other Word of God members to open a cooperative store in the head-town of the township where fellow Pedranos could buy staples at fair prices. In 1993 some Catholic neighbors formed a nonviolent social justice group called Sociedad Civil Las Abejas (Civil Society The Bees).[6]

The organizing work that Antonia and Domingo took on in the Word of God was on top of their subsistence farming. Complicating the increased workload were Domingo's headaches, which were so debilitating that he often spent whole days in bed. On these days Antonia was forced to send her 7- and 9-year-old sons to work in the fields.

Antonia fulfilled many roles during these years—mother, wife, daughter, sister, farmer, weaver, co-op leader, Catholic organizer, and household manager. Her compassion for Domingo's health problems complicated her growing awareness that her workload was more than double his. In meetings with other Word of God members, Antonia learned to connect her personal troubles to political issues. For example, she reflected on how her children working in the fields or at home while Ladinos'children went to school and "had birthday parties," as she put it, was a consequence of social inequality. She also considered how her having to work harder than Domingo, even when he wasn't sick, was connected to a gender ideology that privileged men. Antonia listened to the madres speak of the need for equality between men and women, of women being involved in the public affairs of their communities, not just in cooking, weaving, and child care, and how men should help their wives more with their housework. Antonia co-facilitated discussions with a man when it came her turn, and spoke up in services and public meetings when she had something to say.

During this time of consciousness-raising, Antonia developed a more assertive and independent style, which threatened some people in her community who felt that this was inappropriate for a young woman. Summing up the conflict she faced during this time, Antonia said:

> For example, if I want to put behind me something that's not so good about our traditions, the Traditionalists say, "What she's doing is no good." But if I want to act on something good in the traditions the religious ones will say, "Ah, she's still doing things according to traditions. She doesn't believe in the Word of God." This way the two ways collide.

---

[6]For indepth discussions of Sociedad Civil Las Abejas see Kovic 2003 and Moksnes 2003.

In the following years material and psychological suffering took its toll in Chenalhó. In the early 1990s when I visited I rarely heard Antonia and her children sing. During July 1993 she told me that she had stopped going up the hill on Sunday to the chapel and that she didn't pray much. Her children and co-op demands were taking all her time and energy. In addition to her increased workload, the personal risks involved in individuating herself from the other women had become too much for her. Antonia confided to me that she was pregnant with her fifth child and that she felt so desperate about finding a way to feed it that she considered giving it away. But she kept her daughter and has since had one more daughter, born January 3, 1994, three days after the Zapatista uprising.

Despite one more mouth to feed, the Zapatista uprising was a turning point for Antonia. Hope seemed to come back into her life the year following the uprising. I didn't see her in1994 but I received letters. One letter expressed how she felt when she first heard about the Zapatistas:

> I am very content that there are people called Zapatistas. Because I didn't know how we could struggle to make the government hear us. For years only the Catholics went to San Cristóbal or Tuxtla to march. And the government didn't pay any attention to us . . . It's been two years since I went to Tuxtla to march with thousands of people. We came together in Chiapa de Corzo. Walking by foot from there we arrived in Tuxtla. It was really hot and I was carrying my Zenaida [her 2-year-old daughter]. But the government only treated us like animals, like monkeys, like flies, like flies that fill up the streets . . . I don't complain to the government anymore . . . It doesn't understand anything. It treats us like animals. But it is more animal than we are . . .

In a letter that came a few months later, Antonia told me that she had been working more intensely with other Zapatistas in a support base.[7] Being a Zapatista was becoming her most important identity. She kept weaving and meeting with the weaving co-op, but she resigned her leadership position to become the president of a bakery co-op that 20 women in her Zapatista support base started. Explaining why she entered the support base Antonia said:

> I entered into the Zapatista base because there's a lot of poverty. We poor people want to unite. We don't want injustice. Before the Zapatistas we already knew that there was injustice because we had heard the word of God. It happened this way in Christ's time; there was a lot of pain then, too. The governor of that time did the same as the governor today. . . . That's how the words of the EZLN easily entered into my heart. Because God doesn't want his children to suffer. Jesus

---

[7]The Zapatista support base to which Antonia belongs is composed of about 150 men, women, and youth over 14 years of age who meet twice weekly or more often to discuss the agenda of the EZLN and its relevance for their lives. Traditionalists, Catholics, and a few Protestants belong to the base. In the summer of 1995 bases throughout Chenalhó agreed to form an autonomous township through which they would be free from the social inequality that the PRI agenda promoted.

Christ did the same thing we are doing now when he came to earth. He worked together with poor people.

As much as the Zapatista movement has come to mean to Antonia, each time I have spoken to her about being a Zapatista she has emphasized the complementary relationship between being a Zapatista and a Catholic. On one occasion in 1995 she explained:

> Well, the struggle in which we are now . . . we call it a "holy struggle" . . . for example, one can't give up the Word of God when one gets involved in the struggle. One can continue with the two, because the struggle is connected with the Word of God. When I entered in the Word of God I always talked about injustice, about the government's exploitation. We talked about this before the struggle came. That's why when the struggle arrived, well, then we compared it to when we were in the Word of God. The Word of God is like our flashlight . . . it's my flashlight to see my way, where I can walk with my struggle.

From Antonia's perspective, the Zapatista movement extends the Word of God. As she explained, although the Word of God lit the path for those seeking justice, a big log lay across the path blocking the way. This log was the Ladinos and the government. The poor people seeking justice could only go so far because they had no way to break the log that blocked them. Finally, the Zapatistas came and gave them the tools to move the log. Some of these tools were guns. When first formed, Zapatista support bases were not meant to be armed. But with the escalating violence from paramilitaries in 1997, base members began to train young men to defend their communities with arms. Antonia's eldest son took this training.[8]

Frequently, Antonia has made analogies between her fellow Zapatistas, Jesus Christ, the Virgin Mary, and the early Christians. Both Zapatista members and Las Abejas members view themselves as following in the paths of the earliest Christians who were persecuted for their beliefs.[9] They often speak of St. Peter and St. Paul, men who suffered to bring justice to the world, just as

---

[8]Pastoral agents and Bishop Ruíz do not share Antonia's close link between Zapatismo and Catholicism. Although the diocese recognizes the EZLN's demands as legitimate, it does not condone the use of arms for any reason. The diocese holds that a Catholic man or woman cannot serve as a catechist if he or she is a Zapatista. As a prayer leader and a representative of a Zapatista support base, Domingo symbolizes the efforts of indigenous people to make Catholicism their own, sometimes without regard for directives from the diocese.

[9]Over the past few years opponents of the Word of God have used the following means to persecute Catholics: press campaigns against them; ransacking and closing Catholic temples; and threatening the lives of priests, lay people, and former Bishop Samuel Ruíz and Coadjutor Bishop Raúl Vera. Since 1997 over 31 Catholic temples were closed by PRI authorities with paramilitary backup. On February 15, 1997 Father Michel Chanteau (Padre Miguel), the priest in Chenalhó for 32 years and a defender of Pedranos' rights was expelled. Under President Vicente Fox, Padre Miguel was allowed to return to Chiapas. He is currently ministering to Tzotzil residents of San Cristóbal.

they are suffering. Once Antonia compared the struggle for social justice in Chenalhó with the battle between David and Goliath:

> Do you know that there was a prophet, David, who defended his people's rights? There was this soldier, called Goliath. It says in a text in the Latin American Bible, that he [David] confronted the government soldiers. But David was a poor man; he was a little man, a soldier of the poor people. But, he won. And it's the same today. It's what we have to do. . . . It's necessary to defend ourselves. If there was nobody to defend us, everyone would die. And the life of the children would end through injustice. That's why, to love is to defend. It's true some are going to die, like it's happening now. There are many who have fallen in the struggle . . . but we must defend ourselves.

Most of Antonia's relatives feared joining Zapatista support groups for the sacrifice and risk entailed. Some joined Las Abejas and others remained independent, although opposed to the hegemony of the PRI. Before the escalation of violence in 1997, Antonia and her relatives did not understand the great similarities between the goals and methods of Zapatista and Las Abejas support groups. However, events in 1997 made these similarities all too clear.

The violence in Chenalhó that began in 1995 and intensified in 1997 was the direct result of the spread of the low-intensity war in Chiapas. Constrained by their truce with the EZLN, the Mexican military worked through paramilitaries to repress alternatives to the PRI. Paramilitaries took hold in 17 of the 99 hamlets in Chenalhó. During 1997 more and more members of Civil Society and even PRI supporters had to choose between fleeing for their lives or assisting paramilitaries to oppress their fellow Pedranos. Under these conditions thousands of Pedranos fled their homes during 1997 to refugee camps in and around Polhó, the center of the autonomous township. By the summer of 1998 the numbers of Pedranos in internal refugee camps reached one-third of the township population.[10] In 1997 Antonia took on a cargo in her Zapatista base to help hundreds of women refugees in and around Polhó to market their weavings.

Despite efforts to bring an end to paramilitary aggressions, the unthinkable occurred on December 22, 1997. On that day at Acteal, a hamlet in the north of Chenalhó, 9 men, 21 women, and 15 children were massacred by the paramilitary group *Mascara Roja* (the Red Mask). The shooting started at 11:30 while people were fasting and praying in the chapel and lasted until 4:30 in the afternoon. Army personnel standing on a hill above Acteal saw the shooting but did nothing to stop it. The 45 men, women, and children killed were members of Las Abejas.

When I spoke with Antonia in June 1998 six months after the massacre she was still saddened by the tragedy. But her faith in the struggle was unshaken:

---

[10]In December 2001, most Pedranos left their refugee camps to return home. Although paramilitaries remain a threat, the state government has pledged itself to disarm them.

What we have is our faith. It's that we want to support each other because here there are many people who don't have anything. For example, I have a house, although it's not very elegant. But there are some who don't have a house, who live in a cave. The one who doesn't have a house, I want him to have a house, too. We aren't afraid if there are people who don't understand. We aren't afraid . . . I am a Catholic and a Zapatista sympathizer. I am in a support base, no? But I continue and I will continue being Catholic because God is the rock. Although at times there is sadness, at times there is pain, God is watching over us. When there is sadness, God gives us the strength to do good things.

In a Room Without Windows

When I met Gabriela in November 1986 she had two jobs, one in a government office in San Cristóbal and another in a boutique owned by a relative. Eventually Gabriela quit the boutique job because she was always tired. But without the extra income she had a difficult time making ends meet. Over the next two years Gabriela experienced added stress in her government job trying to master the new computer technology that was being introduced. Eventually in 1989 she and 70 other employees were laid off permanently. Along with her co-workers, Gabriela protested the layoff to government officials, including the President of Mexico, but to no avail.

It took six months for Gabriela's severance check to arrive. Meanwhile she had to change her lifestyle dramatically to survive. When I visited Gabriela during this time I found her living in one small room, all the other rooms in her house rented. Gone was Gabriela's refrigerator and much of her furniture. Where roses grew in her backyard in 1987, chickens roosted in 1989. Gabriela raised the chickens to make tamales, which she sold from her door. During this time she considered selling the house and moving to Tuxtla Gutiérrez, the state capital, where she could live with relatives and look for work. Later she considered joining a niece and her family in Puebla, but as of this writing she is still in San Cristóbal.

When he was alive, Gabriela's father had been an *enganchador,* a man hired by plantation owners to procure indigenous workers. Gabriela remembers her father as being fair and kind to the men whom he recruited, unlike the German plantation owners. The world in which Gabriela grew up rigidly separated Ladinos from indigenous people. Recalling childhood visits to her father on the plantation where he worked, Gabriela describes being carried on a chair by indigenous men into the jungle. The image of Gabriela held high on a chair, long hair brushing huge-leafed trees, always comes to mind when I think about Ladino/Indian relations in Chiapas during the middle of this century.

Although Gabriela considers herself a Coleta,[11] her economic and social circumstances made it difficult for her to maintain the life associated with

---

[11]"Coleta" is a term for a Ladina living in San Cristóbal. It refers to the pigtail (cola, literally "tail") or hank worn by Spanish colonists, especially bullfighters in the eighteenth century. Ladino men are called Coletos, women Coletas.

well-established Coleto families. Gabriela's mother died when she was 8 years old and her father when she was 17. Gabriela managed to finish *secundaria* (equivalent to U.S. middle school), but could not study further because she had to work to help support herself and her family. School was an "extra" for most Ladina girls growing up in mid-century San Cristóbal. Their brothers, in contrast, continued in school to obtain professional training.[12]

In her early twenties Gabriela married a man whose wife had died leaving him with two babies. Gabriela loved the babies as if they were her own. But her husband drank and there were problems with her in-laws. After only a year her husband told her he wanted a civil divorce and took the babies to give to his mother to raise. Gabriela was devastated. Although many Catholic men and women remarry after divorce, Gabriela maintained that she could not divorce and still be a good Catholic. Gabriela resumed the life of a single woman in a society that in the 1960s restricted such women to lives of celibacy in service to their families and the church. While holding down a job, Gabriela kept busy helping elderly neighbors and relatives and serving as godmother to many children at baptism, graduation, and marriage.

Although her nieces and nephews help her, Gabriela says she often feels un-fulfilled and lonely without her own children. Like most Ladinas, Gabriela sees children as the heart of life (Rus 1997: 29). Children bring joy and consolation and take care of you when you are old or ailing. However, having taken care of herself without a husband or children's help for most of her life, Gabriela is mildly critical of her sisters for obliging their children to be there for them when they could find fulfillment in work or activities outside their families. Gabriela concludes, "Mexican society is very cruel to women like me."

Describing her experiences with the Catholic Church, Gabriela divides them into the pre–Vatican II period characterized by considerable physical and emotional distance between priests and laypeople and the post–Vatican II period in which Catholics have developed a more intimate relationship with Christ and the church. In the earlier period, the priests in the churches of San Cristóbal gave mass in Latin with their backs to the people. Few Catholics dur-ing this time read the Bible. Attending mass, praying, especially to the Virgin Mary, and participating in feast-day celebrations were the focal points of Gabriela's religious experience before the reforms of Vatican II. Since these re-forms, Gabriela has been reading the Bible, sometimes in groups that meet in parishioners' homes. In her studies of the Bible she has been inspired by the life of Jesus Christ and his mother. Both Jesus and Mary provide Gabriela with comfort and insights about how to live her own life. Throughout her life, the

---

[12]For oral histories of Ladinas that incorporate information about schooling and reli-gion, see Diane Rus 1997. For a study of both rural and urban women see Barrios Ruíz and Pons 1995. For discussion of the role of religion in the lives of indigenous women migrants to San Cristóbal see Christine Kovic's chapter in this book and Sullivan 1998.

Virgin Mary has been a source of comfort, especially during difficult times, such as when she had cancer and when her mother died. Speaking of the Virgin, Gabriela stresses the complementary role she plays as mother, to God's role as father.

> The Lord is the redeemer of the world and the Holy Virgin is the co-redeemer. She is the best lawyer we could have to reach God. When I have a very great need I say it first to God, but then I ask the Holy Mother to help me, that she pray for me.

Gabriela's awareness of gender oppression coupled with her desire to find the good in others, has helped her to see the commonalities she shares with indigenous women. Gabriela's openness to others led her to befriend several North Americans who came to learn from and work with indigenous people. In the 1980s through these foreigners she met many indigenous women and men who talked about their struggle to support themselves and their households. Antonia and a few other Pedranas came to visit me in Gabriela's home. Each time Gabriela was kind and helpful to the women, sharing their concerns about their children's health and advising them on teas and medicines.

Gabriela has begun to appreciate more than most Coletos how class oppression can unite poor people across ethnic lines. Losing her job when she was in her early forties, raised her consciousness about class oppression and political corruption. During our first visit after the uprising Gabriela told me that Zapatista sympathizers ransacked her brother's ranch taking all his cattle and almost everything he owned. But rather than being angered by this, Gabriela surprised me by saying that she understood why the poor campesinos had done it, that in their place she might have done the same thing. She said that the Zapatistas were right to protest land inequalities and to try to democratize the Mexican political system:

> The government must recognize that there is a lot of injustice, that there must be more equality. Yes, it's not [right] that some people live in a much greater misery, while others live in opulence. . . . The government has committed terrible mistakes, terrible. It has neglected some groups and favored others. It hasn't acted with honesty and honor.

My discussions with Gabriela about religion began in earnest in 1995. At this time we talked about how the Zapatista uprising had affected her. We also talked about classes that I was taking for adults seeking reception into the Catholic Church. Although I have not since converted to Catholicism, these discussions were helpful to me on my spiritual path, as well as to my understanding of Catholicism in highland Chiapas.

My visit with Gabriela in July 1995 was intense. I suspected that she had been living with much fear since the uprising. I had been concerned about her and meant to write or call, but I never did. Between cups of tea and tears,

Gabriela recounted her feelings since the uprising. As I suspected, foremost was fear. Before the uprising Gabriela had enjoyed her daily trips to the market, to work, to church, or to visit family and friends. Since the uprising she has been afraid to walk on the streets or go to the market because at any moment a confrontation could occur between Zapatista sympathizers and their opponents. Rumors of bomb threats at Ladinos' events keep her from going out socially. Gabriela said she feared that Indians were trying to drive the Ladinos out of San Cristóbal in order to turn the city back into the Indian country that it was before colonization.

In June 1998 when I visited Gabriela I wondered if, now almost four years after the uprising, daily life had normalized for her. Her nephew and his family were now living with her and with their help she was able to make some repairs to the house. On a tour of her newly remodeled bedroom I saw the familiar pictures of her favorite saints on the walls—*La Madre del Perpetuo Soccorro* (The Mother of Perpetual Help), *La Madre Medalla Milagrosa* (The Mother of the Miraculous Medal), *El Niño de Atocha* (The Christ Child of Atocha), and *El Niño Fundador* (The Child Founder) of the Franciscan Mothers. These images were the only brightness in the windowless room. Although rooms without windows are common in San Cristóbal, Gabriela made a point to explain that she had decided not to put windows in this room because it bordered the street; since the uprising Indians marching through the streets have sometimes thrown bricks through Ladinos' windows.

As we talked, Gabriela related several stories of what has happened to some Ladinas who ventured into the streets. She told me of a friend who had been in the market and saw an elderly Ladina accidentally knock some fruit off an indigenous man's stand. In the past the man would probably have picked up the fruit, perhaps grumbling a bit, but definitely not complaining loudly to the woman. But since the rebellion the marketplace has become a site and symbol of Indian resistance to Ladino domination and, according to Gabriela, any unlucky person might be the target of it. Gabriela's friend reported that rather than pick the fruit up, the vendor yelled at the Ladina, complaining that she had ruined his fruit, that now he couldn't sell it, and that she had to pay him for it. The man demanded an exorbitant amount of money and the woman could not pay it. Sympathetic bystanders, both indigenous and nonindigenous, dug into their purses and pockets and collected enough to buy the fruit. Another incident Gabriela related to me convinced her to stop going to the market: An Indian alledgedly knifed a Ladina in her side as she strolled, basket on her arm, by the market stalls.[13]

---

[13]In the fall of 1998 the city moved indigenous vendors from their stalls in the market to a site in the southern part of the city. For one indigenous man's account of conflicts in the market, see Pérez Tsu 2000.

Although Gabriela said that she could tell me many more stories, she seemed anxious to tell me about her changed relationship to the church. I had never seen Gabriela as agitated in conversation as she appeared describing to me how she had lost faith in the church's mission in Chiapas under the direction of Bishop Samuel Ruíz. Gabriela said that she feels that the church has abandoned her and other nonindigenous parishioners to devote itself to indigenous people. However, as a single woman struggling to survive, Gabriela says she still very much needs the church's guidance and support.

For the first year after the uprising Gabriela reported being so angry at the church that she stopped going to mass. She worshipped in homes of other parishioners or at her home altar. In deciding to worship at home, Gabriela answered the call of the "Civic Front Against the Destabilizers," a Coleto group that began a crusade soon after the uprising against Bishop Ruíz and all priests who opt for the preferential option for the poor.[14] During a demonstration at La Merced Church in San Cristóbal in February 1994 members of this group placed a seal on the door that read (Russell 1995: 70):

> Fellow Catholics, beginning today, this church and all those of the city will remain closed until Bishop Samuel Ruíz leaves the city, Chiapas, and Mexico. He is responsible for land takeovers and war in the region. . . . Pray and worship at home. God knows you are with him, and God is everywhere.

In 1997 Gabriela began to attend mass again, but in a church where the priest is not closely aligned with the diocese. She is now working full time in a store owned by a friend. Her life has not normalized, but she seems to have found a zone of safety in and between her home and workplace.

Despite reports to the contrary, Gabriela remains convinced that Bishop Ruíz and his staff support the EZLN through obtaining guns for them, that the church uses money that should be going for pastoral work with all its parishioners to provide material and spiritual support only to those Catholics who support the Zapatistas. Nothing I said to Gabriela about my understanding of Ruíz's love of peace and justice, swayed her conviction that he and the church have betrayed her and the majority of Chiapanecans.

At the same time as Gabriela has criticized Ruíz, she said that she has been anxious about her inability to love and forgive him. Since Vatican II, Gabriela has been reading and reflecting on the life of Jesus and the other apostles in the Bible. From this experience she has tried to follow their example to love one's enemies. She has also reflected on God's will for people in Chiapas:

> God loves us all here in Chiapas and he wants the rancor and hate to end. . . . God wants us to reflect on his commandment of love that is the greatest of all. He says, "Love one another." Through this commandment we're going to resolve

---

[14]Gabriela does not agree with fellow Coletos who have armed themselves against indigenous peoples.

all the problems, all the differences that there are. And it doesn't matter if you're Indian or Spanish. No, everyone, all of us are equal in God's presence. Before [the uprising] we all had a normal relationship, I feel. I feel we had this until the church started dragging up things from 500 years ago. We all saw Indians as our brothers, as each in his half. And I think that we lived in peace.

Commentary

Living in highland Chiapas today poses tremendous challenges for Gabriela and Antonia. Being Catholic strengthens the women to confront these challenges even as it poses problems for them. In their efforts to reconcile the conflicts of their faith, each woman sustains a spiritual core influenced by moral values and a relational view of Christianity that pivots on strong connections to human and spiritual others, past, present, and future.

Gabriela and Antonia both struggle to balance their personal visions of equality and unity with images of life in Chiapas conveyed through rumors and religious and political discourses. Zapatista slogans assert that "the bad government" is the source of all problems. This assertion contradicts local knowledge about the multifaceted nature of experience that Antonia grew up with. Her elders taught her that it takes each person, working hard every day, to keep individuals and their societies in balance to achieve a sort of unity. Traditional beliefs about a collective soul that outlasts individual souls has given Antonia a view of herself as refracted in the world such that what is herself is no less than other selves. These understandings, combined with beliefs about collective struggle that she has acquired as a Zapatista and as a Catholic, have enabled Antonia to see herself in all oppressed people, as well as to see the potential for both good and bad in everyone and in everything (see Gossen 1994: 553–570 for an overview of key Meso-American ideas).

Gabriela has also experienced the potential for good and bad in everyone. Nevertheless, in the upheaval of the aftermath of the uprising, Gabriela has sought comfort mostly among fellow Coletos. Gabriela seems more reticent than Antonia to explore the contradictions between her received wisdom about the complexity of social life and rumors that circulate about Bishop Samuel Ruíz and the diocese. But to her credit, Gabriela rejects the rhetoric of racist Ladinos who talk about Indians as lesser beings. She struggles to live out the Biblical commandment to "love thy neighbor," even if that means loving people whom she sees as making her suffer, including her former husband, Bishop Ruíz, and the men who ransacked her brother's ranch.

Although being Catholic strengthens the women in important ways, patriarchal and male-centered beliefs and practices of the church constrain them. Because she is a devout Catholic, Gabriela could not defy the church's proscription against divorce. Consequently, after her husband abandoned her, she could not remarry and have her own children with another man. Meanwhile, her former husband remarried in a civil wedding. Like Gabriela, Antonia has found the church's ideas about women's marital and reproductive rights oppressive and difficult to reconcile with her own experience of organizing women to gain greater control over their lives. However, in Word of God, she has been able to gain a sense of personal empowerment through sharing power in decision-making and leadership with men lay leaders.[15] In contrast, Gabriela attends mass in churches where the priests do not welcome women's participation in decision-making or leadership.

Antonia and Gabriela differ most in the practice of their faith and in their feminist consciousness. Antonia's faith encompasses a syncretic religious tradition that includes both the beliefs of the ancestors about the responsibility people bear to keep the world going and a commitment to struggle for social justice, which she acquired through participating in the Word of God. The Word of God movement has provided Antonia a collective context within which to practice her faith. Her faith forms the core of what she calls a "holy struggle" with her fellow Zapatistas for social justice and women's rights. In the weaving and bakery cooperatives, Antonia uses her faith in the holy struggle to seek ways to improve life for people in her community. Cooperatives are a context in which Antonia can work with other women to seek more equality with their kinsmen while bolstering values that stem from meaningful roles as mothers, wives, daughters, sisters, weavers, household managers, religious leaders, and cash earners. In contrast, Gabriela has not been interested in collective work with other women in the church focused on increasing women's rights. Gabriela prefers to express her faith more privately by helping women friends and relatives on a one-to-one basis. For emotional and moral support she turns to the Virgin Mary who, like herself, has suffered many losses. Through her boundless love and maternal ministrations to suffering souls, the Virgin Mary symbolizes the heart of Catholicism to Gabriela.

Exploring Antonia's and Gabriela's expressions of their Catholic faith reveals several issues that pertain to the church's role in the peace and reconciliation process in Chiapas. Although these issues merit in-depth discussion, I briefly mention two in order to suggest the important critiques that women offer the church. Gabriela's experiences highlight an imbalance in the pastoral and social justice missions of the Diocese of San Cristóbal. She criticizes the church for being more concerned about the wounds of colonization endured by indigenous people than by the wounds endured by all poor or marginalized people, regardless of their ethnicity or political commitments. Gabriela's story suggests that the Catholic Church underestimates the complexity of people's identities and allegiances in its effort to address stark inequalities between classes and ethnic groups in Chiapas.

---

[15]For background on women's religious roles in highland Chiapas communities, see Eber 2000 [1995]; Moksnes 2003; Nash 1970; Rosenbaum 1993; and Linn 1976.

Antonia's experiences underscore the importance of historical continuity in efforts to formulate religious identities and to struggle for human rights. In light of the colonial legacy, Antonia finds collaboration more empowering than evangelization. Catholic priests and nuns have only recently begun to collaborate with women like Antonia as their equals and to respect indigenous women's integration into meaningful local cultures.[16] Antonia and other Zapatista Catholic women ask that before people advise them how to confront oppression or to become enlightened Christians, that they learn about daily life in indigenous communities as well as about traditional beliefs and practices. A deep historical consciousness and many meaningful local traditions are powerful ingredients in Antonia's conception of being a Catholic, a Zapatista, and a woman.

As poor women, Antonia and Gabriela occupy precarious positions. Through their marginal positions, the women have come to understand oppression and to care about other oppressed people. This understanding, coupled with a concern for equality and unity, seems to help the women shift their points of view in order to see those of others. Research in other regions of the world has shown how the capacity to shift one's perspective in order to find points of alliance with people often on the other side of conflicts, can act like cement between the building blocks of peace. The dialogues initiated by Italian feminists with Croatian, Serbian, Palestinian, and Israeli women suggest that women participants in peace dialogues bring with them their rooting in specific memberships and identities as well as the capacity to shift their points of view in order to put themselves in situations of exchange with people who have different memberships and identities (Yuval-Davis 1998). In the back-and-forth movement between rootedness and shifting, participants find connections and compatible values and goals while resisting homogenizing those with different alliances and identities. Antonia's participation in collectives has given her a social context in which to express her rootedness while shifting her perspective to find points of alliance with other women in her own community and outside. Gabriela's shifting seems more tentative and situation-specific, no doubt influenced by her privileges as a Ladina and a Coleta and the more private expression of her faith. Whereas Antonia may feel that she has little to lose by shifting, Gabriela may fear losing privileges and social supports if she shifts too far from her Ladina identity. Both women harbor fears and dreams rooted in their unique lives. Their different struggles and strengths

---

[16]See Kovic's chapter (10) in this book for a discussion of CODIMUJ (Coordinación Diocesana de Mujeres/Diocesan Coordination of Women), a women's group in the diocese that makes dialogue between women central to its work. Also, see María Pilar Aquino (1998) for a regional perspective of feminist movements within the Catholic Church.

suggest the importance of understanding the multiple and often contradictory identities and alliances of the participants in the peace process in Chiapas.

Note

The first draft of this chapter was prepared for "Gender and Religion Across Time and Space, Social Class and Ethnicity in Mesoamerica," a panel co-organized by Patricia Fortuny and R. Aída Hernández Castillo for the 1998 meeting of the Society for the Scientific Study of Religion in Montreal, Canada. I thank the organizers and panel participants for their encouragement and support. I am also grateful to Christine Kovic, Milagros Peña, Mary Kerwin, and Cookie Stefan for insightful comments on an earlier draft. I owe a debt to Antonia and Gabriela (not their real names) that is impossible to repay.

10

Demanding Their Dignity as Daughters of God

Catholic Women and Human Rights

CHRISTINE KOVIC

We women, like the women in the Gospel, are called to announce the Word [of God],
but also to denounce that which is unjust, the exploitation in which we live.
—Reflection on Matthew 28, 1–8, Women's Workshop
Diocese of San Cristóbal de Las Casas, Chiapas

Supported by the Catholic Church and inspired by their faith, indigenous women and mestizas of the Catholic Diocese of San Cristóbal de Las Casas have participated in local women's groups where they reflect on the Word of God, work to "know themselves as women," and build self-esteem; form cooperatives to grow vegetables, bake bread, and sell their artisan products; organize as midwives to attend to pregnancy and childbirth in their communities; and encourage women to participate in local assemblies and vote in national elections. In all of these activities, women defend their rights as women and demand their dignity as daughters of God. At the same time they fight to resist the poverty and oppression they experience as poor *campesinas* and as indigenous peoples.

The defense of human dignity is supported by Catholic theology, which asserts that God created all humans in his image. As children of God, humans are deserving of respect and have the right to a dignified life, which extends beyond Western European notions of rights as individual guarantees. In their struggle for dignity, women fight oppression that comes from various levels: their husbands, brothers and fathers; the historical-structural situation in which they are economically and politically marginalized; and racism persisting from the colonial period. Hence, the actions women take are not centered exclusively on protecting their rights as women, but extend to defending their rights as members of impoverished indigenous and campesino communities. Their struggle is at once individual and collective; women move back and forth between a defense of individual and community rights without distinguishing between the two. As they constantly negotiate and renegotiate their own relationships with their communities, they simultaneously work to defend their rights as women and to further the social, political, and economic demands of their communities. For women, the defense of their dignity and the struggle for justice are an integral part of announcing the word of God.

This chapter explores some the ways in which Catholic women in Chiapas are working to defend their rights, and draws on examples from several sources. The first is the work of the Coordinación Diocesana de Mujeres (the Diocesan Coordination of Women or CODIMUJ) a grassroots group that brings together Catholic women from throughout the diocese to participate in local discussion groups, regional workshops, and meetings.[1] In these settings women share their reflections on the Word of God; analyze the political, economic, and social situation in which they live; and discuss their experiences with other women. They also participate in workshops on health, literacy, and human rights, among others. Thousands of indigenous and mestiza women (primarily members of impoverished communities) take part in CODIMUJ; it serves as a powerful example of one of the ways in which women in Chiapas are organizing. CODIMUJ participants include Zapatista supporters, PRI supporters, and PRD supporters, among others (CODIMUJ 1999: 153).

The second source of information for this chapter is interviews and testimonies of indigenous Catholics of Guadalupe, the name I have given to a *colonia* located on the edge of the city of San Cristóbal de Las Casas.[2] Indigenous Catholics and Protestants who were violently exiled from their native communities for political-economic and religious motives inhabit the community. Perhaps due to their experience of human-rights violations in the process of exile and their involvement in the struggle to create a new life in an urban setting, they have developed an awareness of their rights, which is informed by Catholicism, indigenous tradition, and Mexican law. Catholic women of Guadalupe demand specific rights within their families, their church, and their community. I do not attempt to describe all Catholic women in Chiapas or in the Diocese of San Cristóbal, but rather I use specific examples to show how women's shared Catholic faith, economic situation, and indigenous identity are linked to their struggle for dignity, and to demonstrate the obstacles women face in working to defend their rights.

---

[1] I observed a number of CODIMUJ workshops—both diocesan-wide and regional meetings—as part of a broader project on indigenous rights and the Catholic Church in Chiapas from 1994–2000. Information on CODIMUJ in this chapter comes from my observations of workshops, *memorias* (literally memories, the minutes summarizing meetings) of additional workshops, interviews with CODIMUJ advisers, and the group's publications.

[2] I conducted ethnographic fieldwork in this community for more than 16 months between 1994 and 2001.

Reading the Bible with the Eyes, Mind, and Heart of a Woman

On visits to rural communities, Samuel Ruíz Garcia, Bishop of the Catholic Diocese from 1960 to 1999, noted the stark contrast between Chiapas's wealth of natural resources and the impoverishment of the majority of the indigenous and campesinos.[3] The bishop and pastoral workers of the diocese committed themselves to construct a church that works to defend the dignity of the poor; defending women's rights is part of the work of respecting the dignity of each human being and the equality of all people as children of God. Profoundly influenced by the meetings of the Second Vatican Council (1962–65) and the Latin American Bishops meeting in Medellín, Columbia (1968), which emphasized the structural roots of poverty and called on the church to take concrete actions to end injustice, Bishop Ruíz slowly underwent a process he calls conversion. As he states, "When I came to Chiapas, I really had no choice. So many people in the diocese were Indian. 'The option for the poor' was not an intellectual question here. It was a factual situation. I came to San Cristóbal to convert the poor, but they ended up converting me" (Womack 1998: 30).

For the bishop and the pastoral workers of the diocese, conversion represents a commitment to the *pueblo* (the poor) and its process of liberation; this entails accompanying the poor in their struggles and taking on their struggle as one's own. The influence of Liberation Theology, which recognizes the poor not only as the subjects of their own history but as the *preferred* subjects for the revelation of the Word of God and the history of salvation, is also evident in the work of the diocese. An integral feature of the process of the conversion of pastoral workers involves supporting indigenous peoples in directing their own history, respecting the creation of their own path to liberation rather than imposing Westernization as the only means to end poverty and exploitation. In his later reflection on the diocesan process, Bishop Ruíz noted:

> One of the things that we can say is an achievement in our diocesan work is that indigenous communities and campesinos are no longer the objects of the decisions of others, but have begun to be subjects of their own history.
>
> Ruíz García 1993:33.

Although local women's groups have existed in the diocese since the 1970s, the diocese's commitment to women's rights was not formalized until 1992 with

---

[3]In 1999 Samuel Ruíz Garcia formally retired as Bishop of the Diocese of San Cristobal at age 75 in accordance with canonical law. On March 31, 2000 Felipe Arzmendi, former Bishop of Tapachula (Chiapas), was named his successor. Monsignor Raul Vera served as coadjutor Bishop from 1995 to 1999. CODIMUJ continues its activities under the new bishop.

the creation of CODIMUJ. Committees focused on women's issues are not common in such a traditional and patriarchal institution as the Catholic Church, especially the Mexican Catholic Church. The diocese's work with women is carried out in the context of the biblically inspired promise to accompany those who are historically the most excluded and oppressed in their struggle for liberation. The women of CODIMUJ believe that work for women's dignity is based in the Word of God; through its inspiration they can organize and unite to help one another. Currently, thousands of women from throughout the diocese participate in the activities of CODIMUJ, and there are over 400 local women's groups.[4] This means that CODIMUJ is one of the largest women's groups in all Chiapas. About half of CODIMUJ participants are indigenous women, and half mestizas; the vast majority (over 90 percent) are campesinas.[5] The women in the group are poor; to mention just two indicators of poverty, around 55 percent of the women have lost at least one child and over 40 percent of the mestizas and 65 percent of the indigenous women do not know how to read or write.[6]

A booklet describing the group states that one of its most important goals is to create a space and context for reading the Bible "with the eyes, mind, and heart of a woman" (CODIMUJ 1999). At local and regional meetings throughout the diocese, discussion groups, and workshops, women examine passages from the Bible, particularly those of the New Testament, and discuss the relevance of these readings in their own lives.

The quote at the beginning of this chapter comes from the women's reflections on Matthew 28, 1–8 where Mary Magdalene and another Mary (mother of James) witness the appearance of an angel at Jesus's tomb after his crucifixion. The angel says to the women, "Do not be afraid; I know that you are looking for Jesus who was crucified. He is not here; for he has been raised, as he said. Come, see the place where he lay. Then go quickly and tell his disciples, 'He has been raised from the dead, and indeed you will see him.'" Jesus later appears to women and says to them, "Do not be afraid; go and tell my brothers to go to Galilee; there they will see me." At the April 1997 CODIMUJ workshop in San Cristóbal de Las Casas, women broke into groups to discuss the reading and then shared their thoughts. I quote the women's reflections in their own words as they reveal the process by which they learn to value themselves and their work through reading the Bible:

---

[4]Participants at regional and diocesan CODIMUJ meetings report the number of local women's groups in their region. The memorias from the CODIMUJ meetings of May and October of 2000 list a total of 420 women's groups.
[5]These numbers come from study carried out by Begoña Abad in 2000 (cited in Santana Echeagary 2001: 11–12).
[6]Abad (2000) (cited in Santana Echeagary 2001).

- It is our turn to announce, Jesus gives important work to us women. Today we must have courage like the women who went to the tomb.
- The work of women is important. Some have strength, but those who stay in their homes do not have sufficient strength.
- The women of earlier times had strength. We can also have this strength. The women went to visit the tomb and the angel asked them, "Whom do you look for?" Jesus brings peace to the women, because of this. The reading is important for us because through the women we are given the notice to take the message to our brothers and sisters.
- It teaches us to not be afraid, to take the message to our communities: it tells us to be without fear, like Mary Magdalene and other women.
- If we go out [of our homes], if we come to the meetings, we wake up, we learn, and we gain courage.
- If we learn from this text, we have hope and the clarity to walk. We are the first messengers for the rest of the *compañeras* [women] in order to encourage them.
- We need to have more faith, courage, and confidence; we must be steady and determined in our work so that the announcement of the Kingdom [of God] advances.

> —Memoria from CODIMUJ Workshop, April 1997

Many of the principles of CODIMUJ and of the diocese are evident in the women's responses to the reading. It is clear to them that God gives women and men the task of announcing His Word. Without rejecting their roles as wives and mothers, the women note that they are also called on to "take the message to our communities." They repeat many times the importance of having courage and not being afraid. CODIMUJ participants are at risk of being criticized for not remaining at home to care for their families, even if they are only away for a few hours. In small communities gossip abounds about women who travel: their motives are questioned, and some are accused of leaving to look for boyfriends, husbands, or sexual adventures. Even a male, who in principle supports his wife or daughter's work, may discourage her from traveling to avoid being the subject of gossip. As Catholic women participate in CODIMUJ meetings and as other women in Chiapas participate in a variety of social and political movements, their honor and their reputation as wives and mothers (or as potential wives) is at risk.

Helen Safa notes that women's participation in human-rights groups during the military dictatorships in Chile and Brazil was supported by the Catholic Church; however, these women did not tend to question traditional gender roles, and "appealed to Catholic symbols of motherhood and the family in legitimizing their protest. . . ." (1998: 142). Although the women of

CODIMUJ value their roles as wives and mothers, they are demanding that these roles be renegotiated and that as women they be permitted to serve in other roles as well. They are redefining what it means to be a woman in their communities.They clearly state that those who "stay in their homes" do not have sufficient strength.

In a meeting of CODIMUJ representatives held in August of 2000, participants read Matthew 9, 20–22: "Then suddenly a woman who had been suffering from hemorrhages for twelve years came up behind [Jesus] and touched the fringe of his cloak, for she said to herself, 'If I only touch his cloak, I will be made well.' Jesus turned, and seeing her he said, 'Take heart, daughter; your faith has made you well.' And instantly the woman was made well." The CODIMUJ advisers pointed out that the laws of the times prohibited a woman defined as impure from touching a man's cloak. In a discussion of this reading, the participants reflected that perhaps this woman "lost her fear, was filled with courage, and pushed away any obstacle to be near Jesus." The participants went on to note that after the woman touched Jesus, "She was filled with happiness and felt free to go to Jesus, even though the law did not permit it." Again, the women emphasize the necessity of having the courage to break social norms (and even laws) to be close to Jesus.

The observations that Jesus has given them important work and that they must have courage are clearly linked to raising perception of their own agency. The very structure of CODIMUJ promotes women's agency because it is the participants themselves who take the message to other women and share what they have learned in workshops and meetings. The structure is comprised of four levels: the local, regional, zonal, and diocesan. At the local level there are hundreds of women's groups, for the most part in rural communities, where women meet as often as once a week to read and reflect on the Bible. It is in these small groups of around 15 women where participants speak in front of others, sharing their experiences as wives and mothers (Santana 2001). Each local group is led by a coordinator selected from the community. At the regional level, coordinators from various local groups meet to share their experiences and information on upcoming CODIMUJ events. The next level is that of zones (the diocese is divided into seven zones that loosely correspond to ethnic groups) composed of representatives from the various regions within it. Finally, representatives of the seven zones come together for diocesan meetings. At each level, it is the women of CODIMUJ who organize and conduct the meetings, and participants select their own coordinators or representatives, who make a three- or five-year commitment. Because of this structure, information from local communities reaches the diocesan-wide meetings, and new information from diocesan meetings reaches local communities. Occasionally, massive diocesan-wide meetings are held, where all CODIMUJ participants are invited. The group's structure facilitates networks among women from different communities, and allows women to see the commonalities in their experiences.

The women of CODIMUJ face limits that have been set by the men in their families, as well as the structural situation in which the indigenous and mestizo poor lack basic necessities and are essentially excluded from political participation. At the individual level, the women search for strength and courage, and this, in turn, supports their ability to work in other projects. For example, at the local level many women are involved in small cooperative projects such as bakeries, vegetable gardens, or stores, which serve to better the nutrition of themselves, their families, and other members of their communities. They also return from meetings and workshops with the desire to be heard and to take part in political decisions. As women develop leadership abilities (e.g., organizational skills, learning to speak in groups, learning to analyze political and economic situations) through their participation in CODIMUJ and other groups, they may decide to participate in other political and social movements. Women's involvement in these projects builds their self-esteem and changes their role within their communities, at the same time that it advances the communities' struggles against poverty and oppression.

Around a dozen women serve as advisers to the group and there are significant differences between these advisers and the CODIMUJ participants. Many of the advisers are Catholic nuns, whereas the women in the group are married with children. There are obvious differences in economic class between participants and advisers who are mestizas, foreigners, or urban women. Although advisers assist in organizing and presenting material at zonal and especially diocesan-wide workshops, women participants themselves decide which issues are most important to them and how they wish to present these to other women. This was illustrated to me in a 1998 workshop that I observed in San Cristóbal when an adviser from Mexico City asked the women to place blankets or mats on the floor and to lay on their backs. While the women participated in a period of relaxation, the adviser asked them to concentrate on taking deep breaths, to imagine that they were in peaceful place, among other images. These suggestions prompted giggles from the women, but the exercise continued. During the short coffee break that followed, the participants told me that they had enjoyed the exercise, but that they would not share it with other women in their communities. "We don't have time for that," they explained. It was clear from this exercise that it is not specific activities, but the structure of CODIMUJ that strengthens women's agency and allows them to decide what shape the local women's groups will take.

Conversion to Catholicism and the Practice of Women's Dignity

Although the Catholics of Guadalupe do not participate in CODIMUJ, they explained to me that they have learned about their rights and dignity, as well as women's rights, through study of the Word of God. Men and women of the community insisted on the equality of all human beings, rich and poor, mestizo and indigenous, men and women. As one male catechist (lay preacher) expressed: "In the beginning there were only two people, Adam and Eve. Hence, we are all equal, we all share the same blood. Rich and poor, mestizo and indigenous, men and women, all are equal." The seemingly simple statement that all are equal in the eyes of God is empowering. It supports women's own consciousness of their dignity as human beings. This belief challenges the status quo in Chiapas where a small group of mestizos have held political and economic power for decades. For women, it provides religious support for the idea that they should have the same rights as men.

The practice of respecting family members is central to the understanding of respect in the community. In the interviews I conducted, men and women told me that a husband who "respects" his family works in cooperation with his wife, provides food and other necessities for his family, does not fight with or beat his wife, and will not abandon his family. Likewise, a wife who respects her family cooperates with her husband to support her children and does not fight with her husband. Both men and women in Guadalupe explained to me that women's work is just as important as men's work; that domestic violence is wrong and must be punished by serving time in jail; that girls should not marry at an early age and should never be forced to marry against their will; and that women should participate in community decisions. As to be expected, the ideal and real did not always coincide. But the strong support for women's dignity—rooted in the Word of God—provides a moral defense for women's rights. This focus on women's dignity resonates with the indigenous notion of gender complementarity and interdependence in which men and women work together as partners in many aspects of life (see Eber 2000 [1995]; Nash 2001; Rosenbaum 1993).

The majority of Guadalupe Catholics are recent converts who have been violently exiled from their native homes in the highland township of San Juan Chamula. When a family is exiled (or expelled), they may be jailed, beaten, or threatened; their home may be robbed or burned; and their crops may be destroyed. Then they are told that they must leave the community or suffer further violence. Those responsible for expulsions are *caciques*, or locally entrenched indigenous leaders. Currently, well over 30,000 indigenous peoples have been expelled and live in poverty in San Cristóbal and other towns where they have initiated a new life separated from their land, homes, and communities of origin (Kovic in press; Robledo Hernández 1987). Some of the explanations given for the phenomena of expulsion are: the exiles are Protestant or Catholic converts who threaten traditional religious beliefs and community cohesion in Chamula; the exiled threaten the economic power of the caciques by their refusal to buy alcohol and other items sold by the leaders themselves; the exiles are political dissidents who are affiliated with opposition parties.

The overall process of urbanization in Chiapas and the scarcity of fertile land in rural communities provide important contexts for expulsion.

Many residents of Guadalupe have converted from the traditional religion of Chamula in which Mayan gods are worshipped alongside Catholic saints and Mayan rites co-exist with Catholic sacraments. Some are now Roman Catholics who participate in the pastoral activities of the Diocese of San Cristóbal. When I asked them about reasons for their conversion, the treatment of women was an important subtext in their narratives. A number of people in Guadalupe told me that, in contrast to Chamula, men respect their wives and families. Strong disapproval is expressed for drinking alcohol, domestic violence, abandoning one's wife and children, or taking a second wife, customs that they claimed were quite common among the traditionalists of Chamula but rare among the Catholics of Guadalupe. Hence, the process of conversion itself entailed a change in gender ideology.[7]

The most often-cited change that accompanies conversion is the rejection of alcohol. Anthropologists have documented the important role that drinking plays in social interactions in indigenous communities and in rituals to create and maintain relationships between people and the deities (Siverts, ed. 1973; Gossen 1974; Eber 2000 [1995]). They have also detailed the problems that it creates when it is abused (Eber 2000 [1995]; Rosenbaum 1993). In Guadalupe, Catholic converts, both male and female, reject all use of alcohol.[8] They contrast drinking with the ability to think clearly and say that it leads to fighting. In interviews and conversations, men and women recounted the problems that alcohol created in their families when they were young. They remember seeing their fathers beat their mothers while intoxicated, and some even remember seeing their fathers die from excess alcohol consumption. Women recall being beaten by drunken husbands. Memories of the problems caused by alcohol—including violence, poverty, and illness—override recognition of its ritual significance. For people living in extreme poverty, spending money on alcohol rather than on food and other necessities is an issue of tremendous concern.

In Guadalupe, domestic violence is not accepted. If a man beats his wife, an *agente,* the local authority, can jail him for 24 hours.[9] During the time I con-

---

[7]Some of these same changes have been described for women who convert to Protestantism. See for example, Brenda Rosenbaum (1993), Christine Eber 2000[1995], and Kathleen Sullivan (1998) on Chiapas; John Burdick (1993) on Brazil; and Elizabeth Brusco (1995) on Colombia.

[8]Catholic women in other areas of Chiapas have mobilized to limit the use of alcohol in their communities. For example, Christine Eber 2000 [1995] notes that Catholic women of Chenalhó rallied to prohibit the sale of alcohol in their township in the 1980s.

[9]The agente is a local official who responds to the township president (Guadalupe forms part of the township of San Cristóbal de Las Casas) and has the power to mediate local conflicts.

ducted fieldwork several men were jailed for this reason. In addition, both men and women express strong moral disapproval toward domestic violence.

At the same time that Guadalupe residents reject many customs of Chamula, they are building a community that respects some traditional customs and creates new ones. The local government often bases its decisions on customary law rather than national legislation, privileging community rather than individual interests. In some cases, like the one described in the following, these decisions can serve women's interests.

One morning in Guadalupe I found families talking about a recent fight between two women (both Protestant).[10] After inquiring about the event, I learned that the women had been yelling at one another and pulling each other's hair. Such fighting was rare in Guadalupe and to make matters worse, the fight had taken place in front of one woman's home and many had witnessed the event. Community members decided to assist in resolving the conflict and the local agente called a public meeting. Later that day, Protestants and Catholics gathered in the town hall where the two women were asked to explain what had happened. It turned out that one woman's husband had left her to live with a second woman. After attempting to sort out the story, the agente asked the people in attendance to make a decision as to what to do. Much discussion ensued, but eventually all agreed that the man who had left his wife had made a mistake and should return to his wife. He agreed to this and in addition, agreed to pay a fine of three truckloads of sand that would be placed on the road in the community to help prevent erosion. His "punishment" prevented the erosion of the road during the coming rainy season, at the same time that it prevented a symbolic erosion within the community, by reincorporating the man into community life. Of course, the man could have refused to abide by the community decision; divorce is legal in Mexico, and he could have gone to live with the second woman. Yet, it probably would have been necessary for him to live in another colonia, to escape the strong disapproval from the community.

A major factor behind the decision in this case is communal responsibility for single, abandoned, or separated women. Hence, the man's punishment served the entire community, reflecting the fact that his action had implications for all. Because the case was decided in a public audience, it served as a warning to all men about the consequences of failing to provide for their families. This story illustrates the complexity of gender relations in Guadalupe. For although Catholic and Protestant women are at once dependent on and protected by men, the new gender ideology maintains that they are equal part-

---

[10]Although the families involved in the case are Protestant, Catholics and Protestants worked together to resolve the conflict. This particular conflict involved a Protestant man who had left his wife, yet, I also observed similar cases involving Catholic men.

ners with men. Community controls on drinking, domestic violence, and abandonment have dramatically altered gender relations in households.

In another case, Verónica, a single mother in Guadalupe, explained that she left her husband in Chamula because he did not respect her or carry out his obligations to his family.

> According to the Word of God, one must respect his/her spouse. Husband and wife must live together united. A man should not hit his wife.
>
> Here [in Guadalupe] there is much suffering because I have to support my children alone. We need food, there are not enough clothes. I left my husband in Chamula four years ago. My husband beat me a lot. He beat me even when he wasn't drinking. When he returned [from the fields] in the afternoon, I said to him, "Here is your food, your *pozol* [a drink made from ground corn], your tortilla and beans." But he didn't want to eat. He hit me and kicked me. My face swelled up from being beaten.
>
> He didn't give me money to buy maize, beans, and clothes. He would go to work in the *finca* and return to scold me. However, I forgave my husband. But he continued to beat me. So I left him. I left him because I didn't want to be beaten any longer. I was without food and went to live in another hamlet in Chamula.

Verónica is not criticized for leaving her husband; instead her decision to "follow the Word of God" is praised. Although Verónica prays for forgiveness for leaving her husband, Catholics of Guadalupe criticize a man who does not provide for his wife, "looks for another wife," or beats his wife. Verónica is considered an upstanding member of the local chapel and regularly sits on the front bench, a place reserved for the wives of catechists and other honored members. She earns money from a small store where she sells such items as rice, oil, and soft drinks to members of the community. Her oldest son, married with two children of his own, also offers financial support. The fact that the catechists and other members of the community of Guadalupe will take the side of a woman who is being mistreated is perhaps the strongest sanction against abusive husbands. Women's rights are enforced by the community's disapproval of mistreating women.

The types of solutions to domestic conflicts achieved in Guadalupe are common in other communities, even in those that do not follow Catholicism. Scholars studying Protestant conversion in Chiapas note the ways Protestants respond to women's needs in criticizing alcohol abuse, domestic violence, and abandonment (see Chapters 14 and 15). Likewise, in Zapatista base communities, women collectively resist domestic violence and alcohol abuse at the same time as they construct new gender roles that encompass their identities as wives and mothers (see Chapters 9 and 22). These similarities suggest that broader political and economic changes in Chiapas play a critical role in the reconfiguration of gender relations. This is not to downplay the significance of religion; men and women in Guadalupe constantly refer to their faith in underscoring the importance of gender equality. They find in Catholicism powerful ideas that reinforce community norms and supports the resolution of domestic conflicts.

A Day in the Life of a Woman: Valuing Women's Work

As the other chapters in this book illustrate, gender inequality within indigenous communities of highland Chiapas is the norm; in many cases women's domestic work allows men to work for wages outside the home and to spend their money on their own needs. It is rare for a woman to remain single, and widows and women who have left their husbands depend on the assistance of their older sons or other men in the community. However, both men and women have power in the community and are profoundly interdependent in daily life and production. As Christine Eber notes for women in the highland township of Chenalhó, "Although no patriarchy allows women to act freely, the kind of patriarchy I saw in Chenalhó makes men and women partners in most aspects of life, not just those necessary for survival" (2000 [1995]: 239).

As noted, women in Guadalupe are protected and have rights; men are expected to provide money for food and other necessities. The distinct yet complementary roles carried out by men and women are evident in the division of labor at the household level in Guadalupe. Women's work starts before sunrise when they must prepare the tortillas for the day; they may also prepare beans, greens, rice, and other foods if these are available. They obtain water for cooking, cleaning, and drinking from one of the two tanks on the road of the community, carrying it home in plastic jugs. Firewood for cooking is cut from the forest above the hill and carried back. Women are also responsible for washing clothes, cleaning their homes, caring for animals, and making clothes for themselves and their families. Child care is for the most part women's work, though older children of both sexes help out in many household tasks. Women also participate in income-producing activities, making bracelets, belts, woven cloths and wool jackets, vests, and bags that they then sell in local tourist markets for small amounts of cash. The income from these ventures is used for household expenses such as the purchase of food staples and materials for clothing. In the context of impoverished living conditions, women's work is more burdensome: women carry water and firewood to their homes in the absence of piped water and gas or electric stoves.

Men's household responsibilities include building their homes and repairing them when the roofs and walls are in need of replacement. Sometimes men help in gathering firewood. Men work in the city in paid occupations, bringing in cash. They work mainly as *peones*, unskilled day laborers who perform menial work in the construction of homes and public works; others sell items in the market or the streets, or rent land to cultivate. The money they earn is expected to go toward the maintenance of the family. Spending money on alcohol, described as "wasting" money, is strongly criticized. The jobs performed by the majority of men provide irregular employment at best, whereas the artisan work sold by the women provides regular, if very small, sums of money.

In Guadalupe, as in other indigenous communities, the work of both men and women is considered indispensable for the family's survival. Both husband and wife have responsibilities to carry out to support the family and there is strong disapproval if either fails to comply. Even though men and women in Guadalupe have complementary roles, structural inequality is evident in gender relationships. Several single mothers and widows live in Guadalupe; however, they are dependent on the economic assistance of men. In the community's chapel, men occupy the *cargos* (duties performed in service of the community) of prayer leaders, treasurer, musician, and secretary. In the family, women receive the protection of men, and, as I describe in the foregoing, widows and single mothers receive protection of the community itself.

In CODIMUJ women assess and evaluate the work they do in their homes, their church, and other areas. In the workshop of April 1998, participants carried out an exercise called "A Day in the Life of a Woman" in order to evaluate the work they perform. Working in groups, each woman answered the following questions: What do I do during the day? How much am I paid for what I do? Who benefits from my work? The responses showed that the majority of the women awoke at 4:00 A.M. to prepare the corn, the fire, and the coffee. Then they take the corn to the mill, and prepare breakfast and the lunches of the men who will go to the fields. They are also responsible for feeding animals and working in the orchards. The day does not end until 9:00 or 10:00 P.M. when the women finally rest. All of the participants carry out domestic work within their homes, and several also perform salaried work. The women concluded that if their domestic work were paid, they would earn between 1050 and 4500 pesos a month, or $130.00 to $562.00.

The purpose of the exercise was to help the participants realize how hard they work and to appreciate the value of their work. The women noted that because their work is unpaid, it is not considered to be as valuable as men's work. The women's conclusion from the exercise was not so much the need to involve men in domestic work as the need to elevate their own self-esteem. In assessing who benefits from their work, the women noted that for wage labor, their bosses benefit, and that for domestic work, the family benefits. In addition, the government and the wealthy who own stores benefit because the poor often pay high prices for staples such as cooking oil, salt, and soap even though campesinos receive little money for the products they sell. Without money for transportation, people are dependent upon the *coyotes* (middlemen) and stores in their local communities. In this analysis, the women link their oppression to the context in which they live. They note that their bosses, the wealthy, and the government benefit from their work, pointing to the ways that structural factors constrain them as poor indigenous women and campesinas. Their husbands suffer this same oppression in their waged work and in selling products. However, the women at the workshop also noted that "the men benefit the most because the women go to their homes to work when the men rest," expressing awareness of the oppression that they experience as women within their households.

Conclusion: Sources of Oppression, Sources of Resistance

The women of CODIMUJ struggle against poverty at the same time that they struggle against gender discrimination. As Cheryl Johnson-Odim (1991: 315) notes:

> While it is clear that sexual egalitarianism is a major goal on which all feminists can agree, gender discrimination is neither the sole nor the primary locus of the oppression of Third World Women . . . Thus, a narrowly defined feminism, taking the eradication of gender discrimination as the route to ending women's oppression, is insufficient to redress the oppression of Third World Women . . .

In CODIMUJ women analyze their economic and political marginalization and address the need to organize at the community level to gain access to basic services such as health care and education, and the need for broader organization to change the fundamental situation of inequality in the state of Chiapas. A 1998 CODIMUJ booklet explains that women work together "to find new models for responding to the situation of injustice in which we live, and to meet the urgent necessities that we have in our communities." As noted, the women have carried out diverse projects in their communities: they establish small stores or cooperatives to sell goods at affordable prices; raise and sell chickens; bake and sell bread; and grow fruits and vegetables to better the diet. The stores are one of the most important projects for rural communities since working together the women can pay for transportation to the nearest town in order to buy in bulk, saving a great deal of money. Involvement in these projects is empowering for the women; they learn the necessity of participating not only in community decisions, but also in activities to improve their economic situation. The productive activities also serve their families' needs at the same time that women redefine their roles as wives and mothers.

For the case of urban Brazil, John Burdick (1993) notes that the progressive Catholic Church is not very successful working with women, in part because the model of small discussion groups intensifies gossip in the urban arena, but also because the church's emphasis on structural change "places responsibility for domestic conflict on the complainant herself" (115). Burdick states that women's immediate needs in their households are not adequately addressed. I would like to suggest that CODIMUJ is attractive to poor women of Chiapas because it handles everyday issues differently than the church in urban Brazil; CODIMUJ does not separate the personal from the political. At local, regional, and diocesan meetings, women in Chiapas share their concerns about alcohol abuse and domestic violence as they share strategies for alleviating these abuses. Through small stores and cooperatives they make improvements in their family's diet and economic situation. They are involved in weekly activities in their local chapels, even as they complain that male catechists often fail to listen to them or to take their views seriously. Indeed, a number of women's rights activists of San Cristóbal are critical of CODIMUJ for placing so much emphasis on the household level of change and for not placing sufficient emphasis on broader structural issues. Yet, CODIMUJ advisers are careful to assist women in linking distinct levels of analysis. For example, in a meeting for CODIMUJ representatives held in San Cristóbal in July 1999, women spent the greater part of a day discussing violence and poverty. The women began by describing the kinds of violence they experience within their households. Then they described the ways that the economic crisis impacts them. The advisers presented information on the regional and national economy, and explained the role of neoliberal policies in the Mexican economy. A small group of women designed a skit to show the ways international leaders and organizations (such as the International Monetary Fund) impact the national and regional economy. Finally, the advisers presented information on plans for the year 2000 World March of Women, an international event to denounce violence and poverty. (Women of CODIMUJ would later support this event by collecting over 19,000 signatures for a petition and sending two representatives from Chiapas to the United Nations meeting in New York City.) Information on the march served to link the struggles of women in Chiapas to the broader struggle of women in the world.

In this way women's practical (or feminine) needs as wives and mothers, are linked directly to strategic (or feminist) needs of working toward structural change.[11] Many women are initially attracted to CODIMUJ for the potential to make concrete changes in their daily lives, and many become increasingly involved in politics through the group. Yet, women's participation at any level—be it in a small Bible study group in the local community, in a small bakery or garden, or in a regional meeting—can be empowering to them. As women travel to meetings they leave their households and communities, share their experiences with other women, participate in discussion groups, and assist in organizing diverse projects. In their actions, the women themselves change, the terms of the struggle within their communities change, and the respect women receive from men increases.

In contrast to women in CODIMUJ, women in Guadalupe seldom struggle for anything beyond their quotidian feminine needs. Their struggles center on gaining access to food and education for their children as well as on eliminating men's drinking and violence. Yet, it would be a mistake to underemphasize the importance of such acts as leaving an abusive husband and curtailing problem drinking or domestic violence, especially in a social context where the

---

[11]Lynn Stephen (1998) demonstrates that women in Chiapas simultaneously work toward both sets of needs.

idea that men and women are equal is becoming commonplace and is reinforced through religious belief. These small acts illustrate some of the ways that the Catholic women are attempting to change their lives as they struggle to live with dignity. Their actions fly in the face of common stereotypes of indigenous women as stoic and fatalistic.

In July of 1998 I observed a CODIMUJ workshop that illustrates a major understanding about how Catholic women intertwine their notions of individual and collective rights in the process of renegotiating their roles and identities. In one exercise, all participants were asked to draw five concentric circles. They were then instructed to label the center circle with the person whom they consider the most important, in the second, they were to write the second most important person, and so on to label each of the five circles. Next, the labeled drawings were posted on a wall where all could see. In the center circle the women commonly wrote "God," and in the next circle "my children," followed by their parents, their spouses, and their friends. One woman wrote "my pueblo" as the people most important in her life. The next day, following several additional exercises, the women observed that no one had listed herself as the most important person in her own life, nor had any woman listed herself *anywhere* on her own diagram. With the assistance of one adviser (a middle-class mestiza woman from Mexico City), the women reflected on this omission, and later one of them noted that "God loves us and we should love ourselves. If we begin to place ourselves in the center of our lives, we will have more strength to do other things—to support our families, our pueblos."

This exercise illustrates that individual and collective rights are not necessarily separate and conflicting categories, but can exist simultaneously. Women's actions in their Catholic groups are at once individual and collective; women observe that through valuing their own dignity and respecting themselves they can best work to help others. The women's groups are successful because through them participants are able to raise their self-esteem and find strength at the same time they are able to further the social, political, and economic aims of their communities.

Note

I thank Ruth Chojnacki, Christine Eber, and Kathleen Murphy for their careful readings and comments on this chapter. In addition, I would like to thank the women and advisers of CODIMUJ and the families of Guadalupe.

11
Today, the Women

**Translated by Christine Kovic
and Francisco Argüelles Paz y Puente**

The Catholic women of the Diocesan Coordination of Women (CODIMUJ) have written a number of songs in Spanish to express their hopes, problems, and struggles. The songs are sung to animate local meetings and regional workshops. "Today, the Women" is sung to the tune of "La Cucaracha," the popular song of the Mexican Revolution. The words of the song emphasize the ways women are working together in their communities to liberate themselves.

> **Refrain:** Today the women, today the women,
> we want to liberate ourselves.
> From the oppression and the lies
> that the past has left to us.
>
> Since the time of creation,
> people blamed Eve
> as the cause of all evil
> that exists here on earth.
>
> **Refrain**
>
> But little by little,
> the truth begins to appear.
> From the mouths of women
> you hear us express our thoughts.
>
> **Refrain**
>
> We women just like men,
> from the hands of God were born.
> The two have power and help one another
> because the two are equal.
>
> **Refrain**
>
> Since times of the Old Testament,
> women have been struggling
> to bring down the powerful
> and lift up the lowly.
>
> **Refrain**

Christ showed to the Samaritan
the path he had to walk.
Communicate with others
and share the Water of Life.

Refrain

Today in our communities
something new is happening.
The women are participating,
and we've begun to move forward.

Refrain

From our homes we go
thinking about the needs
of the poor and the abandoned.
And we begin to remedy them.

Refrain

This illness called alcohol
takes away the life of the pueblo.
But with our strength and courage
we are freeing ourselves little by little.

Refrain

12
Irene
A Catholic Woman in Oxchuc

PILAR GIL TÉBAR

My own view is that the group is very good, we are united as women, we are not isolated, each one in her own home. And now the Sisters say that the women have dignity the same as the men. And now the men let the women participate in the group.
—Irene

Irene was one of the first women to befriend me when I arrived in Paraíso, a community in the township of Oxchuc, in June of 1995. Irene is the coordinator of a small women's group that she and other women in Paraíso formed with assistance from Catholic nuns of the Diocese of San Cristóbal de Las Casas. In the new space for organizing and reflection that they created, the women bake bread, plant small vegetable gardens, and learn additional skills. They also pray together and read and reflect on the words and lives of women in the Bible. Through these diverse experiences they begin to value themselves as indigenous women.

This chapter presents Irene's words about her involvement in the women's group. Her words are prefaced with a brief background on Paraíso and the Catholic Church's work in the community.

Ethnographic Background

Paraíso, the pseudonym of a Tzeltal community of about 700 inhabitants, is located in Oxchuc near the border of Altamirano and Ocosingo. According to the elders and teachers of the community, Paraíso was founded 30 or 40 years ago. At that time, the land was one man's private property. He employed the *mozos baldíos* (sharecroppers) to work on the *finca* from 12 to 14 hours a day while the women did housework in the landowner's home and took care of their own families.[1]

---

[1]For more information on fincas in Chiapas see Castellanos (1952), García de León (1985), Ruz (1992), and Stephens (1949). The works of Bruno Traven, particularly *The Rebellion of the Hanged* (1952), offer stark accounts of the appalling conditions on the fincas.

In the 1960s young men in the community decided to try to buy the land. After overcoming numerous political and economic obstacles, they managed to purchase the land and founded the village of Paraíso. Over time, the population has grown and land has become scarce due to plots becoming smaller as fathers divide their land among sons. Due to land shortages, the residents repeatedly asked the government to annex the adjacent plot of uncultivated land. In 1991, tired of receiving no answers, they occupied the land. The government authorities and the landowner reacted violently. Spurred on by the repression, some residents of Paraíso formed a peasant organization. The current residents of Paraíso belong to this organization. With its help they have been able to buy the land. However, they still do not have the deeds legitimizing their ownership.

The Catholic Church has been present in Paraíso since it was founded. The school and the chapel were the first buildings constructed. Initially, the residents limited themselves to reciting the prayers and hymns that they learned, as well as listening to the catechist read from the Bible. Beginning in the 1980s, in accordance with the pastoral objectives of the Diocese of San Cristóbal, the community abandoned its attitude of formal assimilation of doctrine in order to participate actively, contributing with their own words. In this process, the catechist ceased to be a *teacher* and became more of a *facilitator,* promoting reflection on the realities of poor peasants.

In the process of collective reflection, the residents of Paraíso transformed the Word of God into an expression of unity, commitment, respect, nonviolent struggle, mutual collaboration, and personal dignity. Commentaries that followers of the Word of God make during the celebration of the Word of God[2] stress the unity of the community, and the need to abandon "diseases"of laziness, division, confrontation, indifference, apathy, envy, and hate.

The Catholic chapel in Paraíso is the only democratic platform in the community.[3] The first women to benefit from this new democratic space were the catechists' families.[4] The catechists refer to the necessary role of women to construct the Kingdom of God on earth by their active participation. The women are expected to contribute equally with men to a new social order based on values of justice, equality, and dignity for all. Reading the Bible, at times accompanied by Catholic nuns, the men receive continuous messages with the

---

[2]This expression refers to the mass celebrated by priests, and the meetings of indigenous women where the Bible is read, although the priest is absent.

[3]At least up until now, there is only one non-Catholic family, of Presbyterian faith who hold their meetings in other communities.

[4]The catechists are pastoral agents recruited from the indigenous and peasant population who ensure the progress of the apostolic work. They act as community leaders and as important agents of change by introducing values of living together in accordance with the new Catholic perspective. One of these values is the recognition of women's dignity, as well as women's right to actively participate in all aspects of social life of their communities.

goal of strengthening their attitude of openness and respect toward the women, comparing their situation with the treatment Jesus Christ gave to those women who accompanied him during his apostolate. For example, the catechists underscore the roles of women in the Bible immediately after the resurrection of Christ, emphasizing that women were the first to witness such an important event in the Catholic doctrine.

The Catholic women's group of Paraíso could be defined as being halfway between a survival movement and a women's rights movement. It is a survival movement (focused on women's feminine or practical needs) because it is searching for alternative food products. The population lives on a meager and precarious diet of corn, beans, and coffee. In response to the difficulty of surviving off of subsistence crops in the context of the implementation of neoliberal economic policies such as NAFTA, the women of the group, advised by the nuns, are initiating a change in their traditional diet, introducing the bread and vegetables that they themselves produce. The women also sell some of the bread and vegetables to earn small amounts of money.

In addition to their applied projects, the women's reflections on Bible readings and the teachings of the nuns are slowly facilitating an increased awareness among the women of their dignity as human beings. Women are using the church as a resource, as a forum where they can express themselves and find their own sense of dignity and identity.

Another important function of the women's group relates to the patrilineal-patriarchal system that defines the social organization in Paraíso. This system requires women to break with their family and friendship ties when they marry. Many women have to abandon their place of origin in order to move to their permanent residence. In response, the women's group facilitates friendship and collaboration among the women creating networks outside the limits permitted by the norms of patrilineality. The women's group creates its own identity so that the women are no longer only *wives of, sisters of,* or *daughters of* some man or woman.

The members of the women's group in Paraíso say that they feel more confident knowing that their words are taken into account, respected, and valued. Irene's words, which follow, exemplify this confidence and the changes in women's lives related to their participation in the Word of God and in the women's group.

Irene's Testimony

Ever since I've been a child, I have only one memory—that I've suffered a lot. [When I was young] we didn't have food, just one tortilla and a little *pozol* for the entire day.[5] Life in the finca was difficult. The men worked and worked, but

---

[5]The corn tortilla and *pozol* (a drink made from corn and water) are basic ingredients of the indigenous diet.

when their work ended they went to the landowner's home to drink alcohol and waste their money. The men returned home without money and hit their wives and children. That's what I remember. But the women also worked a lot. And the landowner abused the women [sexually].

José's parents noticed me and wanted me to marry their son. So they went to ask for my hand. My grandmother said that they were going to give me to José's parents. When they gave me up, everyone was drunk. I hadn't been to school at all, and I cried and cried because I wanted to study. I was 15 years old and José was about 22 or 23.

So, I had to leave my home. I lived in José's parents home for a year. The house was far away; it was difficult to walk there on foot and there wasn't any water there. I was sad when I got married because there was a lot of work to do: grinding corn; walking for more than an hour to bring water; gathering firewood. About 10 years ago we got our own home, separate from my in-laws. Before then they shared their food with us, but now I am in charge in my home. It used to be worse because mothers-in-law treat their daughters-in-law poorly.

In the community it is custom for the women to marry; a single women is looked down on. The men always want to marry because they always want to order around the women; they want women to serve them. When a woman asks a man to help her carry water, he answers, "Do you think I'm a woman who carries water?" When a woman is alone or single it is dangerous because bad men may come to hurt her or abuse her [sexually]. When a woman stays with her children because her husband died or left her, she will never again marry because she knows that another spouse would treat her badly for having other children with another man. Furthermore, if a woman remains single, she has to stay with her parents or siblings, and can only eat what they want her to eat. If a woman doesn't want to get married, she has to leave the community because if she doesn't, the men will come to mistreat her.

When Sister Laly first came here she brought the women together in the chapel and spoke to us about how the men dominate us women. The women commented that what the Sister said is true.[6] But the women thought that these meetings weren't of any use because the men weren't there and because after, when they went to their homes and told their husbands about the meetings, their husbands forbid them to go ever again. The men always order the women around, the men always want the women to have everything ready for them. If not, the men get angry and hit the women.

Before, José used to hit me a lot. We would sit down to eat, I served him and I had to take care of my son because he cried. If I forgot to put salt in his food, he hit me. José drank a lot. Later on he began to follow the Word of God. Then

---

[6]In Chiapas, the Catholic nuns are known as *Hermanas* (Sisters in English). Despite there being a Congregation in San Crístobal formed by indigenous novices, the majority of nuns are mestizas.

he dreamed that he saw that God wanted him to be a catechist. When José began to seriously follow the Word of God, well, then he began to change, and now, he does help me somewhat and he never hits me anymore. The men who follow the Word of God change, they help their wives.

I think that the women work more than men. We always have to clean the house, care for our children and animals, carry firewood and water, but we also have to go to the cornfields. We do everything the men do. Only the women don't plant corn because the men don't want them to. The men say that this work is only for men. But the men don't plant beans because they say that they only do the most important things.

Around 1991, Sister Doro came to work with the women and to look for the coordinators for a women's group in each community. They pulled out my name and said that we're going elsewhere to see how the groups are formed in other communities. The women began to organize themselves. Sister Miriam said that we'd organize the woman to bake bread and plant a vegetable garden. First, we planted a vegetable garden and then we baked bread. For the oven, we asked the sisters for help. The husbands of the women in the group made the oven and a little house for the oven. José prepared the earth for the garden. The land belongs to the chapel, but the chapel gave its land for the garden.

To get the seeds, we all contributed. The bread and garden project helps the women in the group a little bit because it gives them a little bit of money and we can eat a little bread and vegetables and not only corn and beans.

We meet every Wednesday in the chapel to reflect on the Word of God. We look at the actions of the women in the Bible and how we are in comparison. Sister Laly came to accompany us and to speak with the women so that we don't get tired, so that we work together.

Now we are more than 40 women in the group. Beginning in 1995, Sisters Nuria, Justa, and Salud came and we had a workshop to learn to sew and knit. We pray in the chapel. There the sisters speak to us about the readings in the Bible and we share our thoughts on the problems that exist in our community, in Chiapas, and in all Mexico, and on what we have to do as women. It is good to pray because it helps to wake us up. We learn a lot because the sisters tell us about the government, about the PRI and PRD, what has happened with organizations, with the Zapatistas, the soldiers, Tatik Samuel.[7] The sisters always say that one has to be wide-awake.

The women's group also wants to serve the community, but the men don't really want this. Once we wanted to give our word, but they didn't pay attention. We said, "You've seen that we always gather firewood for the *temescal*, to make food, to boil water.[8] You've seen that we have to cut lots of trees." So we

---

[7] Tatik is a term of Tzeltal origin meaning great father. It is commonly used to refer to Samuel Ruiz García, Bishop of the Diocese of San Cristóbal.
[8] The *temascal* is a small adobe hut where the indigenous peasants take vapor baths.

told the men and the authorities of Paraíso that it would be good if we also planted small trees, because there is already a lot of bare land. The men laughed and said that they would plant corn. They didn't want to change their way of thinking and said that the words of women aren't of any use. Another thing we did is that we don't want alcohol to be sold in Paraíso, and we've been able to achieve this and that is a good thing. If a man is drunk the authorities put him in jail.

My own view is that the group is very good. We are united as women. We are not isolated, each one in her own home. And now the sisters say that the women have dignity the same as the men. And now the men let the women participate in the group. I don't want my daughter to have the difficult life that we women live. I want my daughter to study to become a doctor or teacher, but there isn't any money. When my daughters marry, it will be because they want to. José and I will not force them. We won't give them away without their knowledge. We will share our thoughts and tell them, "Think about it carefully if you want to marry."

I think that if all the woman unite we can change our way of thinking. But it is very hard because it just makes some very tired. Their husbands don't want to come and they say bad things about their wives. I like the group because I've learned a lot. Also, I now know women in other communities. It makes me happy to go to a meeting in San Cristóbal. I have friends who live very far away, and I learn about the women from Marqués de Comillas, from Chamula, from Sabanilla. All give their word and all see themselves with respect. And we also look at the obstacles of every woman in her community and we say everything up front. When we are only women, no one laughs at our words. There, the sisters listen carefully to the women's words. It's really nice when we are together sharing.

13
Prayer for Carly

MARGARITA PÉREZ PÉREZ
Translated from Tzotzil to Spanish by Augustin Ruíz Sánchez
Translated from Spanish to English by Christine Eber

The following prayer by Margarita Pérez Pérez, a traditional *ilol* (Tzotzil for healer) from San Pedro Chenalhó, demonstrates the adeptness of women to use traditional forms of healing to respond to complex social problems and to reach across languages and cultures to share healing knowledge. Healers of highland Chiapas often use prayers to help their fellow townspeople stop drinking. Pérez's prayer is unique because she offered it for a 16-year-old from the United States who was struggling with a drug and alcohol problem. At the time (1987) that Pérez prayed, I was researching women's experiences with their own and others' problem drinking. I had learned that alcohol plays a complex and contradictory role among Pedranos (the native inhabitants of Chenalhó). Pedranos describe *pox* (Tzotzil for rum, pronounced "posh") as a harbinger of hope and a powerful healing agent, on the one hand, and as a principal cause of suffering and sorrow on the other. To invoke its healing role, elders refer to pox as the drops of water from the leaves of the Maya World Tree, which in ancient Maya cosmology stood at the center of the universe and constituted the fifth world direction. In healing ceremonies that still occur today, iloletik (plural for ilol) sprinkle pox on pine branches to simulate World Tree shedding water from its leaves to nourish Earth, a Maya diety. The actions of iloletik also recall how Sun, another Maya diety, shed its blood each night when it journeyed to Xibalba, the Underworld, to fight with the forces of evil in order to rise again. As they sprinkle rum in healing ceremonies, iloletik seek the blessings of both Maya gods and the Christian God and Saints. God's grace or healing power in the form of drops of pox or water reflects the layering during colonization of the Christian God's sacrifice of his son, Jesus, on a cross onto the image of Sun sacrificing its life each night as it moves down the veins of the World Tree (Eber 2000 [1995]).

Pox is also the "water of sorrow." As the chapters in this book illustrate, women throughout Chiapas share tales of the suffering alcohol brings, their struggles to check its harmful powers, and their appeals to God to heal its victims. Women's testimonies provide convincing evidence for why Pedranos sometimes refer to rum as "the devil's piss." Like many women, Pérez has developed a critique of alcohol's negative effects. She has joined a movement among iloletik throughout highland communities to substitute soda for pox in all prayers.

While conducting fieldwork I lived with Pérez's niece, Flor De Margarita Pérez (see her song for International Women's Day, Chapter 21). When I asked Flor de Margarita how I might learn about the use of prayer to treat problem drinking, she suggested asking a healer to pray for one of my relatives or friends. I immediately thought of Carly (not her real name), a teenage relative. Flor de Margarita suggested that her father's sister, Margarita Pérez, might be willing to pray for Carly. In addition to being an ilol, her aunt was also a member of OMIECH (Organización de Médicos Indígenas del Estado de Chiapas, The Organization of Indigenous Doctors of the State of Chiapas), founded in 1985. Other Pedrano friends suggested additional iloletik, both women and men. After asking several iloletik to pray for relatives and friends, I came to appreciate the important roles they play in maintaining and restoring physical as well as emotional and social well-being. Through serving their communities as healers, women gain status and heat, a sign of spiritual strength. They also enjoy more independence than most women, traveling alone on paths to their patients' homes and on unseen paths to the places where powerful spirits reside.

Since 1987, Margarita Pérez has continued her activities as an ilol and as a member of both the Catholic Church and OMIECH, which operates a museum of traditional medicine and a herbarium in San Cristóbal de Las Casas. She also works with COMPITCH (The Council of Indigenous Traditional Midwives and Healers of Chiapas).

Carly is now a 32-year-old mother of a 12-year-old son living in Buffalo, New York. She is clean and sober and planning to attend college. At the time that I told her that I had asked for a traditional Maya woman to pray for her, Carly didn't say much. Looking back, she says that she is amazed that someone who was so poor had empathy for a person who had so much. She is touched that Margarita wanted to help her when Margarita had her hands full just trying to survive.

—Christine Eber

Prayer for Carly

oy ka'yej tal un	I have something to say to you.
oy jlo'il tal un kajval	I have something to take up with you, my Lord.
yu'un avantsil,	for your daughter,
ol yu'un avantsil tojben,	for your daughter whom you bought,
yu'un avantsil manben	for your daughter whom you bought,
un kajval nichimal riox jesucristo kajval.	my Lord, flowery God, Jesus Christ, my Lord.

mu xu' puro pukujetic ta sujun
   une kajval
ta anichimal ba,
ta anichimal sta une kajval

jech komen ta avivia.
jech komen ta ta ats'ib,
mu xu' ta jsujbatic ta uch' pox
   une kajval.

jech avaloj ta ava'yej.
jech avaloj ta alo'il un kajval,

anichimal riox
jech avaloj ta ava'yej, jech avaloj t avun
nichimal jtot, jesucristo jtot ta vinajel
   javjal.

"cuxubinabaik, mu xu' xa tunik,
mu xu' xa bainik ti jun poxe xachi,"
la avaloj une kajval.

chavok'bun ta o'lol ta ye,
   ta sti' une kajval.

ak'o aba ta ilel atsatsal une kajval.

ta snamal osil une kajval,
ta snamal banamil une kajval.

mu yu'unikuc schij o ta sba axalu'

ta sba ameril un kajval
nichimal riox jesucristo kajval.

jun ti jkoltavanejot une kajval.
ja' la akolta ti koxo.
ja' la akolta ti ma'sat.
ja' la akolta ti k'a'al chamel.

te chlaj ta lo'lael une kajval
a' ti puro pukuj ta s'abtej,

a' ti puro satanas une kajval.

a' ta xlo'lavan te cholol une kajval

e nitil une kajval,

It can't be that the demons make her do
   it, my Lord,
before your flowery presence,
before your flowery face, my Lord.

Thus it is written in your Bible . . .
Thus it is in the scripture,
That we mustn't drink a lot of rum,
   my Lord.

That's what you said in your story.
That's what you said in your talk,
   my Lord,
flowery God.
That's what you said in your book,
flowery Father, Jesus Christ, Father
   who art in heaven, my Lord.

"Respect yourselves, you can't use rum.
You can't take possession of rum,"
that's what you said, my Lord.

For this reason, my Lord, here, put a part
   of it for me in her mouth and in her
   lips, my Lord.
Grant her your healing power,
   my Lord . . .
there in distant mountains, my Lord,
there in distant lands, my Lord . . .

Let her be educated well about your
   first pitcher,
your first portion, my Lord,
flowery Jesus Christ, my Lord . . .

You are the savior, my Lord.
You cured the lame.
You cured the blind.
You cured the leper . . .

There they deceive her, my Lord,
they are demons who are at work in
   her life . . .
It is pure Satan, my Lord.

There the bottles of rum are lined up,
   my Lord,
and he is there with them, my Lord.

vax'elan une kajval.
ta stun
ta sbalin o une kajval
ti sba ap'is
ti sba xalu'
ti sba amerira une kajval nichim.

mu' j'ip o'ntonal van un kajval

mi jti' o'ntonal van un kajval

ja' mu xtoj sc'u.

ja' mu xtoj yich
ja' mu xtoj yats'am;
ja' mu xtoj k'usi ta stun bi.
mu xtoj ti k'usi tsbaline une kajval

ta anichimal ba
ta anichimal sta une kajval.

toj utsuts sba un kajval.

axe'lan une kajval.
ak'o me stsak sbek'etal
ak'o me stsac stakipal ek un kajval.

toj olol to une kajval
ta stun ta sbain,

ti sba ap'ise
ti sba axalu'
ti sba ameril une kajval.

ti mu sve'eluk ti mu yuch'omukuk,
mu xchi'ieluk
mu sc'opajeluk,
mu sak'be sba vokol ti bu javal xkom

ta jun kaya ta jun xoral un kajval ti pobre
kirisyano une kajval.

pero manbil chava'i pox ne une kavjal,
mu ta smotonuc bu ta stun,

mu ta smotonuc bu tsbain.

Look, how she is, my Lord.
She indulges herself.
She makes herself owner, too, my Lor
of your first cup,
of your first pitcher,
of your first portion, flowery Lord.

Perhaps it's because of some envy, m
    Lord,
or perhaps it's because of some ang
    my Lord . . .

Because of it she can no longer buy
    clothes;
she can no longer buy her chile,
she can no longer buy her salt;
she can no longer buy what she ne
She can no longer buy things that
    her well-being then, my Lord,
before your flowery presence,
before your flowery face, my Lor

Well, this abandoned one makes
    her, my Lord.
Look how she is then, my Lord.
Let her flesh become strong.
Let her body become strong, to
    Lord . . .

She's just a child, my Lord,
to be using rum and becoming
    of it,
of your first cup,
of your first pitcher,
of your first portion, my Lord

Don't let them be like food, o
They don't serve her well-bei
nor for her upbringing.
Don't let this poor Christian
    herself
by passing out in some stree
    my Lord . . .

But as rum is bought, my lo
where she drinks it they do
    to her.
They don't give it to her to

ora mo'oj xalok'esbun ta sjol un kajval.

xalok'esbun ta yo'ntonun kavjal.
Mu xu' puch'ul o,
Mu xu' nitil o une kajval

ja' yu'un avokolikuk une kajval.

ti sjoybinel,
ti scha'tij.
ti scha'vok'inaj.

Ti scha'ayinaj eke kajval.
xcha'och ti ich'ay une kajval
nichimal riox, nichimal jkaxlan
muk'ul riox, jesucristo kajval.

ak'o yo'nton une kajval;

ak'o x'abtej ta sna;

ak'o x'abej ta sk'uleb.
me oy ston une kajval.
me oy stak'in une kajval.

ak'o sman sve'el
ak'o sman me span.
ak'o sman me sopa.
ak'o sman svakax.
ak'o sman k'usi,
k'usi sna' stuel ek ta slumal eke kajval.

ak'o sba ta skaxa.
ak'o sba ta skajon une kajval.
me oy ti stone une kajval,
me oj ti staki'in une javajal.

k'uxi ta sta ti ton une?
K'uxi ta sta ti tak'in une kajval?

Amuk'unuk te sa'eluk ti jun alurasil
ti jun apaxional une kajval.
Avokol ta sa'el une jajval.

Now cast rum out of her mind for me
there, my Lord.
Cast it out of her heart for me, my Lord.
She can't be always lying down,
nor continue with drinking then,
my Lord.

For this reason do me the favor,
my Lord.
Let her mind turn around.
Let her demons be defeated.
And let her be re-born, my Lord.

Let her get back on the good path,
because she has been lost, my Lord,
flowery God, flowery Ladino,
great God, Jesus Christ, my Lord . . .

Grant her a heart capable of everything,
my Lord.
Let her work in her house;
[Let her have enough food or money
not to have to work on a plantation]

Let her work in her home.
if she has a stone [money], my Lord
if she has money, my Lord.

Let her buy something to eat.
Let her buy bread.
Let her buy soup.
Let her buy beef.
Let her buy whatever,
whatever she eats there in her land,
my Lord . . .

Let her know how to keep it.
Let her know how to value it, my Lord,
if she has money, my Lord,
if she has money, my Lord . . .

How does one earn money, then?
How does one find money, my Lord?

Well, it's not easy to find your blessings,
my Lord.
It takes a lot out of us to look for it,
my Lord.

ja' to ti mi ibak' yak une kajval.

ja' to ti mi ibak' sk'ob une kajval.
ta sta ti akurusil une, ta sta ti apaxional
une kajval.

avocoluc me ka'itik un kavjal.
ja' yu'un tana un vo'ot xava'anaba:
ja' xak'ejbun ti jun pukuj
Ja' xak'ejbun ti jun satanas
ta sjol
to yo'onton.

Jech bu xvak jun musico xa'i

Bu xvak jun k'usi xvak xai'i
mu xa sna batel.
mu xa ja' st'un batel.

ja' yo' xikejet
o ta xipatet o ta,
ta yolon avok une kajval,
ta yolon ak'ob une kajval.
ta akeoval ta avaxinal une kajval
jalame' maría santisima, jalalme' rosario

k'elbeikun un kajval,
ta avol anich'on.
Ak'bun tal atsatsal
yalesbun talel ts'ujesbun
talel ta atsatsale ta avu'el une ta stojol

ti pobre Carly une kajval,
nichimal riox, jesucristo kajval.

She will obtain it if she moves her feet,
   my Lord,
if she moves her hands, my Lord,
then she finds your blessings, my Lord.

Please do me the favor now, my Lord.
That's why, thou who standest erect:
Throw out the demon!
Throw out the Devil,
from her mind,
from her heart.

So, too, if she hears some music
   somewhere,
or hears something,
don't let her go,
don't let her follow it . . .

This is why I come,
kneeling with my face to the ground,
beneath your feet, my Lord,
and under your hands, my Lord,
under your shadow, my Lord . . .
Holy Mother Mary, Mother Rosario . . .

Look at me, my Lord,
at your daughter.
Send me your healing strength.
Lower it to me.
Let your strength fall and send your
   power
to your poor Carly, my Lord,
flowery God, Jesus Christ, my Lord . . .

Note

Margarita Pérez's prayer was originally published in *Women and Alcohol in a Highland Maya Town: Water of Hope, Water of Sorrow* by Christine Eber 2000 [1995], pp. 166–171. The prayer is a condensed version of the original prayer which Pérez prayed in two churches over the course of three hours. It is reprinted here with permission of the University of Texas Press.

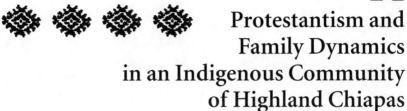

14
Protestantism and Family Dynamics in an Indigenous Community of Highland Chiapas

GABRIELA PATRICIA ROBLEDO HERNÁNDEZ
Translated by Christine Kovic and Christine Eber

Introduction

Religious conversion, among other forms of economic and social change, transforms families, households, and private life. This chapter examines the relationship between religious affiliation and social life in a rural community. I present some results of a larger research project that examines the reproduction of domestic groups of diverse religions in highland Chiapas.[1] This chapter examines Protestant households, especially those practicing Pentecostalism.[2]

My research indicates that women are more affected than men by the cultural change resulting from religious conversion. Although Protestant women do not occupy leadership roles in their churches, they constitute the largest part of the faithful who attend religious services. Many of the women search for refuge in religious congregations in order to confront challenges in their subordinate relationships with their spouses. The ties created through religious groups give women the possibility of weaving new support and solidarity, networks that are indispensable for widows, single mothers, or those who are ill. Women who have grown up under the influence of the new religions have acquired a new way of thinking that includes gender role expectations that differ from traditional ones. Participation in Protestant groups allows women to create a new type of life.

---

[1]My doctoral dissertation, "Religiosidad y estrategias de reproducción de grupos domésticos en una comunidad indígena" (Colegio de la Frontera Sur 2002), compares the numerous religious groups of the region, namely, Catholics, Protestants, and Traditionalists.
[2]In my research, I followed Richard Wilk in examining three dimensions of the reproduction of domestic groups: (1) morphology (which considers family composition); (2) activities (which include the paid and unpaid activities of household members); and (3) culture (which considers the family dynamic). By family dynamic I refer to the relations between genders and generations that are created in daily and generational reproductive processes of domestic groups. In this chapter, I use other terms that are more helpful for comparison with chapters in this book.

Conversion to Protestantism has taken place in the context of dramatic economic and social changes in highland Chiapas in the 1970s and 1980s. During the '70s indigenous workers were recruited from highland communities to build hydroelectric dams in the Central Valley. Cancian (1992) describes how the development policies of this period transformed the occupations of the peasant farmers of Zinacantán (a highland township), deepening the social differentiation between members of the community and impacting the political and ceremonial life of the community. Additionally, women's insertion in the labor market in the 1980s through the sale of artisan products or salaried work, brought a new element of change into the family interaction patterns in the Highlands.

This study was carried out in the *ejido* (community) of Campo Santiago located in the township of Teopisca, in the southwestern region of Highland Chiapas. The community was formed in the mid-1960s by indigenous families from the nearby townships of Chanal, Huixtán, Oxchuc, Amatenango del Valle, and Venustiano Carranza who had worked as *baldíos* on the plantations of the zone.[3] These families formally requested that the Secretary of Agrarian Reform grant them an ejido. This request was met in 1981.

Conversion to Protestantism is common in the region surrounding Campo Santiago. In the 1980s, various groups of expelled Protestant Chamulas[4] acquired land in the zone around the ejido and mobilized to gain the rights to the land that they had worked as sharecroppers. They began to divide and sell the property. Toward the end of 1997, there were 22 hamlets in the area surrounding the ejido. The increased importance of these settlements influenced the growth of Evangelical congregations in this zone.

I initiated fieldwork at the end of 1999 with periodic visits to the community over a two-year period. Between December of 1999 and January 2000 I carried out a census that revealed that the population consisted of 398 people distributed in 62 domestic groups. Residents are Tzotzil and Tzeltal Mayas. Some residents speak more than one native language, others speak only Spanish. In terms of religious affiliation, 80 percent were Catholic; Pentecostals, Seventh Day Adventists, and Evangelicals made up the other 20 percent. The Catholics in the community are divided into those who practice a traditional religion revolving around communitarian festivals and those who participate in the pastoral work of the Catholic Church. The former is by far the largest group. The religious life of this group centers around the Fiesta of La Santa Cruz (The Holy Cross), a Mesoamerican agricultural ritual with a long tradi-

---

[3] *Baldíos* refers to indigenous peoples who were allowed to cultivate their cornfields on a small piece of land in exchange for working long hours for landowners of fincas.
[4] Thousands of indigenous peoples have been expelled from their homes in the indigenous township of San Juan Chamula for complex political, economic, and religious reasons.

tion among the Mayas (Friedel, et al. 1993). The Fiesta of Señor Santiago (Saint James), patron of the community, is organized by the local authorities of the chapel who participate in the pastoral work of the Catholic Diocese of San Cristóbal de Las Casas.[5]

The Multiple Productive Activities of Protestant Women

One element characterizing Protestant households in Campo Santiago is the wide range of productive activities carried out by women. In contrast to Catholic women, Protestant women tend to diversify the types of productive work that generate income. Throughout highland Chiapas female income has played an important role in the survival of indigenous households (Nash 1993). The crisis of Mexican agriculture in the 1980s forced indigenous women to look for income to support their families. Since then, women's contributions to the domestic economy have transformed gender roles, which in turn have affected other areas of the social reproduction of the family (Rus 1990; Eber 2000 [1995]; Rosenbaum 1991).

My survey of activities in campesino homes revealed that 86.3 percent of the women carried out some type of activity to earn income. Protestant women's most important source of income is making tostadas to sell in the markets of Teopisca and San Cristóbal. In addition, Protestant women engage in salaried work and agricultural labor in cornfields. The large number of female-headed households explains the high percentage of women who must earn money to support their families.

Marriage

Female Heads of Households in Protestant Families

Although nuclear families predominate in Campo Santiago, comparing Catholic to non-Catholic households reveals that the Protestants have a higher percentage of female-headed households, i.e. households that lack a spouse and are headed, in most cases, by widows or divorced or separated women.[6] Female-headed households also exist that are not recognized as such. These include households headed by women who return to their parents' homes to support their children without a spouse. This type of family arrangement permits young single mothers to earn their own income through working, without placing the survival of their children at risk because they can count on the support of their natal family. The following testimonies from Flor and Dorotea, two Pentecostal women, illustrate how joining a Pentecostal community helped the women better their own and their children's lives.

---

[5]This type of Catholicism is referred to as "Word of God" or the preferential option for the poor in other chapters of this book.
[6]In Catholic households, the percent of female-headed households is 11.3%, while 30.8% of Protestant households are female headed.

Flor is a 52-year-old leader in her community. Daughter of one of the founders of the ejido, she participated with her father and brothers in negotiations to gain access to the land. She collaborated in community programs, the most recent being Progresa and was named a promoter of the program two years ago.[7] Women of the community respect her because she knows some medicine and attends postpartum women.

When Flor left her husband, she moved to San Cristóbal where a friend helped her and took her to an Evangelical church. There, together with her friend, Flor decided to devote herself to the new religion. In the new congregation she found the spiritual strength necessary to live without her husband. Flor tells the story of her marriage:

> [My marriage] went very badly for me because we lived together for only a year. After getting married, he [my husband] began to drink a lot. He was very bad. He hit me. He was jealous. We couldn't live in peace. He wanted to kill me. Three times I endured this abuse, but then the fourth time, I left him in peace.
> . . . I was Catholic when I was with him. But then I became Evangelical. . . . He stayed single, and I stayed single. . . . As the Bible says . . . I didn't get married again. Neither he nor I married. And later, my children were given to me. [Flor refers to the two children she adopted and who now make up her family].

After a while, Flor returned to live in Campo Santiago, but as a converted woman. She did not return to live with her husband, in spite of his insistence that she do so. Years later her husband died of alcoholism.

Dorotea, a 32-year-old woman, currently lives with her children in the home of her widowed father whom she cares for. Like Flor, she left her husband because he abused her.

> I married at age 20. Well, I didn't get married. . . . we started to live together, nothing more. Later, my husband treated me badly, he hit me a lot, he had a lover. I had my son, my son was 1 year old when I left my husband. . . . We divorced because I didn't want to continue with him. And so, that's how our life was before . . . After so much upheaval and so many problems I didn't like it anymore and went to live in San Cristóbal to work for a time, to raise my son. . . . I worked there as a servant. . . . I found a woman who treated me well. I stayed with her for 2 years. . . . That is when a man deceived me and "brought me" this child. After I was pregnant, after I couldn't work anymore, I came here [to Campo Santiago] where my [second] son was born.
> [I used to be Catholic . . .] and my father was president of the chapel. When my father left that position, I studied catechism and began to teach catechism to children. But I was discouraged, I didn't like it that people were talking about me again. . . .

---

[7]Progresa is an aid program for campesino families begun under the administration of President Ernesto Zedillo (1994–2000). In contrast to other programs, aid is directed toward women and children who regularly attend school in rural communities.

It's been about four months [since I changed my religion]. I didn't like having problems [with the people], I couldn't put up with it anymore. They talked a lot; it is worse when you are Catholic, worse because they didn't understand the readings [from the Bible] and the catechists don't explain them very well, and we don't know anything. When we were Catholic, we didn't know anything, nothing about the fiesta. . . . We would say that we were good Catholics, but we were lost. We would dance [laughs] but it was the dance of the demons. . . . Now we are learning, before we were lost. We will raise ourselves up, little by little. I don't like being Catholic any longer.

Flor and Dorotea each separated from their spouses and found a support network in the religious group where they were not shunned for being separated from their husbands. They negotiated their personal difficulties by joining an Evangelical congregation where they found other women in similar conditions who offered mutual support in quotidian tasks such as cutting firewood in areas far from the pueblo, or selling tostadas in the market of San Cristóbal.

Selection of Marriage Partners

Freyermuth Enciso (1999) notes that the attitude of new religious groups—for example, Pentecostals and Presbyterians in Chenalhó—are more open in relation to the role and participation of women and youth in the society. This openness has transformed women's participation in selecting a marriage partner.

Below I relate the marital experiences of three daughters of a Pentecostal family—Carmen, Berenice, and Gertrudis. During childhood, the girls lived outside the ejido for several years in a colonia of the township of Venustiano Carranza. Later they moved to Betania and Jerusalem (two Protestant communities in the township Teopisca), and finally back to Campo Santiago.

Upon finishing secondary school at age 18, Carmen found work as a community teacher. She was assigned to El Cambray, a community in Teopisca. She did not work there for long before she met a man who would become the father of her first two children.

. . . I was 18 years old [when] I met him [my children's father]. He worked on the buses of the route San Cristóbal–Teopisca–Comitán. I met him there because I traveled a lot. He asked me [to go out with him] and I said yes, and so we began our relationship. It lasted until after the second daughter was born.

. . . He had another woman. He told me that he didn't, but at the same time, people told me that he did, that he was married. I didn't believe it, but after I saw it myself, I knew that it was true.

. . . From the day I saw him [with another woman] I didn't want anything to do with him. But, since I was pregnant already, he told me that he wouldn't leave me because of the child, that we should stay together until the child was born, and that he would pay child support . . . When I was five months pregnant with my daughter [Sarita, her second daughter], I stopped seeing him. . . .

At age 14, Berenice, married a man from her community. He was a traditionalist and asked permission from Berenice's parents to marry her. Dalia, Berenice's 39 year-old mother, explained:

> The man came to ask permission because he liked my daughter. He wanted to marry her. We gave our permission. When my daughter came she said yes, that she agreed to marry him. We told the man that they should have a civil wedding and he accepted. . . . A few days later the father of the young man came because his mother had advised him not to marry. The mother started to give bad advice to her son, saying that they shouldn't get married because one day they could break up. The couple ran away. . . . For three months [my daughter] was with the man and then she came back already pregnant with her daughter . . . The mother started to gossip that the child was not her son's, that the girl was the child of Carmen's husband . . . So they started to conspire to kick out my daughter. . . . They kicked her out when she was three months pregnant. . . . To this day the man insists that he is not the father of the girl . . . They even asked us to give back what they had spent [the gifts given to the wife's family when a marriage is arranged]. But I said that I wouldn't give back the money because my daughter now has a child. . . . The custom [in our community] is that the [newlyweds] don't stay long [with the husband's family]. But he [my daughter's husband] told her, "Ten years we will live here, you will obey my mother." And his mother said, "For ten years you have to lend a hand here."
>
> No, my daughter didn't agree. So they called us to a community assembly. The people united. The people said, "Better that they live apart, that they have their own home. . . ." [The man said] "No, I don't want to leave, I am going to stay for 10 years in my mother's house." So they separated again. After they separated, he took another girl like this and three months later he left her. . . . So then he asked my daughter's forgiveness, he said, "Yes, I admit that I'm guilty. Yes I admit that this daughter is mine." But my daughter didn't want him. "Not anymore," she told him. "Get yourself another woman. I don't want you anymore.". . . Now he has another woman and a baby who was just born.

After completing high school in San Cristóbal, Gertrudis, the youngest sister, went to live with the son of her boss. She was determined to go to the city and did so, eventually living with a Catholic man. She was certain, she told me, that she didn't want to marry a *ranchero* (man from the countryside). Gertrudis was attracted to urban life. She dressed in pants in the city, but changed out of them before going to her parents' home to avoid scoldings or beatings. Currently, she has a son and lives with her husband and mother-in-law in San Cristóbal. Her parents allow her to visit them with her son.

The experiences of these three sisters demonstrate the independence of Protestant women in selecting marriage partners. Two of the sisters chose spouses against the wishes of their parents, passing over the practices of bride petition, and choosing men who not only were from another community, but who worked in the city. Carmen and Berenice returned to their parents' home as single mothers with their children. To support their respective families, they make tostadas, and Carmen, the eldest, has salaried work while her mother cares for her two children. The degree of independence that the three daughters exercised in their marital decisions is greater than young women typically experience in traditional families.

Building a New Family Dynamic in Protestant Homes

Rejecting alcohol and domestic violence are the most important factors influencing changes in gender and generational relations in Protestant households. Alcohol use has become one of the most important parameters of differentiation between traditional religious groups and the Christian groups, especially Pentecostals and other Evangelical groups.[8]

Traditionalists consider alcohol as sacred; alcohol is present in public and private social transactions uniting all participants with "one heart."[9] Drinking *aguardiente* (rum) during community fiestas is part of local custom in Campo Santiago. For example, in one community fiesta people began to drink during the ceremony at the waterfall and continued doing so during the night when the ceremony was moved to the chapel. By then, some of the participants were rather drunk. Nonetheless, the community does not condone excessive drinking. A traditional religious leader who had participated in the prayer at the cross was removed from the festival because of excessive drinking.

Disputes and conflicts are frequently associated with alcohol use; alcohol is feared for its connection with envy and resentment (emotions believed to precede any illness) that result from these conflicts. Residents of Chenalhó say that deities come to them in dreams condemning alcohol abuse and requesting that soft drinks be used instead of rum in festivals in their honor (Eber 2000 [1995]: 211). Experiences such as these have encouraged the prohibition of alcohol sales in some highland Chiapas *cabeceras* (the administrative and political centers of townships). In Campo Santiago local authorities in the community assembly prohibited the sale of aguardiente in the community, and one community member was jailed during 2001 for breaking this law.

Research in Chiapas suggests that domestic violence is linked to alcohol abuse and is a mechanism of female subordination (Miranda Arteaga 1998; Freyermuth Enciso 2000). Women's perceptions in Campo Santiago are similar to those of researchers—they see alcohol and domestic violence as linked. Alcohol abuse has had negative effects on indigenous families where women and children suffer from a lack of money, mistreatment, and illness. Although women and children also drink during rituals and ceremonies, alcohol abuse and dependence is generally limited to men.

---

[8]Eber, Kovic, and Gil in this volume note that Catholic women, particularly in indigenous communities, have also worked to curb the use of alcohol.

[9]According to Eber (2000[1995]:25), alcohol has substituted the sacrifice of human blood in contemporary Mayan rituals. Alcohol is considered to represent "the drops of blood from the hands and feet of Jesus Christ."

In my interviews with families who have converted to new religions, women repeatedly stated that their husbands' and fathers' giving up alcohol has led to better treatment of themselves and their children. Below are Dalia's and Dorotea's stories.

Dalia was married at age 16 in the Catholic Church. Eladio, her husband, converted to Pentecostalism a year after marriage. Dalia links alcohol with abuse, and notes that her husband changed after his conversion.

> Yes, I saw him as different because he didn't drink so much. [Before] he drank every week, he drank and there was no money. But he managed to study the Bible, then he changed a lot, he didn't drink, he didn't come to hit me. . . . First he accepted [the new religion] and then I did.

In her opinion, when a spouse drinks, the wife suffers a lot, "Well, I hear that many women are beaten, their husbands grab them by their hair, there is no money, just alcohol. . . . Life is sad."

Eladio "looked for his religion" as an exit from the violence that imprisoned him when he drank. Men, especially older men, may become ill after years of drinking alcohol, and religious conversion serves as a mechanism to help them end their drinking. "Finding religion" permits them to create a social environment that distances them from regular drinkers, and at the same time, strengthens their will to feed the sacred part of their personality. Such is the case of Gustavo, who was already old and ill when he "looked for his religion." His daughter, Dorotea, gave her testimony of the violence of her father when he came home after drinking.

> [My father] used to drink a lot. My younger sister used to live here and my father would come home very drunk. He would hit us with a stick, almost killing us. He threw chairs; they flew by our heads. He would become furious with us. We wanted to go far away to work; we wanted to leave him alone because we saw how he was when he drank excessively. Later, two brothers who lived here came by every week to explain the word of God. When [my father] was very ill and he couldn't get out of bed, his knees got cold, and he couldn't even walk. . . . All of the siblings gathered together and we told him to follow the new religion, that he shouldn't give up because otherwise, he would continue there lying down. He accepted. In time, he was able to get up, little by little. The brothers came to pray with him every afternoon, and he got up and finally recovered. . . . He changed. Now it is more peaceful. We are content now; we don't see him drunk anymore. Yes, we changed as well. I thought, "We have to leave these bad things behind . . . because they are not good."

Barrios and Pons collected similar testimonies from Evangelical women who live in the city of San Cristóbal. "All women pointed out that their relationships with their husbands improved after conversion because the spouses used to drink and hit them. Now the men only drink 'every once in a while' and when they do they do not 'come to scold or hit us, they fall asleep, nothing more'" (1995: 78). These testimonies from San Cristóbal reveal that women are treated better when alcohol is not consumed. However, the absence of drinking in Protestant households does not mean the absence of violence against women.

Another element that affects the position of women in the family is polygamy, a practice tolerated in highland indigenous communities. Although monogamy is the model for marriage, a man may have several wives who live in one or several households. This type of union carries a high economic and emotional cost for the male given that he has to support several women with their respective children, and it frequently involves tension between the wives who compete for the resources provided by the husband (Rosenbaum 1991).

Ethnographic information reveals that men in polygamous unions frequently take the sister of their spouse as a second wife, which generally leads to the breakdown of the siblings' relationship. Nonetheless, Freyermuth Enciso (2000) gathered testimonies of women who affirmed that the presence of another wife could be advantageous if the two wives created an alliance based on the distribution of domestic tasks and if they supported one another in cases of illness or domestic violence.

In the testimonies I collected, women associated polygamy with abuse. In the following testimony Dalia relates the difficulties she experienced as a child.

> Because my father had two women, we could never live well. We didn't have enough clothes. He wasn't responsible. He had children with the other woman. My first stepmother said that he gave us more than her. We suffered, the women fought. . . . We lived separately but there was jealously over the food, money, everything. So, I asked my mother why she married my father when there are single men? Why did they fight for my father? . . . It was very ugly. It shouldn't be that way.

Protestant groups preach monogamous and lasting unions as one of the distinct elements of a new ethic opposed to traditionalism. The indigenous women I spoke with favor monogamous unions and link them to the well-being of their families.

Conclusion

From examining the daily life of Campo Santiago households, we can see that Protestantism is shaping indigenous families' search for alternatives in the face of household and community changes resulting from policies developed at the regional and national level. Religious groups have facilitated both collective and individual responses to the most important problems facing indigenous families—alcoholism, illness, violence, and the extreme poverty that accompanies these ills. For indigenous women, a husband's drinking typically means abuse, lack of money, and family illness. The ethic encouraged by Protestant groups directly affects their quality of life and the well-being of women and their children.

New gender identities, both masculine and feminine, are being constructed through Protestant conversion. Men, whose central activities revolved around public community life, cede much of this space for the home and interaction with their families when they convert to Protestant churches. Public life, which culturally has been masculine par excellence, becomes centered on the cargos of the new religious group.

Women are making use of new religious ideologies to transform customs—such as domestic violence, alcoholism, and polygamy—that mark their position of subordination to men. Nonetheless, women who have opted for this path also confront new difficulties. Their conduct, often considered as transgressing social norms, can cause tension in their marriages and lead to separation and divorce. As female heads of household, women rely on networks woven around religious congregations for their social support.

The social change shaped by religious conversion does not radically question indigenous women's status. For example, women do not hold leadership positions within Protestant Churches. However, the new churches do give women a tool to transform some aspects of subordination in their lives.

15
Women's Empowerment through Religious Change in Tenejapa

SUSANNA ROSTAS

Introduction

Maria and Antonia are two teenage Tzeltal girls who live in one of the *parajes* (hamlets) of the rural indigenous township of Tenejapa. To the anthropologist who has known the community for some time, the most striking thing about them is how well turned out they are. Their traditional clothing is neat and clean, their skirts immaculately pleated and belted, their hair combed, braided, and tied with bright new ribbons. Although their families are, like all families, *campesinos* (peasants), the girls give the impression that they no longer have to work on the land but lead a more leisurely life. As they approach me, they begin to giggle, but stop briefly to exchange greetings. They are on their way to attend the midweek service in the nearby temple and are clearly in a hurry. Their new religion is the consuming interest of their lives. They *know* that they have a special relationship with God and are amongst the chosen who will be saved. They carry themselves with self-assurance and give the onlooker the clear message that all is well with their world. They have a degree of self-confidence that those who have not yet "found the way" rarely show. These girls are typical of the way in which women are gaining a new sense of self but not one that aims to give them access to or a position in the male world.

In Tenejapa, new social space is being created by women as they become involved in the various Protestant religions that have recently gained representation.[1] Although the proselytizers who bring in the new religions are always

---

[1] In the late 1980s, throughout Latin America a wave of conversion to Protestant and other churches began to occur on a previously unprecedented scale (Stoll 1990; Martin 1990). Although religious change of this kind had been underway for decades in some indigenous communities, it has been only in the last 20 years that the rate has accelerated. For recent work on religious change in Chiapas (where in many communities converts have been forced to leave), see Sullivan 1998; Giménez 1996; Robledo Hernández 1987; Hernández Castillo 1989. For overviews of the literature and the churches, respectively, see Hernández Castillo 1992; Pérez Enríquez 1994; Rivera Farfán 1998. For religious change as situated in its broader social context see Hernández Castillo 2001 and Eber 2000 [1995]. The significance of conversion for women's empowerment remains, however, a largely unexplored area.

local men, it is women who make up the greater proportion of those who are active in the recently built places of worship, as attendance at any service quickly reveals. The new social community formed thereby, although it links them with the wider society, is strengthening indigenous identity rather than weakening it, and giving new impetus to their ethnicity.

In part, this chapter asks whether this change in religion is predominantly about religious conversion, or whether it is not as much about affiliation: a means for women to develop new forms of agency in a community that is being rapidly drawn into the global economy, but where, at least at present, women have far fewer opportunities than men. Which of the new churches now available in the community is chosen is often of less significance than the fact that religious change is sought. For what is occurring often seems to be as much about the taking up of a new lifestyle, as about an inner religious transformation, at least in the first instance. One woman, for example, admitted that her family had joined the Baptist Church less for reasons of belief or even practice, than because of the kinship ties that her family had with other new members. I thus explore how the self-gendering of women alters as they take up the new religions, which is reflected in the greater freedom that younger women in particular enjoy in everyday life.[2] It should be borne in mind, however, that this autonomy is achieved at the price of being brought into a subordinate position with respect to the men who dominate the hierarchical structures of the Protestant churches to which the Tenejapans are turning.

The Community

The Tenejapans grow maize and beans for subsistence, supplemented with the cash crop of coffee by those who live at lower elevations. The population was some 27,217 in 1990 (according to the Census) and they are predominantly monolingual Tzeltal speakers, although boys usually learn some Spanish at school. For most of the time, the Tenejapans are to be found at the *ranchería*, as they have begun to designate their simple homesteads. Located on the land that they farm, these are usually fairly isolated from one another although there are occasional hamlets. The men spend their time working in the fields with the assistance of their wives and children, although principally a woman's life is centered in the home, where she works intensively in the early morning to make the tortillas and beans for the day. In the afternoon, a family will usu-

---

[2]This type of appropriation probably happens more frequently at the grass roots, in largely preliterate, comparatively isolated indigenous communities than in cities or towns. In the latter two, the process of religious affiliation can be more tightly controlled and those joining can be drawn into an already existing community of believers. Detailed studies on the mechanisms and effects of conversion and/or affiliation appeared in the 1990s (Rostas and Droogers 1993; Droogers, et al. 1991; Stephen and Dow 1990; Garrard-Burnett and Stoll 1993; Burdick 1993. For Mexico, in particular, see the work of Garma Navarro 1987; Fortuny Loret de Mola 1989).

ally work close to the house as the younger children return from school. Then the woman may settle down to weave before preparing the evening meal. Her husband often assists with collecting and carrying firewood or bringing the water. Aside from these tasks, a woman makes occasional trips with other women to wash clothes in the nearby river, and to make purchases from the small shops in neighboring houses. The latter may involve conversations, but women, unlike men, do not just go out and about (*pasear*) for the sake of it.

On market days, women often travel to the *cabecera* to sell, accompanied by their husbands. The cabecera is the politico-religious and administrative center of the township inhabited largely by Spanish-speaking mestizos, who number some 1000 persons. Here the Catholic Church is located where an indigenous couple goes to pray. The practices of the indigenes are, however, completely separate from those of the Catholic mestizos and until recently, most Tenejapans knew little of mainstream Catholicism. They venerate, rather, a number of immanent deities, the sun and moon being the principal ones. These and others are represented in the church in anthropomorphic form by images of Catholic Saints: San Alonso (known as Kahkanantik in Tzeltal, which glosses as the sun) and Santa Maria (Halame'tik or the moon) (Rostas 1987). The practices associated with the Saint-deities constitute a so-called cargo system. By taking a religious cargo, a woman and her husband undertake to look after, as part of a group, one of the ten Saint-deities. A fiesta can last for up to eight days and engenders a community of interest among the participants. Women have a chance to talk openly with women from other parajes, contacts that, later on, can be used in other spheres of life. The religious cargos thus help to create ties for a couple, which, although not those of kinship (and they are never likened to them), are based on a trust developed with people whom they would not otherwise have had the means of meeting. Taking a cargo was, until recently, one of the few significant roles that a woman could have in her life, outside her house.[3] Catholicism amongst the indigenes in Tenejapa has only been Catholicism of the most popular kind.[4] Although mass is held in the church by a resident priest, who baptizes, confirms, and marries the mestizos, these services are not part of the practices of, nor offered to the indigenes, nor is the priest present at any of the ceremonies that the indigenes hold there.[5] The Bible in Tzeltal, let alone the New Testament, has

---

[3]Information from other townships indicates that women can also act as midwives and curers.

[4]In Latin America in general, much of so-called Catholicism has for many centuries been little more than a veneer that has appeased the Catholic Church. Many of the present conversions are of rural (or newly urbanized) peoples previously practicing such forms of folk-Catholicism (see Rostas and Droogers 1993:1–16).

[5]This has apparently changed recently. Currently there is a priest working with the indigenes as indicated in the postscript.

never been made easily available by the Catholic Church and few until recently have been literate.

A woman's role as a religious cargo holder is essential although ancillary to that of her husband: a married couple usually take such cargos together.[6] Although in general, during ritual, the boundaries between men and women are as strongly emphasized as in everyday life, these tend to break down a little as the ceremonies progress. On a quotidian basis there are very clear differences between the sexes; women do not go out alone but take an accompanying child. On the footpath a man does not greet a woman. If a man comes to a house and the woman's husband is out, she will stay inside and reply to his greetings in a high falsetto voice, displaying the "kinesics of deference" (Brown 1981). Women by tradition have only a muted voice outside the home. Although personal autonomy is highly valued, women have never been able to develop much agency outside the sphere of the house, whether this be their home in the paraje, or the cargo holders' house in the cabecera. They do not (and cannot) politicize in the world of men. Although the religious cargos are linked to the political cargos, women participate here only as wives. But the difference between indigenous men and women is still much less than the difference between them both and the mestizos in the cabecera, who have exerted a form of moral control and economic exploitation over the indigenous population for centuries.[7]

In the last few decades, participation in the religious cargos has become increasingly difficult to secure, as the number of positions in relation to a growing population, have become few: at present less than 5 percent can actively participate.[8] They have also increasingly been filled by a small number of regu-

---

[6]However, I know of cases where an older woman took cargos with her married son.

[7]Although only a tiny percentage of the overall population, mestizos often earned their livings as middlemen between the indigenes and the wider mestizo world, learning only as much Tzeltal as would further their interests. The transcendence of the mestizos has gradually been eclipsed by the emergence of a class of indigenous caciques. They mostly reside in the cabecera and have become rich and powerful by means of the high-ranking political cargos. Typically, during his term of office, a cacique pockets considerable sums of federal money, overriding the pervasive code of reciprocity and trust and ensuring his subsequent economic and political hegemony. The caciques' religious affiliation, if any, is to the cargo system and their attitude to the converts is at best ambivalent. In other Chiapas communities, such as Chamula, the caciques have expelled the converts, whereas in Tenejapa they have not moved against them.

[8]In the last few decades, the population of Tenejapa has risen hugely. According to the 1960 census, it was 9768; for 1980, 20,642, consisting of 3010 families (1982 Censo general de padres de familia del municipio de Tenejapa). In the '80s, approximately 150 to 200 families would have been involved in the cargo practices each year (i.e., 4.5 to 6.5 percent of the population or from 12 to 16 percent of the traditionalists who amounted to 40 percent of the total (see footnote 10). In 1961 Medina (n.d.) calculated that approximately 500 families were involved each year. If we can assume that the average family size has remained unaltered at 6.8, then in 1961 there would have been 1425 families in the township and involvement would have been occurring at the much higher rate of 35 percent.

lar devotees. This is partly because overall perceptions of what life should be about have been changing, which is linked to why so many people have switched their allegiances to the various new religions.

The Intrusion/Encroachment of Modernity

During the last four decades of the twentieth century, the countryside increasingly saw the emergence and sustenance of a more differentiated (and secular) way of life as the developed world gradually made inroads into the community. In the parajes, schools were built. Not only has the school system interfered with the pace of family life; families often want their children to be educated but also tend to keep them at home in order to have enough person-power for the work on the land. But the schools have also provided a new social focus for paraje life. Teenage boys play basketball on the adjacent courts and small shops have sprung up in the vicinity, where men congregate to talk and drink in the evenings. In the mid-1900s, drinking *chicha* (fermenting sugar-cane beer) and *pox* (cane alcohol) only occurred in the cabecera, and then usually only in connection with a fiesta. Now as transport has become easier both pox and more especially bottled beer are readily available. The new roads that enable the school teachers to come and go easily, also give access to officials from the various federal agencies. Some come to inspect housing conditions; there is a strong correlation between the incidence of illness and thatched roofing. Many houses now have tin or asbestos roofs and some, rather than having timber walls, are constructed from concrete block. Other agents have brought the possibilities of cash crops. Many living at lower elevations have converted much of their land to growing coffee and no longer grow enough maize and beans to be self-sufficient. Other agents have brought fertilizer to assist the growth in the first instance of coffee.

Success for the new crop is thus ensured by chemistry rather than prayer which has also become less important for subsistence crops. Previously prayers would be offered to *kaxaltik*, the female protector and sustainer of the earth, to ensure a good harvest. The old beliefs in this sphere, as in many others, no longer have the power or significance they once had. Those aspects of local community care or social control once under the auspices of the local male shaman (*cabildo*), have either lapsed or been taken over by others. The cabildo carried out ceremonies not only for the fertility of the fields, but also for rain, for the building of houses, and acted as a healer. It was a position of respect held for life. Each paraje now has a group of local men known as committees who, elected for one year, meet at night in the school. They take responsibility for the various affairs of the paraje; there is a representative for fertilizer, for water, for public works, and for lighting. Rather than seeking traditional healing, many now buy Western medicines from a small range stocked by one of the shops. Dispute settlement in the school is preferred to witchcraft, but more serious cases that have gone for some time are heard in the cabecera.

With better roads, mestizos can now come in and out more easily to buy and sell, and the distance to the closest Spanish-speaking town (San Cristóbal de las Casas) has been reduced both temporally and subjectively. Many people have transistor radios to listen to Tzeltal-speaking stations and electricity has recently been installed in most houses. Some families have even acquired sufficient capital from the sale of coffee to buy their own vehicles. Many now have bank accounts in town.

The Growth of the New Religious Community

During the period of the growth of the new institutional facilities, the religious picture did not remain static. Even before the roads had been completed, evangelists were starting to make forays into the community. Their success was marked by the appearance of various temples and chapels. Protestant Evangelists refer to their places of worship as temples and the other religions as chapels, except the Catholics who call theirs *hermitas*. All are built from durable, mestizo materials—concrete block—and are usually decorated with brightly colored inscriptions from the Bible in Tzeltal. But the incursions of the new religions have taken time and met with more initial resistance than the other changes described earlier.[9]

Currently evangelization in Tenejapa is carried out by indigenous men, predominantly from Tenejapa, who preach in Tzeltal. This is undoubtedly one of the keys to the success of the present wave of conversions. The Evangelical Presbyterian Church of Mexico, represented by the Dutch Reform Church has obtained a firm foothold, but so too to a lesser degree have the Independent Baptists, the Seventh Day Adventists, and the Jehovah's Witnesses.[10] The local evangelists were frequently converted while working outside the community (on the finca, teaching in a school, or working in Mexico City, for example). They have received training in their respective faiths at centers set up by Amer-

---

[9]Americans from the SIL (Summer Institute of Linguistics, otherwise known as the Wycliffe Bible Translators) arrived in Chiapas in the 1940s (Stoll 1982; Rus and Wasserstrom 1981). They were not able to make much headway in Tenejapa as conditions were then too stable. But they prepared vocabularies that were used in the translation of the New Testament into the Tzeltal spoken in other neighboring, lower-lying communities, such as Oxchuc. The New Testament was first published for that community in 1956 (Jarvis personal communication; Turner 1979; Siverts 1981). There has, however, been a Catholic hermita and a Protestant Evangelist temple in La Cañada, a paraje near the cabecera of Tenejapa since the early 1970s.

[10]A survey carried out in 1982 indicated that the approximate affiliations were as follows: 30 percent Protestant; 3 percent Baptist; 27 percent Catholic; 40 percent were involved in or still believed in the religious cargo practices (Censo general de padres de familia del municipio de Tenejapa, Chiapas 1982). The percentages have changed considerably since that survey. Support for the cargo practices, according to the 2000 census, amounted to only 21 percent of the population (described as "without religion"); Catholics had risen to 36 percent, Protestants to 36 percent, and "others" to 5 percent.

icans and/or other foreigners outside of the community. It is thus their interpretations of the new religions that are being offered in Tenejapa.[11]

In the various chapels and temples built by the different churches not a
word of Spanish is to be heard. The New Testament has been translated into
Tzeltal by the Mexican Bible Society (Catholic) while other religions have
more recently published their own versions.[12] Some Presbyterians own copies
of a hymn book published in 1977 with 324 hymns. A translation of the Old
Testament was recently produced by the Evangelical Presbyterian Church. The
Tenejapans are now achieving literacy by means of the Bible. The mytho-
poetic power of the story of a man, Jesus Christ from a foreign land unimag-
inably far away who "died to save us all," should not be underestimated.
Although the male preachers are much better educated than the majority,
other young men are beginning to read and are the proud owners of the various different versions of the New Testament. "Books" to them mean the Bible.
Teenage youths are frequently seen rushing along the path, with huge tape
recorders in one hand, clasping their Bibles in the other. If talked to, they will
tell you that neither the sun, the moon, nor corn should be perceived as alive
(*kuxul*) and that there is only one God up there (pointing at the sky).

For understanding to occur, however, not only is a literal translation of the
Bible required, but a further translation, which is conceptual. The decades of
syncretic Catholicism can be seen, in part, to have paved the way. For the indigenous (syncretic), beliefs are to an extent permeated with Catholic imagery.
Christian concepts are thus not entirely new. But not only must Tenejapans
change their way of thinking: the earth, the elements, and nature itself must
lose their anthropomorphism. More important, their practices need to be
shaped to fit the "Protestant Ethic" (as I will indicate).

Some have gone for Liberation Catholicism because they do not want to
give up saintly representation.[13] Others prefer Protestantism as the idea of a

---

[11]In an indigenous community, such as Tenejapa, although the local proselytizers have
had contact with an established branch of the church and have possibly had a conversion experience, those in the community are modeling their practice and belief on the
learned expertise of these proselytizers. The practices and beliefs found in a place such
as Tenejapa are thus often very different from those propagated in a town, let alone a
city.

[12]For example I have copies of the *Ach' Testamento* published by the Sociedad Biblica de
Mexico in the Tzeltal of Oxchuc (n.d.) and the *Yach'il Testamento*, Sociedad Biblica de
Mexico, in the Tzeltal of Bachajón (1964), of which, 2000 copies were printed for the
first edition, 15,000 for the fifth.

[13]The indigenous Liberation Catholicism community is separate from the mestizo
Roman Catholic community. (Liberation Catholicism is labeled Word of God in other
chapters of this book.) Liberation Catholicism has its places of worship in the parajes
whereas in the cabecera a separate hermita for indigenous worship has been constructed; the main Catholic Church is never used. On the whole, affiliation to Catholicism is less attractive to the Tenejapans than to Protestantism. This is partly because of
the association that Catholicism has with the mestizos and the church in the cabecera
and because some Liberation Catholics continue to drink.

God who tells you that you cannot depend on a saintly intermediary. Tene-japans have always displayed a tough self-sufficiency. Many, however, are not certain about why they have chosen their new religious affiliation. In the initial stages, the differences in the beliefs and practices of each church are often not immediately apparent. Even those who bring the churches into the commu-nity, have not necessarily joined the new religions for their particular repre-sentation of Christianity but rather from a sense of the inevitability of socio-religious change.

Women especially are taking on the new religions for a range of rather dif-ferent reasons. Often both more religious and more conservative than men, their reasons for conversion are also, frequently more pragmatic.[14] A woman may have heard about the Seventh Day Adventists from a sister, and the Jeho-vah's Witnesses from a neighbor. She follows the sister; kin ties are still stronger, more trustworthy. In another instance, the Catholic hermita is a hun-dred yards away, the temple of the Evangelical Presbyterian Church a mile away in a different paraje. So the hermita is chosen for its convenience and be-cause this is where most of those living close by go.[15] The Independent Baptists are showing a film, which attracts a lot of people, young and old, because this is a novel and exciting occurrence; this may or may not lead to longer term links with the organization. Or, the eldest son has heard about a musical group organized by the Presbyterians and persuaded the whole family to join that congregation. Affiliation occurs by the trickle effect (Fallers 1954). Families talk about what is going on, who is doing what, the effect it has had on them, evaluate, and act accordingly. Each woman and/or her family makes its deci-sion with the information available to it, which is often very limited. Some parajes only have one religion represented and a family may thus join that church. The effect of charisma or more straightforwardly, individual effort and dedication, should not be left out of the networking equation. It is often because of the efforts of one man, initially, that a religion has come to the com-munity. The Jehovah's Witnesses, for example, were brought in by Juan, a young man who had encountered them while working outside the commu-nity. When Juan returned, he started services in his house wanting to carry on with his new faith. With time he had enough adepts to collect money toward the building of a temple (funded predominantly by the wider organization); the religion became established and its following grew.

The Attraction of the New

But why is it that so many Tenejapans are ready now to abandon a long-term socio-religious form when in the 1940s they were not? How is it that evangeliz-

---

[14]Conversion experiences seem to be rarer for women than men (see Walker Bynum 1984:111; Ozorak 1996; Gallagher 1990).
[15]As indicated in the findings of a small survey I conducted in the paraje of Kotolté.

ers of local origin have managed to convince so many people—especially women—to give up so much of what was considered sacred and inviolate such a short time ago? The answer, in large measure, is due to the changes already discussed. Capitalism is slowly but surely creeping up into the mountains to engulf indigenous notions of community in general, but more especially of spiritual communality. Where previously there was no choice, there are now alternatives available. Celebrating a Saint-god's fiesta as a cargo holder involved not only drinking strong alcohol in excess but also eating, dancing, prayer making, and when someone was drunk, singing—all classic methods of achieving *communitas* (Turner 1982). This was, however, costly in terms of time and money; many couples who wanted to take a cargo could not finance it without taking out loans. The work involved required their presence in the cabecera, not just on weekends but also on weekdays, taking them away, from the daily round often for considerable periods. Too much alcohol is not conducive to work either. After a fiesta in the cabecera, the cargo holders were often seen struggling home, carrying their various bundles, often very hung over, if not physically ill, and incapable of work in the fields for several days.

The cargos, however, only involved a few people. The majority suffer because they live close to nature: contrary to Western romanticism, it is a very tough mode of existence. Most still do not have an adequate water supply and it is often only available in small quantities at a tap located in a public place. Tenejapan cosmology does not see any connection between dirt and disease: all illness is caused by spirit entities. The new religions are, however, awakening people to the germ theory of disease and propagating the idea that "cleanliness is closer to Godliness." The proselytizers also explain that beds are better for sleeping on than the floor—many families by necessity still sleep on straw mats on the floor, in the room in which they cook and eat during the day. These kinds of messages are an important aspect of religious change. When asked why they have converted, Tenejapan's often answer that there was a need to change daily practice. But they also refer to money.

Fulfilling a religious cargo was an enormous drain on resources. Even those who never took one (because they were so few in number) spent a lot on alcohol and other ceremonial prerequisites for related activities, such as frequent prayers or during Carnival. Achieving communality and perhaps as important, sociability by this means was thus restricted to the few who could raise the money. The rest were predominantly thrown back on their own resources—another factor contributing to religious change. For not only have the religious cargos in the cabecera increasingly failed to provide sufficient spiritual support to the majority, but the cabildoetik in the paraje are no longer carrying out those ceremonies formerly linked to essential aspects of everyday life. The new religions, on the other hand, provide the possibility for active participation by all. They encourage money to be channeled toward the self and consumer-styled consumption rather than toward communal religion (although converts are asked to donate on a small scale at every single service they attend). They forbid drinking, which when the husband's conform, saves money and reduces domestic violence: it is not unusual, before conversion, to see women with terrible bruises or a black eye, the result of batterings from their husbands when drunk. The new religions persuade affiliates to invest in furniture and other equipment for their homes, which are then more likely to have a place for everything. Traditionally, house floors are cluttered with all the objects that cannot be hung from the ceiling, lodged on precarious shelves or stacked. Some have even acquired commercially made sideboards, which contrast strongly with the small scale of indigenous furniture. Women usually sit on blocks of wood to eat, after serving their men, who sit on small chairs. The new religions encourage women to also sit on chairs, bringing them up on the same level as their husbands.

Age is also a significant factor. The older generation of Tenejapans almost without exception had one set of beliefs and associated practices (or to use one of their metaphors: one place to "put their hearts"). Because of the lack of choice that characterized life, they are much less likely to be lured into a new religious affiliation. People of a younger generation are already accustomed to more heterogeneity. Few young people take cargos even if their parents did. They have a self-consciousness in a way their parents do not, and are interested in looking around and making choices. They are prepared to try something new, especially if it is already on hand in their community.

Time is also an important factor. For the new religions, the place of worship is literally just down the road. Services are timed to fit in with other aspects of life whereas the fiestas centering around the Saint-gods are at some considerable distance from home. They often clash with the school timetable, the visits of representatives from government agencies or the purchasers of commodities such as coffee. The schoolday is between 8:00 A.M. and 2:00 P.M. five days a week. Combined with the activities of the new religions, attitudes about the workday are changing. Converts work throughout the week and see themselves as having earned a day of rest on the weekend. Women, in their enthusiasm, often go to two services per week. On a Wednesday, the congregation will be smaller because it is predominantly female. Although the women come for the service, it also provides them with an opportunity to meet up with other women (otherwise impossible during the week), to talk, exchange gossip and information. The services are held in the mornings or early afternoons, at a time when children are usually at school. Men rarely attend midweek services, although more turn up on a Sunday but, even then, often as appendages to their wives. It seems that women are frequently the first to be convinced that there is something to be gained from joining a new religion, especially when it has already become established locally. The husbands often then follow suit.[16]

A woman goes to the temple as often as she does because as she joins her new religion, she will disband the altar in her homestead. The house has always been the woman's domain and in times of difficulty, it was usually she who prayed there. At that altar or at the various wayside crosses, contact could be made with the deities. As affiliation to the new spiritual community begins, the house ceases to be the repository of religiosity. It moves instead to the local chapel or temple. Private communication with the deities is thus replaced by a more public and communal form of prayer. Women no longer obtain spiritual strength predominantly by themselves in their homes. They can begin to rely on a community of others with whom they can discuss their difficulties. Where previously some might have allowed their kin to know their problems, but would have kept these assiduously hidden from outsiders (for reasons associated with witchcraft), membership creates both a kinship of interest as well as some of the ties previously only associated with close kin. Co-congregants tend to refer to each other by new kin terms, part Spanish, part Tzeltal. They use the Spanish *hermana* or *hermano* in the singular, and add the Tzeltal suffix -*etik* to form the plural, viz *hermanoetik*. When neighboring and closely related families begin to belong to different religions, it becomes increasingly difficult to share intimacies. A Catholic family I visited frequently had little to do with their immediate neighbors because their religion differed, even though they were cousins. The temple thus begins to be relied on to fulfill needs previously associated with the home and kin and this may in part be why it is that women attend whenever there is a service. However for most of the week such buildings are locked, and religious observance is beginning to be not only compartmentalized spatially but also temporally.[17]

Despite this, for the first time women have a location to go to that they can, at least before and during the weekday services, call their own. They can attend in their own right and talk to others without being accused of misdemeanor by their husbands. Before the arrival of the new religions, if a woman was reported to be spending too much time out and about, she was chastized by her husband. Still today, if a single woman goes out much alone it is assumed that she is "looking for a husband." Women can now begin to get to know other women who hold the same beliefs about the world as themselves. The temple

---

[16]Children often encourage a woman initially (cf Burdick 1993) and it is usual for all the family to convert. I heard of a number of families split by conversion in other communities (Menegoni personal communication), although during my work in Tenejapa I came across very few.

[17]Increasingly time, rather than being related to the cycle of nature, to maize and to the landscape, is being seen as an abstractable entity that can be turned into money (Thompson 1967).

provides a locus where they can have agency without their husbands, where they can find empowerment at a spiritual and perhaps as important at a secular, social level too. The partying of the cargo system never met with as much enthusiasm from women as it did from men. The women were always too aware of the terrible drain on their physical and their psychological resources. The ready acceptance of the ban on drinking is probably part of a pendulum swing reaction to the excesses associated with the religious practices of the cargo system.

However on Sundays, the congregation in the temple is clearly segregated. A family walking to the temple will go as a group, led by the father, but as they wait outside, the men will tend to converse in one group while the women will sit together separately. Both only enter as the service begins, the women sitting on one side of the aisle (with the children in front), the men on the other. Although in the ceremonies of the cargo system, men and women also sat apart, overall these occasions usually brought men and women closer together for their duration (Rostas 1987; Stephen 1991). In the temples and chapels they are, if anything, further apart, reflecting the increasing social distance between the sexes. Not surprisingly, there are as yet no women who are preachers. It would be too difficult for a woman to gain the necessary training outside the community. The desire to do so would probably meet with strong male opposition.[18]

When men go with their families to be inculcated and more widely educated for a period by the Evangelical Presbyterian Church, their wives are not directly involved—although they are taught hygiene and Western childbirth techniques. The hierarchical posts associated with each religion are held by men. These local functionaries are continuously on the move, attending a meeting here, invited to preach there.[19] Again women would find this very difficult. This contrasts strongly with the religious cargos where each position had to be filled by both a man and his wife (or mother) together. Overall women had a more equal status with men. Not only has the center of religiosity moved to the chapel from the house, where women had autonomy, but the services, unlike the cargos in the *cabecera*, are ceremonies dominated by men. Women, rather than being active participants, are now more passive as they

---

[18]I came across one exception, an older woman who took a cargo in a Catholic hermita. She spoke Spanish and had been a schoolteacher when younger. It was her age (postmenopausal) that probably enabled her to adopt this position.

[19]Each temple of the Evangelical Presbyterian Church has a secretary, treasurer and president, positions supposedly held for one year but in practice held for longer. In addition there is a deacon who deals with practical matters. The anciano, who has more status than any of the former, has to be literate, but has less power than the pastor who is in charge of a church, which is the center for a number of temples. In Tenejapa, there are two centers with some 13 temples subordinate to them. Weekly meetings are held at each centers to discuss business, such as who will go to which temple to preach in the coming week.

listen to men's sermons, which provide a male interpretation of Christianity, which, of course, the New Testament is itself.

What is it, then, about these strongly male-directed churches that seem to draw women inexorably but that paradoxically give some men more religious power and prestige than the religious cargo system could ever have done?[20] Why are these new affiliations so attractive to women? And perhaps more important, why are they choosing an apparently spiritual path?

A New Source of Agency for Women

The many recent changes have created a new local community in which women cannot fully participate. The world of the school is a male one, almost mestizo, of which women are wary; it is only with reluctance that married women ever go to the school. Women, cannot take positions as committees because they cannot go out alone after dark when committees generally meet. For cultural reasons they cannot just hang out. The last decades of rapid change have been exciting perhaps and disrupting for most, but have been much more confusing for women than for men. Women understand the new even less than the men because of their lack of familiarity with the mechanisms of the outside world, their lack of knowledge of Spanish, and their lack of literacy. The distance between the sexes has been increased by the various new institutions. Women are more alone and excluded locally than they have been in the past and are suffering an unprecedented insecurity. In search of a new social space, women find that the new religions provide them with one, which gives new spirit to their lives and helps them too to break old taboos.

I return now to Maria and Antonia mentioned in the introduction of this chapter. They come from neighboring families, not closely related by kinship. Their companionship is based on shared membership of a congregation. Maria's mother converted some five years ago after the death of her father who had always taken religious cargos. (Maria's eldest brother continues to do so.) This had meant that the family had often been in debt for long periods and had little to eat. The mother emphasizes how she doesn't need alcohol anymore to enable her to talk to the deities but can now converse directly with God. Antonia's family have been Presbyterian for longer. Her parents joined because of an illness in their family when Antonia was very young. They talk proudly of no one having been ill or having died since! Her mother found it difficult to stop her husband drinking, at least initially, as from time to time he took political cargos, which required him go to the cabecera and drink with the others. But he never drank at home in the paraje. If Maria and Antonia

---

[20]There are few men sufficiently experienced in the new religions to take up these positions at present. Although the highest religious cargo could be taken several times, with a break between holding office, ambitious men usually also took political cargos, which gave them secular powers, although these were couched in religious terms.

were from families who still supported the traditional syncretic practices, they would have much less excuse or reason to be together, and would almost certainly not be out and about in the middle of a weekday. The new religions provide a focus for interaction that can take young girls such as these away from the house and the constant supervision of their families to a physical space for a specific purpose (their mothers do not have time to attend every weekday service). By so doing, the new religions make possible a new form of community. For the younger generation it is not a problem that the temple or chapel is locked for much of the time; their upbringing has accustomed them to this kind of temporality.

Although this space is presided over by men, they are indigenous and the language used for the services is Tzeltal. The women are aware that the new religions originate outside the community, in that other "world," but they are nonetheless seen by them to be very much Tenejapan (as indeed the proselytizers make them).[21] The new religions give women's ethnicity a new impetus. They have no desire to become like the dreary mestiza women whom they see when they go to the cabecera. Those aspects of their lives that publicly make indigenous women so different—their language and dress—are viewed as being one of the ways in which they can retain their separate identity. They all dress traditionally, without fail. Maria and Antonia do so much more carefully than nonconverts.[22] In fact, the new religions are valued as highly as they are precisely because they bring the women into a wider community but one that is distinct from that of the mestizo world. There are no mestizos in the cabecera who are members of the new religions.

Yet, the new religions enable women to drop some of the forms of traditional etiquette related to their gender that hamper and lower their status in relation to men. The community of interest created between Maria and Antonia gives them the courage to be defiant. They tend to almost look men in the face while out on the path (previously unthinkable), reply to a man's questioning in their ordinary voices rather than adopting the high falsetto (at least when they are together), and sometimes come to the door when addressed from outside. I have witnessed such girls being cheeky to mestizos in the cabecera. Indigenous women (and men) of an older generation would never have dared to do this. Despite their recent loss of political and economic power, the mestizos do still dominate the indigenes and oppress them, calling them *cochino* (pig) to their faces and chastising them as though they were chil-

---

[21]When people adopt a new religion or sect, they tend to appropriate it to their needs or the communities needs, shaping its form and tempering its beliefs to meet their expectations and/or their ideological preconceptions. Elsewhere I have called this the popular use of popular religions (Rostas and Droogers 1993).
[22]It is worth noting that indigenous female schoolteachers dress in Western clothes and often even in trousers: they have no interest in retaining the markers of their ethnicity.

dren. Surprisingly the mestizos have a new found respect for the members of the new religions.

Finally, why are women choosing an apparently spiritual path while men appear to be moving in a more secular direction? The new religions can satisfy a spiritual need that the old no longer can, but women may have joined because they desperately needed change. The message of most of the new religions "that you must convert now if you want to be saved," speaks more directly to women than it does to men, partly because "saved" is understood in more than a spiritual sense. Women want to be saved from certain aspects of their daily way of life. The corollary to this is that although the new religions are giving women a new found agency in their own right, this is not a form of agency that appeals particularly to older men or even to younger ones as they mature. Although there is no other organization in Tenejapa that provides youths with the opportunity to sing and play the guitar in a group, the new churches are not currently directly linked to community politics and prestige, unlike the religious cargos. Those who become members of the church hierarchies may see this rather differently. But for most, male gendering is not bound up with the new religions. For men in general, the new religions offer little scope for agency in the wider community, let alone in the wider world.

Conclusion

This chapter has shown that the last decades of the twentieth century were a disorienting period for women in the community of Tenejapa. They had little direct involvement with the political and economic encroachments of the more developed world, which were beginning to cause such rapid social change in their midst. By taking up the new religions, women have been able to gain a previously unimagined agency. The focus of their religiosity has moved from the house, linked periodically to the church in the mestizo-dominated cabecera, to the less personal, but twice weekly forms of observance in the paraje. These churches, by providing a base that is both physical and social, as well as a congregation that is spiritually and emotionally supportive, have given women the opportunity to take up new approaches, not only to the ways in which they organize their lives in general, but also to how they represent themselves. When their men take up the new religion too, no longer need they live in fear of domestic violence, violation in the countryside, and the oppression of the mestizos—their larger world (see Brusco 1995). They now know that there is a wider outside world, whose new religions have enabled them to throw off some aspects of indigenous practice that had begun to prove too disruptive, burdensome, or restrictive (such as alcohol, the religious cargos themselves, and certain forms of etiquette that are linked to their gender). The new religions are enabling them to find value (even enhanced value) in certain indigenous cultural practices. They esteem their language more, their mode of dress and their overall way of life, which remains predominantly unchanged.

Away from the negative appraisals of the mestizos, they are beginning to find pride in their ethnicity.

In the early '90s, Tenejapans were in the first throes of post-affiliation euphoria. The new was seen to be bringing everything the old could or did not. But will this last? It is possible that this intense initial religious affiliation that is almost a cleaving, this sense of belonging to a different community (that you know is better than the one your neighbor belongs to), will not necessarily last. Tenejapans will begin to accept that God can be reached by a diversity of paths and that each religion does not need to be in competition with the others: religious pluralism will become the norm (Burdick 1993). The new conception of a more abstract and global God will perhaps lose his novelty as a more materialistic attitude to the practices of daily life replace the previous more metaphysical ones. Once those who were not formerly active, religiously, become quiescent again, once Tenejapan women in particular have become accustomed to the fact that their world will continue to become more heterogeneous and that they need not be isolated from social change, women may well find it easier to be involved as actors in the wider world.[23] This intense phase of religiosity for women may then be seen as a first step in the transformation of how they represent themselves to themselves and to their men. The gender oppression they currently suffer both in daily practice in the home and in wider Tenejapan society will undoubtedly change with time as a direct result of this early but very important phase of religious empowerment.

Postscript

There have been many changes in Tenejapa during the last decade. Not only has globalization proceeded apace, but the Zapatista revolution, which began in 1994, has had its effects. The town of Tenejapa is much less mestizo, a change that had begun as early as the late '80s. Fewer mestizos live in the cabecera; they no longer dominate the transport system—their vans have been replaced by indigenous taxis; fewer of them own the shops. The organizations concerned with indigenous interests are, not surprisingly, headed by indigenes. But the state also has a higher profile: there are now police on duty who do not speak Tzeltal. During my visit I saw only 2, but I was told that there had been up to 40. A bypass is being constructed and the town hall has been ex-

---

[23]If in the late 1980s, the new religions provided the only associations open to women, thereby having to fulfill both a sacred and profane role, more secular forms of participation will emerge, leaving the religions to the more spiritual. At that time there were only two weaving cooperatives in the community and membership tended to be limited to the few women who were particularly fine weavers. In the future, women will probably become involved in an increasingly mechanized and/or commercialized form of weaving as in Oaxaca (Stephen 1991; Leon 1987). As the community becomes further part of the global economy, other forms of employment will undoubtedly draw both women and men into the wage economy.

tended and refurbished. There is even a public library. A wide paved road now leads to the parajes. Federal funding has not been lacking in recent years.

But what of the religious picture and women? The number of chapels has continued to grow and there are three or four instead of just one, even in the previously more inaccessible parajes. The organization of the Evangelical Presbyterian Church has mushroomed: four centers have now been established in the township instead of just two, clearly indicating a continued process of affiliation/conversion. The organization and interests of the Catholic Church have shifted, too. The old church in the cabecera is now not so much a mestizo one, as indigenous. Not only do the traditionalists perform their ceremonies in its interior with greater freedom, but the Liberation Catholics also hold their services there. A mass for the mestizos is now only held there in the evenings. The priests also go out to the hermitas in the parajes where they "assist" at the services in the hermitas. Each is visited about five times in any one year. However priests do not speak Tzeltal and seem disinterested in learning it. Women continue to go to the hermitas and chapels in larger numbers than men. My impression is that the men are beginning to go to services less. For the women, the occasional presence of the priests brings them into closer contact with the Spanish-speaking world than ever before.

Note

This chapter is based on two periods of fieldwork in Tenejapa, Chiapas, Mexico. The first, from 1980–1983 was funded by both the ESRC (UK) and CONACYT (Mexico) and culminated in a D.Phil on religious practice. The second from 1987–1988 was also funded by CONACYT: I would like to acknowledge my gratitude to both. An earlier version of this chapter was published in the *Bulletin of Latin American Research,* Vol. 18, No. 3, pp. 327–341, 1999: I thank the Society for Latin American Studies for permission to reprint it in a modified form. I would also like to thank the Centre for Latin American Studies in Cambridge for funding a brief visit to Chiapas in 2002.

III
Women Organizing
for Social Change

Baking cooperative in a Tojolabal community in Las Cañadas. Photo by Melissa M. Forbis, 2000.

Women of The Chiapas Media Project videotaping events in their community, Las Cañadas (names withheld by request). Photos by Melissa M. Forbis, 1999.

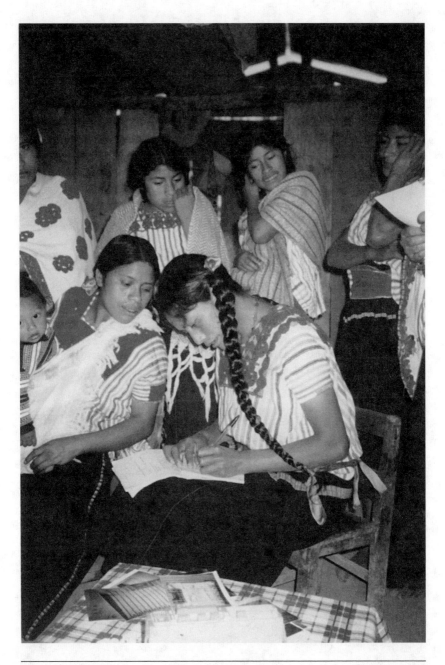

Lucia Pérez and Margarita ("Pancha") Ruíz Pérez of the weaving cooperative, Tzobol Antzetik, San Pedro Chenalhó. Photo by Christine Eber, 1997. (Ruíz Pérez died of cervical cancer in 2001. She was preceded in death by her son, Pedro, who died in 1998.)

Flor de Margarita Pérez Pérez, weaver and cooperative organizer from Tzabalhó, San Pedro Chenalhó demonstrating backstrap weaving to a group of Mexican-American weavers in San Miguel, New Mexico. Photo by Christine Eber, 2002.

Rosalinda Sántis Díaz, former president of weaving cooperative, Jolom Mayaetik, off the coast of Capetown, South Africa. Photo by Bárbara Schütz, March 2001.

16
Overview

CHRISTINE KOVIC
CHRISTINE EBER

The chapters in Part 3 illustrate the everyday settings in which women in Chiapas struggle for their own and others' fuller participation in the political affairs of their communities, the state, the nation, and the world. Women's activism takes various forms—from serving in civilian support bases for the EZLN to participating in cooperatives, church groups, political parties, and nongovernmental organizations (NGOs). Yet, it is important to bear in mind that women's organizing did not begin with the Zapatista uprising. From the colonial period to the present day, women have played important roles in rebellions and nonviolent protests against Spanish and mestizo domination.

Throughout history women of Chiapas show agency through their critical assessments of ideas and practices that come from outside of their communities. Women do not take on new social movements without carefully weighing the benefits and losses for them, their families, and their communities. Many women strive for personal autonomy in a collective of other women and men. For example, in indigenous communities married women often seem loathe to compete with men or displace them from their accepted roles and statuses. These women prefer to preserve valued aspects of their traditional roles while creating alternative all-women spaces in which they can reflect on their lives within their societies and the world. The chapters in this book provide abundant evidence that women in Chiapas articulate their own visions of liberation and autonomy.

Women's groups and mixed groups of women and men that convene to discuss women's rights provide an important arena in Chiapas for women to gain greater control over their work and lives. For example, in weaving co-ops women come together to sell their handicrafts, to support their families, or even to decide to leave an abusive husband (O'Donnell n.d.). Co-op meetings provide women safe spaces in which to reflect on influences that come from their interactions with NGOs and fair traders and then rework them in ways that make sense from their points of view, which are in line with their identities and responsibilities. Women also analyze and protest the political system in Chiapas, both in their local groups and in meetings with women from other regions of the state, such as during the Chiapas Women's Convention.

Women's organizational efforts take place in the context of multiple and overlapping levels and forms of oppression. Their efforts to resist highlight the need to examine the ways that oppression operates at various levels. On the local level, women experience constraints within their families and communities. On the regional, state, and national level broader political and economic forces oppress them. The actions taken by women demonstrate the link between their feminine or practical needs as wives and mothers, and feminist or strategic needs of working toward structural change in the public sphere (Elson 1992). As Lynn Stephen (1998) points out, women in Chiapas effectively work toward both sets of needs simultaneously.

Women's organizations in Chiapas have become integrated into networks that scholars call "transnational civil society networks" or "transnational advocacy networks." These terms refer to the many nonstate actors "that interact with each other, with states, and with international organizations" to work toward social change (Keck and Sikkink 1998:1). These networks have been especially important in debates over human rights, women's rights, the environment, and indigenous peoples. They bring together people who occupy very different social locations and in the process facilitate shared understandings and goals (Keck and Sikkink 1998). Advocacy networks in solidarity with people of Chiapas bring into association church groups, women's groups, public schools, labor unions, human rights organizations, Chiapas solidarity committees, university programs, student organizations, artisan cooperatives, agricultural cooperatives, Zapatista support bases, autonomous communities, *Las Abejas* support groups, and health and environmental organizations (Glusker 1998; Nash 1997; Olesen 2002; Sampaio 2002). The internet has greatly aided communication and collaboration between these groups and individuals. Many organizations have Web sites and send communiques through E-mail lists. These advocacy networks were especially important in the wake of the Acteal massacre by providing an alternative report of the massacre to the one being promulgated by the Mexican government.

Activists in Chiapas and in the U.S. recognize that oppression throughout Mexico is deeply embedded in global capitalism. The World Bank and International Monetary Fund conditioned loans to Mexico on the Mexican government's agreement to implement neoliberal economic policies. These policies have led to a significant cut in public spending in urban and rural areas. Plan Puebla Panama, a continuation of these policies, is predicated on serving the interests of national and international investors rather the inhabitants of the regions to be impacted by the plan. A number of protests and events have been carried out in the United States and Europe to draw attention to the role that the U.S. has played in Chiapas.

In transnational civil society networks participants share their different abilities. In this book we are particularly interested in the articulation between scholars and activists. Typically, scholars are responsible for researching social changes and analyzing them. Activists, in contrast, put their energies into constructing social change movements with grassroots constituencies. They tend to subordinate their critiques of the movements in which they are involved because of their obligation to help these movements survive. Increasingly over the past few decades, scholars and activists have come together in a variety of organizations with common goals.[1] The scholars who have contributed to this book are also activists. Their work must speak for itself, but we suggest that critical analysis has not suffered through their involvement in transnational advocacy networks. On the contrary, in many cases activism has strengthened scholarship through the intense self-reflection that is required to wear two often conflicting hats.

Inés Castro Apreza's chapter, which opens this part, provides an overview of the many state and nonstate organizations in which women have been involved since the 1970s. Castro enumerates the strengths and weaknesses, losses and gains for women of these movements. Despite many obstacles, involvement in social movements brings hope to women. Women's organizations also show a positive aspect of change throughout Mexico and Latin America. Women have forged alliances across differences within their communities and with the broader society through working with nongovernmental organizations, fair-trade companies, and religious and other groups (Stephen 1997). By means of these connections women open up transnational spaces for communication and collaboration.

Chapter 18 by Yolanda Castro describes women's participation in artisan cooperatives and political organizations. In her account of the evolution of the weaving co-op, Jolom Mayaetik (Maya Weaver) and the women's NGO, K'inal Antzetik (Women's Earth), Castro describes how both women artisans and women working with NGOs have been beaten and their lives threatened for being involved in cooperatives. She also addresses the complexity of the relationships between mestiza advisers and indigenous participants. Castro's reflexivity as a mestiza adviser of an indigenous women's groups illustrates her capacity as an activist to be critical of the very efforts upon which she has based much of her identity.

Following Castro's chapter is the song "Compañeras," (Chapter 19), which women sing regularly in meetings of Jolom Mayaetik, K'inal Antzetik, and the

---

[1]Activist scholarship among Maya peoples began in earnest with the formation of the Guatemala Scholars Network (GSN) in 1982 as an outgrowth of the 1981 National Teach-in on Guatemala. This advocacy network of 300 academics and professionals seeks to foster communication among scholars; to share information and stay informed about the situation in Guatemala; to provide a forum for Guatemalan voices to be heard in North America; and to support the renaissance of Mayan intellectual and academic activity taking place in Guatemala. www.vanderbilt.edu/AnS/Anthro/GSN/. Following the Zapatista uprising a Chiapas Scholars Network was created based on the GSN model.

Diocesan Coordination of Women (CODIMUJ). The song rallies women around their shared experiences as poor women and animates them to continue the hard work of organizing. The words of the song link women's oppression at the level of the household to broader political-economic structures. One stanza in the song states that the "individualist, neoliberal system" is the "cause of great destruction." Several stanzas speak of women's significance to their societies.

Diana Damián Palencia's chapter (20) recounts her story of awakening to the effects of patriarchy on her own life and her work with women in gender workshops in Chiapas. Damián explores communication and power and the challenges women face to create shared understandings and agendas across class and ethnic differences. Damián also provides a detailed description of a *taller* (workshop). Workshops are the favored format within NGOs and the Catholic Diocese to help people develop capacities such as critical thinking, self-reflection, and public speaking. Workshops are modeled on popular education, commonly understood as "education for liberation," a participatory process through which people share their own stories and experiences with the goal of building grassroots movements for social change. These workshops reflect the social context in which much popular education has taken place throughout Latin America (Friere 1973).

Flor de Margarita Pérez Pérez, an indigenous woman of San Pedro Chenalhó, voices both anger and determination in the song that she wrote in 1997 to celebrate International Women's Day (Chapter 21). Even though she expresses anger at the government's neglect and abuse of indigenous people, she ends her song with, "We are not cowards," declaring that her people's struggle will continue.

Melissa Forbis examines indigenous women's participation in Zapatista base communities and the movement for autonomy in Chapter 22. Women in Zapatista support bases take the abstract concept of autonomy into their own hands by creating collective projects in which they experience increased control over their work and economic resources. In the context of collective work, women express their identity as both rooted in local communities and as mobile and constantly changing. Forbis also notes that "First World nonindigenous discourses" commonly dismiss the efforts of indigenous women to resist multiple oppressions because the women do not overtly criticize patriarchy. Indeed, some urban-based feminists question women's involvement with the EZLN arguing that feminism is incompatible with the use of arms. Yet, Forbis demonstrates the ways women in base communities work toward a liberation that encompasses their identities as women, campesinas, and indigenous peoples. Her piece emphasizes the dangers of imposing a limited view of feminism on indigenous women and the necessity of understanding women in Chiapas on their own terms.

17

Contemporary
Women's Movements
in Chiapas

INÉS CASTRO APREZA
Translated by Christine Eber and Christine Kovic

Women's organizations in Chiapas have increased dramatically in complexity and number since the 1970s. In this chapter I describe the growth and development of women's organizations and examine the roles of the social actors that have influenced them. Although my analysis is academic, I also write as a participant in some of the organizations and movements that I analyze. I was an adviser to K'inal Antzetik, a nongovernmental organization (NGO) formed by indigenous women and mestizas who advise artisan cooperatives. I was in charge of the area of information and analysis of CONPAZ, a coalition of NGOs that carried out numerous projects in the conflict zone from 1994–1997. Finally, I served as research director for the Instituto de la Mujer (the Women's Institute), created by the state government in 2000 to implement programs and public policies for women in Chiapas.

Some recent studies point to the multiple social and political actors that have influenced women's movements. They pay particular attention to definitions and conceptions as well as tactics and strategies.[1] I follow this approach, yet recognize that through interaction with external agents, indigenous women appropriate knowledge and practices, transforming them and making them their own. I do not examine the process of appropriation in this chapter, but mention it here to highlight the independence and creativity of indigenous women.

A key theme in this chapter is how various women's movements in the state coexist, specifically how the leadership and political programs of these movements overlap, while each maintains its own identity. Another theme is the problems women face working across class and ethnic differences. For exam-

---

[1]Graciela Freyermuth Enciso has analyzed the influence that diverse actors have had on indigenous groups in their organizing and training in the area of health in highland Chiapas. Ana María Garza Caligaris and Sonia Toledo (2002) analyze women's organizations and their links to external groups in the highland and northeastern regions of Chiapas.

ple, whereas *campesina* and indigenous women tend to prioritize economic demands, mestiza women privilege gender demands. The first group tends to support the global program of the Zapatistas, whereas the second emphasizes issues specifically relevant to women. Despite these differences, mestiza, campesina and indigenous women have found it possible to unite.

The Catholic Diocese of San Cristóbal de Las Casas

Under the leadership of Bishop Samuel Ruíz Garcia (1960–2000), the Catholic Diocese of San Cristóbal de Las Casas has supported the organization of indigenous women and mestizas in Chiapas (see chapters in this book by Christine Eber, Christine Kovic, and Pilar Gil). Through its pastoral work, the diocese encouraged a collective process of reflection about the social, political, and economic circumstances in light of Biblical readings. In the Northern Zone and the Lacandon Jungle, the book Exodus is commonly used to provide a framework to analyze the relocation of entire families and the building of new communities in the past 25 years. Through reading the Bible, women find the foundation for action and a source of strength (see Chapters 7, 9, 10, and 12).

Some women who were active participants in the Catholic Church went on to become leaders of social organizations and productive cooperatives. Many of these women no longer participate in the religious arena, although they continue to identify as Catholic. Rather, they work in diverse organizations, including government offices. To strengthen its work with women, the diocese created the Diocesan Coordination of Women (CODIMUJ) in 1992. The CODIMUJ is not an organization or civil association, but an alliance of many indigenous women and campesinas of the diocese. Members of the CODIMUJ participate in a number of important political activities. For example, they have joined other women from a variety of organizations in the state in annual marches for International Women's Day, the Forum against Violence Toward Women (held in November of 2000), and the Zapatista Consultations (of 1995, 1999, and 2000). (See Chapters 10 and 12 for an in-depth discussion of the activities of the CODIMUJ.)

The CODIMUJ has suggested the formulation of women's needs as rights. It has constructed this formulation gradually through discussion of a number of questions, which apply to indigenous women and campesinas and also to men. In these discussions the CODIMUJ participants began to learn their rights and to find their path to *concientización* (political awareness and empowerment). Important questions that workshop facilitators pose include: How do we live? Why are we poor? Why do assassinations and land evictions occur? What do we want to learn about? Through this process, the diocesan pastoral work supported women's learning about democracy and the democratization of social relations within communities and townships.

Social Organizations and Political Parties

Campesino organizations and opposition political parties—that is, parties different from the *Partido Revolucionario Institucional* (Party of the Institutionalized Revolution or the PRI)—have involved women in activities and mobilizations such as marches, sit-ins, roadblocks, meetings, and assemblies. This participation has led to the formation of networks not likely to develop in the framework of traditional socialization within communities.

One could argue that women's incorporation into large campesino groups and political groups was originally a pragmatic strategy, since these groups benefit in numerous ways from women's participation. For example, the numeric force of these groups has increased with the presence of women. The stereotypical image of women as being "inoffensive" and "nonviolent" is advantageous in certain circumstances (Garza Caligaris and Toledo 2002). One could also argue that women's participation was influenced by the patrilineal and patriarchal structures of indigenous and campesino communities. Nevertheless, women's involvement in these groups constitutes a learning process for them. Specifically, through participating in these groups women recognize their *right to have rights* (see Castro Apreza 2000).

Related to the tendency for men to dominate, is the limited participation of women in the directive bodies of social organizations and political parties. Large organizations such as the Organización Campesina Emiliano Zapata (Emiliano Zapata Peasant Organization, OCEZ) or the Coalición de Organizaciones Autónomas de Ocosingo (Coalition of Autonomous Organizations of Ocosingo, COAO) do not have female leaders in their highest posts. However, in January of 2001 a women's commission was formed within the COAO, signaling the gradual transformation that this organization is experiencing. The women's commission is composed of three general coordinators and two representatives for each of the ten organizations that make up the COAO. The women leaders are in charge of carrying out evaluations and creating work plans.

Artisan Cooperatives

Women's empowerment in artisan cooperatives is taking place more quickly than in the previously mentioned groups. In cooperatives, women are gradually taking ownership and developing leadership in each phase of production, from acquiring raw materials to the production and commercialization of their artisanry. For a long time, men controlled the distribution and earnings of the artisan products, as well as the leadership positions in cooperatives. Recently, in many artisan cooperatives women have begun to take administrative control. For example, Desarrollo Económico y Social de los Mexicanos Indígenas (Economic and Social Development for Indigenous Mexicans, or DESMI) and K'inal Antzetik have encouraged the formation and/or consolidation of organizations of indigenous women who produce artisanry (See Chapter 18).

Although incorporating women in the directive bodies of organizations represents an important step, this change does not always guarantee solidarity, democratic decision-making, and transparency in administration. Nonetheless, at this time, women's participation in and of itself is of tremendous importance in the process of empowerment and democratization of social relations in Chiapas.

Government Institutions

By the 1970s a number of government offices had begun to support the organizational and productive processes of indigenous women and campesinas. The most important offices include the Instituto Nacional Indigenista (National Indigenous Institute, INI) and the Casa de las Artesanías (House of Artisans), which have promoted local artisan production, and the Unidad Agrícola Industrial para la Mujer Campesina (Industrial Agricultural Unit for Women Peasants), which has supported projects through offering small loans. Indeed, a new women's program has emerged in each administration. Most significant about these programs is their encouragement of women's organization and participation. In some townships, the most politically and socially active women are also members or leaders of these productive processes supported by the local government.

In this context, the Women's Institute was created in December 2000 under the leadership of Governor Pablo Salazar Mendiguchía. Mendiguchía, of the multiparty coalition the Alianza por Chiapas (Alliance for Chiapas), is the first non-PRI governor of Chiapas. The Women's Institute is a decentralized body of the Secretaría de Desarrollo Social (Secretariat of Social Development), with limited autonomy and resources.

The institute has encouraged what is called the *transversalidad de genero,* a process of incorporating a gender perspective into the public programs and policies of all government offices. During its first year the Women's Institute was limited to holding forums and meetings, publishing their results, and distributing pamphlets on sexual and reproductive rights and the right to social and political participation. However, as indigenous women of the institute noted, because these pamphlets were in Spanish, many indigenous women could not read them.

During its second year, the Women's Institute received funding to support women's productive projects such as baking, artisan production, and raising domestic animals that allow women to have their own earnings. Among mestizas in the institute, a discussion took place over the pros and cons of supporting such projects. These women and their advisers noted that in these projects women stay in the home and that it is only when this circle is broken (e.g., when women move into the public arena), that they are able to initiate a process of autonomy and empowerment.

How do other sectors of society view the Women's Institute? Some of the mestiza leaders linked to mestiza NGOs and large social organizations see the institute as advantageous for women. Others, also linked to mestiza NGOs, distrust the institute and distance themselves from it for a number of reasons. They consider that the state has "co-opted" many of the indigenous, campesina, and mestiza leaders formed in the heat of the mobilizations and protests, which took place since the 1970s. For example, women who were once part of the Central Independiente de Obreros Agrícolas y Campesinos (Independent Confederation of Agricultural Workers and Peasants or CIOAC) are now linked to the institute. Critics argue that it is best to work independently of the government to avoid being limited. Women in the institute are currently reflecting on both the pros and cons of making decisions and exercising power in the framework of relative political distention. While members of the institute sought to democratize decision-making, this process proved difficult for a number of reasons. First, in many cases it was necessary to make decisions quickly eliminating the possibility of consultations. Second, although institute members come from independent and democratic organizations, they do not always follow democratic principles. Finally, democratization is difficult within a hierarchical government structure.

As former research director of the Women's Institute, my greatest lesson was recognizing the existence of women's organizing that urban-based mestizas were unaware of or did not value. Most important are the groups of women of all sizes in indigenous and mestizo regions who meet to work toward common goals such as improving their living standards, learning such skills as sewing or baking, and fighting against alcoholism. None of these groups have urban-based mestiza leaders. The women who make up these groups have completed few years of formal education and do not use the concepts and strategies that mestizas might identify as "feminist" or as coming from a "gender perspective." Nonetheless, in these groups women create empowering spaces for themselves and share a common identity as women.

The Women's Institute shows potential to continue to form a part of the women's movement in the years to come. This group will most likely serve as the government office that "institutionalizes" an important aspect of the women's movement. Such institutionalization will enable groups in different zones to identify in some way with the government and to establish relations with and links to it. Although "institutionalization" carries a pejorative connotation for those who disagree with the institute's policies, those within the institute view it as positive. The latter group maintains that advocating in favor of women is much more efficient and rapid within the government where public policies can be created and changed.

Nongovernmental Organizations

Nongovernmental organizations (NGOs) constitute another important sector of society that has supported the women's movement. Beginning in the 1980s and 1990s, multinational organizations and international foundations began to impact the research and action agenda of NGOs.

Male and female mestizos who work in NGOs often support leftist, and sometimes radical, ideologies. Many NGOs refuse government support and identify themselves as "independent," while labeling groups that receive state or federal support as "official." Some NGOs function with resources from foreign governments. People who identify themselves as part of "civil resistance" refuse most types of government support.

NGOs that depend on funding from multinational organizations and international foundations are influenced to some extent by the interests of these sectors. Indeed, it is the funding from these sources that allows the NGOs to carry out their projects. In the 1990s, human rights, and in particular women's sexual and reproductive rights were key themes promoted by multinational organizations and NGOs. These themes were closely linked to key concerns of civil society and the EZLN in Chiapas—that is—human rights, citizenship, and democracy.

The Zapatista Army of National Liberation

In my opinion, no event has been more important for the women's movement in Chiapas than the public appearance of the EZLN in 1994. In the context of revolutionary processes in Latin America, the EZLN is certainly the group that has most involved women as public and political subjects. Women comprise a large number of those active in Zapatista support bases and hold directive positions within its political-military structure. In addition, the Zapatista movement has had an impact on the broader women's movement in Chiapas. The EZLN Revolutionary Women's Law, made public in January 1994, affirms a broad range of rights for women (see Box 1, p. 23 for this law).

Negotiations between the Zapatistas and the federal government immediately unleashed diverse activities of civil society including (1) the broad mobilization of diverse sectors; (2) the formation of the Consejo Estatal de Organizaciones Indígenas y Campesinas (State Council of Indigenous and Campesino Organizations, CEOIC), made of more than 200 social organizations; (3) the formation of the Asamblea Estatal Democrática del Pueblo Chiapaneco (Democratic State Assembly of the Chiapan People, AEDPCH), which continued the work of the CEOIC; and (4) the convening of the National Democratic Convention (National Democratic Convention, CND) by the EZLN in August of 1994. Indigenous women and campesinas played important roles in all these organizations and events, although they did not always share the same sentiments or opinions. An example of discrepancies in perspectives took place during the negotiations between the AEDPCH and the federal government. As part of the negotiations, the federal government offered 1000 pesos along with chickens and pigs to each indigenous woman participant. Whereas mestizas criticized the government for offering "crumbs," many indigenous women welcomed the money as an important source of economic support. In addition, women in some indigenous communities noted that leaving their homes to attend different types of meetings was important to them.

State Women's Convention

The public appearance of the EZLN was decisive in inspiring the Convención Estatal de Mujeres (State Women's Convention, CEM), composed of indigenous women, campesinas, and mestizas of various organizations. In preparation for this convention, two women's forums were held in San Crisóbal de Las Casas, one convened by the Colectivo de Mujeres de San Cristóbal (COLEM) and the other convened by J'Pas Joloviletik (Those Who Weave), the PRD pottery cooperative of Amatenango del Valle, and the Organización Independiente de Mujeres Indígenas (Independent Organization of Women, OIMI) (see Castro Apreza 2000). In July of 1994 the first session of the CEM took place with the participation of NGOs and indigenous organizations. Participants agreed to take part in the CND and to take up the Zapatista demands. In a second session held in October 1994, approximately 500 women from numerous campesino organizations, the PRD, and the aforementioned groups came together. They agreed to demand women's right to land, to denounce violence against women and militarization, and to support Amado Avendaño, ex-candidate for state governor of Chiapas, in his fight against electoral fraud.

When the final meeting of the CEM was held in 1995 only 100 women attended. During the meeting, the women differed greatly in their positions and decisions. Some members of campesino organizations decided to negotiate with then governor Eduardo Robledo Rincón. Others refused to negotiate, considering this to be a betrayal to the EZLN, which insisted on working toward broad changes for indigenous communities rather than focusing on economic demands. The CEM dissolved due to difficulties among some of the mestiza leaders. Some also cite the low-intensity warfare promoted by the state government as a factor in the group's disintegration.[2]

Independent Women's Movement

In 2001, a group of NGOs decided to support a Movimiento Independiente de Mujeres (Independent Women's Movement). A key actor in this movement is

---

[2]Low-intensity warfare is a counterinsurgency strategy that attempts to destroy popular mobilizations through propaganda, misinformation, threats, and other tactics. Low-intensity warfare has impacted social relations in a number of communities in the Northern Zone, the Highlands, and the Lacandon Jungle. Consequences of this warfare include state violence and paramilitarization in these regions (see Chapter 3). Although low-intensity warfare has certainly impacted NGOs, it is also necessary to recognize that men and women have also erred on the path of mobilization. Envy and resentment as well as fights over leadership, economic resources, and the control of territory have negatively affected social relations in organizations.

the Feminario, a group of mestizas from diverse NGOs who analyze the political situation, study gender theory, and support practical actions. Supporters of a regional assembly held in November 2002 included: COLEM (the Women's Group of San Cristóbal); the Centro de Acción e Investigación de la Mujer (Center for Women's Action and Research, CIAM); Formación y Capacitación (Formation and Training, FOCA); Chi'iltak (Companions/Friends in Tzotzil); Alianza Cívica (Civic Alliance); Casa de Mujer (Woman's House); Ixim Antsetik de Palenque (Women's Corn of Palenque); Centro Cultural Feminista "Casa de Luna Creciente" (Feminist Cultural Center "House of the Growing Moon"); Seminario de Género de la UNACH (Gender Seminar of the UNACH); Colectivo de Educación Popular de Las Margaritas y Comitán (Popular Education Collective of Margaritas and Comitán); Maestras de la Sección VII (Teachers of Section VII); and Na-Snopel (Tzeltal for House of Learning).[3] Many of these groups have a long history of working with women in Chiapas. The members demand equality based on gender, ethnicity, and class. Their immediate program is to fight against violence against women and the Plan Puebla Panama (PPP), a development plan implemented by President Fox and the state governor, Pablo Salazar Mendiguchía.[4]

Regional Coordinators of Civil Society in Resistance

Finally, the EZLN has impacted women's movements through the Consulta Nacional por los Derechos de los Pueblos Indios (National Consultation of the Rights of Indigenous Pueblos), which took place in 1999. Through this consulta, liaison coordinators were created for five regions of Chiapas: the Northern Zone, the Lacandon Jungle, the border, the Highlands, and the coast. Liaison coordinators brought together the many diverse organizations and groups of men and women that support the EZLN, the San Andrés Accords, and the demands of indigenous peoples. A number of the female leaders of the coordinators have a long political trajectory struggling for indigenous and women's rights in Chiapas. The coordinators held two regional meetings in 2001 and 2002 where women's rights were discussed. Participants identify themselves as members of civil society, and in 2001 changed the name to "Coordinadoras Regionales de la Sociedad Civil en Resistencia" (Regional Coordinators of Civil Society in Resistance). In two state meetings, the coordinators agreed to open their doors to mestizo men and women, and not to focus exclusively on indigenous groups. Although mestizo groups had participated previously in the coordinadoras, they began to participate more organically and

---

[3]Diana Damián's chapter (20) in this volume documents the work of FOCA. On the foundation and projects of COLEM see Freyermuth Enciso and Fernández (1995).

[4]Women of this Movement criticize the PPP because it supports the construction of maquiladoras, which have contracted women at low rates of pay on the U.S.–Mexico border. They also criticize the PPP for the damage it will cause to the environment and because the project was put into place without consulting those whom it would impact.

regularly in some regions. These groups continue to follow initial demands linked to indigenous rights. Yet basic struggles against the high cost of electricity, women's rights, and other issues unite this regional rainbow. Members of many organizations including K'inal Antzetik and Jolom Mayaetik as well as teachers and many unaffiliated people participate in the highland coordinators. The majority of the leaders of the Highland Coordinadora are women.

What the future holds for the coordinadoras and the Independent Women's Movement remains to be seen. However, it is clear that these two coalitions, together with church groups, the Women's Institute, and the civilian support bases for the EZLN, currently constitute the most important routes of participation and organization for women in Chiapas.

Conclusion

When we speak of the social and political participation of women we cannot ignore one theme: the positive impact of women's mobilization on human rights and women's rights. Despite the generally positive impact of women's participation, responses from those who oppose change in both urban and rural areas can sometimes be negative. Yolanda Castro's chapter in this volume describes numerous cases where men (soldiers, mestizos, and others) harass women who work in cooperatives. In my own research in the framework of the *coordinadores regionales,* women shared their difficulties breaking away from oppressive traditions, particularly female confinement in the domestic sphere. In indigenous communities, many men and also some women oppose changes that they perceive as going against *usos y costumbres* (the traditions, customs, and normative systems of indigenous pueblos). Men's resistance can retard the growth of the seeds of women's rights, which women have planted. It can lead to family violence and in extreme cases to assassination.

The NGOs comprised of mestizas have documented the violence generated by indigenous women and campesina's who have exercised their "right to participate." COLEM has done the most work in this area. Together with other NGOs, COLEM has encouraged state meetings where the problem of violence toward women has been discussed.

Despite obstacles, women are changing their lives through mobilization for social change. Benefits to women of their mobilization include: increasing their self-esteem; becoming visible as public and political actors; developing their capacities as leaders; obtaining economic independence; learning about their right to have rights; and moving out of the domestic arena into spaces dominated by men. As a result of being active in the movements discussed in this chapter, women have participated in road blocks, sit-ins, and marches to demand the right to land, better prices for their products, and the respect for human rights. In the 1980s and 1990s, women's participation widened to include such areas as statewide women's meetings and women's demonstrations. Particularly important are the annual marches in celebration of International

Women's Day on March 8 and the protests against violence toward women. Women participate in workshops on health training, sexual and reproductive rights, and in women's assemblies in communities, among other events. For indigenous women, participating in a variety of groups has expanded their identities as women at the same time that it has influenced existing identities, such as religious identity.

Although interethnic relations continue to present obstacles, the links between diverse groups of women have grown and strengthened, an important process in all multicultural societies. Despite differences, mestizas, campesinas, and indigenous women have unified around similar objectives, including denouncing violence against women, defending women's rights, and improving the social and economic conditions of their lives.

18

J'pas Joloviletik-Jolom Mayaetik-K'inal Antzetik

An Organizational Experience of Indigenous and Mestiza Women

YOLANDA CASTRO APREZA
Translated by Jeannette Minnie

The history of some indigenous organizations is also the history of those who accompany them in the course of their growth. In the following pages I narrate the history of J'pas Joloviletik and Jolom Mayaetik—artisan cooperatives of highlands Chiapas—and K'inal Antzetik—a nongovernmental organization comprised of indigenous women and mestizas who advise women artisans. Starting with my own experience as a consultant to two cooperatives and as coordinator of K'inal Antzetik, I share moments of our respective histories, and reveal the scope, limitations, risks, and challenges of the organizational process of women of highland Chiapas.[1]

J'pas Joloviletik: Making Spaces for Women

In 1991, after working with peasant women in the region of Marqués de Comillas, the central coordinator of the *Instituto Nacional Indigenista* (National Indigenous Institute, INI) invited me to work with the most important state-run indigenous women's artisan cooperative of the Highlands, J'pas Joloviletik (Tzeltal for Those Who Weave). The cooperative was in crisis. Since the co-op began in 1984, although it had more than 800 members from 23 communities and 9 townships, its members only wove; they did not run their organization. The technical staff of the INI had obtained financial support and an accountant from INI controlled sales and the weavers' pay.

An important person in the co-op was a Tzeltal woman from Tenejapa, one of the first women whom the INI established as a bilingual promoter in order

---

[1] I thank my sister, Inés Castro Apreza, for assistance in preparing this chapter. Inés recorded my oral account that forms the backbone of this narrative and helped me transcribe and construct the written narrative.

to support the work with indigenous women. It is important to remember that the work carried out by the INI throughout the years was ultimately about empowering a few persons to become new bosses, without encouraging them to reproduce what was learned in their communities of origin. Those first bilingual promoters, men as well as women, gradually assumed absolute control in numerous social organizations and production cooperatives due to a variety of advantages that they had, among them a command of Spanish. Being INI workers, they also knew how to manage resources, which permitted them to have a lot of control in some organizations. As soon as they could capitalize on their work at a political level, some of the promoters left the INI and became part of organizations or cooperatives as economic resource managers who controlled and administered resources. This was the case, and a problem, of J'pas Joloviletik.

The years from 1990 through 1991 represent the last phase in the INI when key personnel came from the social sciences, such as sociology and anthropology. These people had supported social organizations and had proposed alternative development approaches, such as forming indigenous organizations and helping them become self-managing. During these years, the INI systematically expelled the progressive personnel that the state government saw as "leftist" and "dangerous." During this period a change in indigenous politics was also taking shape; meetings of indigenous people searching for a new direction were beginning to take place on the national level. It was in this context that I was invited to work with the women of J'pas Joloviletik.

I confronted a difficult reality. In 1991, J'pas Joloviletik was a cooperative of nearly 1000 weavers from 23 communities in 9 townships in the highlands. Then and still today, women had their strongest relationship to their local groups. Weavers worked at home and attended meetings in their local groups, with occasional trips to San Cristóbal for workshops or meetings. They depended primarily on representatives to take their work to the cooperative store in San Cristóbal. The majority of the members were monolingual in their native languages.

The first task I undertook was a study; I began by visiting the place where the power and control of the cooperative was concentrated—the headtown of Chenalhó. There I met María Peso, an indigenous woman, who came to symbolize the organizational expression of indigenous women. She was important to the state government, particularly to several governors, who exploited her image to use the cooperative as an important base of political support. When the director of the INI or important persons such as the President of the Republic came to highland Chiapas, they visited this cooperative. María Peso mobilized the women to attend government events. As she is monolingual in Tzotzil, Maria's son, a bilingual teacher, assisted her. He gained strong political control within J'pas Joloviletik.

In the course of my study, I visited numerous townships where I talked with the women cooperative members. When I had finished my research, I reported to an assembly of the cooperative, which the Director of the Coordinating Center of the INI attended. (This event occurred before he was removed within the framework of institutional policy change.) There I presented a proposal for how we might overcome the cooperative's problems. Among the principal problems I presented was the lack of information available to women about the management of resources within the institute itself and the lack of education and training in accounting and administration for at least the women representatives. I proposed to initiate a series of educational and training courses, principally for the women representatives, which would enable us to evaluate whether it was necessary to change the representatives of the artisan groups. The women still viewed me with distrust, but they accepted the proposal.

Aside from this conflict, another conflict resulted from the deaths of seven cooperative members in an automobile accident in a van belonging to the co-op. The accident occurred in 1991, on the highway from Comitán to San Cristóbal de Las Casas in the region of Teopisca; seven women died. The driver was the son of one of the cooperative representatives. Two of his sons died, as well. This accident worsened the conflict within the cooperative, because the members had to make a series of audits that revealed a financial crisis. The co-op had incurred a debt of approximately 300,000 pesos, about which the members had never been informed. Other types of balances in the red also began to appear after the accident. Financial problems were another element of the crisis in which J'pas Joloviletik found itself.

From the first assembly of the cooperative, there had been a large presence of men. Among them was María Peso's son who tried to mobilize women from Tenejapa and Chenalhó, mainly those living in the headtowns. He questioned whether a mestiza woman (me) should do this work when he, a man, indigenous and bilingual, was well suited to help an organization of indigenous women. In San Andrés Larráinzar, the women strongly questioned this man's role. They criticized his ties to the then State Governor Patrocinio González Garrido. They pointed out the fact that he, an official translator for the governor, was the voice of a woman's organization, when the women themselves should speak and make decisions. Since those early years, the women, especially those from San Andrés Larrainzar, saw the importance of taking the reins to direct and control the cooperative.

K'inal Antzetik: Indigenous-Mestiza Assistance to Women's Organizations

As the months passed, the education and training of indigenous women became a priority. We began to form a team of indigenous women who would work for J'pas Joloviletik. Around that time, we added a Tzeltal woman from

Tenejapa to the team. Micaela Hernández was neither a weaver nor a member of the cooperative. She succeeded in learning Tzotzil (Tzeltal is spoken in Tenejapa) quickly and showed a great sensitivity toward the other women. Soon after she joined the team, she began a process of education and training along with another woman co-op member. These two women made up our first team. With Micaela we later formed K'inal Antzetik.

The step of involving members in the administration of the co-op distinguished us from the public institutions, federal as well as state. Although these institutions had staffs of indigenous women, they still maintained control. By encouraging the members of our organization to agree on which co-op members they wanted to be trained as members of the working team we ensured that the representatives had moral and political authority.

Although there were already Tzeltal women in the cooperative, the majority were Tzotziles. They were pleased to have Micaela Hernández join them, but they "put her to the test." They gave her a predetermined time to see if she could learn Tzotzil and if she was really able to learn and commit to the Tzotziles and their values, as well as to the Tzeltales. Of vital importance to the co-op members in assessing whether a woman could take a leadership position was her behavior with the members, for example, how she spoke to them, how she gave them information. Moral values were the main criteria that the women used to choose a woman as their leader.

Subsequently, Cristina Orcí, a Mexican-American, came to work with us. She appreciated the structure of the cooperative and the women artisans' process and began to translate for us with tourist groups, as well as assisting us with marketing and national and international contacts.

The year 1993 was a difficult because we received death threats against several members, including Micaela, Roselia, the president of J'pas Joloviletik at that time, and me. Those threats included the ongoing destruction of the cooperative store, located on a major street in San Cristóbal de Las Casas. Numerous times the windows facing the street were broken. Anonymous threats were left on our answering machine. We suspected that most of the threats came from the team tied to the state government that now saw our presence as usurping an important political space from them.

From the beginning of our work, we talked about the rights that indigenous women have and the importance of making women's organizations our own space where decisions are made by women themselves. To achieve this goal, it was necessary to replace indigenous men who controlled some weavers' groups with indigenous women. The women initiated this process by claiming the power that they had begun to take in the different groups and at the assembly level. They carried out this process in the most peaceful manner possible. Eventually, men no longer appeared in cooperative discussions. Throughout this process there were many threats made on the building and on our person. With the 1994 uprising of the Zapatista Army of National Liberation (EZLN), the threats intensified. At one point, I was approached by judicial police and the Mexican Army who wanted to question me about the Zapatista movement.

In that same year, the INI drew boundaries for J'pas Joloviletik and began to get rid of all of "progressive" personnel. The cooperative began to deteriorate as a result of members seeing that their negotiations and demands along with their visits to Mexico City had not brought any answers from the federal and state institutions. That realization led us to break relations with the INI and to attempt to work in an autonomous manner. We assumed full responsibility and began searching for markets in other countries and for foundations that could help us financially. But at this point we faced an obstacle—most foundations did not give money directly to production cooperatives, regardless of their longevity and whatever recognition they enjoyed. The foundations conditioned economic support on there being a "bridge" between them and the production cooperatives, in this case a nongovernmental organization.

In 1994 we invited other *compañeras* to join our consulting team—Nellys Palomo and Merit Ichin, the latter of indigenous and mestizo origin, and Dora María Chandomí, a professor. To search for financing to support J'pas Joloviletik, we formed a nongovernmental organization, K'inal Antzetik, A.C., in February 1995. From the beginning, we were aware that K'inal was a space in which we could solicit grants. We also had in mind forming an NGO that in time would be run by indigenous women.

Among the objectives of K'inal Antzetik has been strengthening indigenous women's organizations, basically production organizations of women already in existence. That commitment forms part of our ethics. Now, years after the formation of K'inal Antzetik, our thinking remains the same: to facilitate a transition from reliance on outside assistance to self-management by the members themselves. The formation of K'inal was a joint venture with J'pas Joloviletik. It was not a unilateral decision.

Why the Name K'inal Antzetik?

The workshops, mentioned in the preceding section, were concerned first with accounting and administration. Training included learning how to use an electric calculator and a credit card, to open a bank account, and to use a checking account. For example, members would receive a check signed by their representative, after which they would learn how to go to the bank to cash it. Each representative learned to control the sale of their local group's products. She was responsible, along with her secretary, to return to her community and pay each member of the local group. The new process lessened mistrust that women had of their representatives, because the administrative activities became transparent to everyone.

The women also received basic courses on natural dyes, and on steps in marketing artisan products (e.g., components of a profitable project, searching for markets, labeling products for sale with the price and name of the weaver on each piece, etc.) We traveled with some women to Cancún, where the owner of a restaurant refused to serve us because indigenous people were in our group. We also traveled to Mexico City. On our different trips we encouraged the women to represent their organization. All of these experiences gave the women more self-assurance.

We progressed to another phase, that of discussing Mexico's Constitution. To assist us, we invited Carlotta Botei, one of the women at the national level who had dealt with the Agrarian Reform Law, including its impact on women. Botei spoke at an assembly of co-op members about the Mexican Revolution and the history of Article 27.[2] She placed a great deal of emphasis on the right of indigenous women to inherit land. In previous co-op meetings we had discussed the EZLN Revolutionary Women's Law, which includes women's right to inherit land (see Box 1, p. 23). But it surprised the women to hear someone outside of our group talk about it.

After Botei spoke, Doña Juana from the headtown of San Andrés Larraínzar, said that the same blood, indigenous blood, which had been spilled with the death of Emiliano Zapata, was being spilled today in the indigenous people's struggle.[3] Other reactions to the presentation included those of older women inclined toward the more traditional concept of land. They talked about their love for the land. In all the workshops on rights that we have held, women speak a lot about land. K'inal Antzetik, the name of our NGO that advises indigenous women's cooperatives, came out of this collective analysis. In choosing to call ourselves K'inal Antzetik we built upon the theme of land that is so important to the women, at the same time as we tried to maintain harmony between our work and their ideas. K'inal means land in Tzeltal. For indigenous women, the land means the place where the seed is planted; the land represents fertility. For the founders of K'inal Antzetik, the land is each group of women artisans. K'inal embodies the planting of the seed and planting it on this land, on their land. The women are the seed; education and training signify planting the seed and giving fruits along the way that the women will see and enjoy and use to improve their lives. We did not think of our organization as only serving the members, but also their daughters who were showing indications of being different from the founders of the cooperative. Hence, our NGO in Spanish is Tierra de Mujeres (Land of Women.)[4]

---

[2]This Article in Mexico's 1917 Constitution set forth agrarian reform and established the *ejidos*, or communal lands. Under President Salinas de Gortari the article was reformed in 1992; the reforms declared an end to land redistribution and allowed the once inalienable ejido lands to be bought and sold.

[3]Most older women have never attended school where they could learn about the Mexican Revolution. Even those who have studied the revolution in school, rarely learn about its connection to the contemporary reality of poor Mexicans.

[4]K'inal Antzetik does not have an exact Spanish translation. A priority in selecting our name was to embody the spirit of the assembly in which the name originated.

At the same time, in 1994 the indigenous-mestiza consulting team began to see that we needed to have our own physical space that would permit us to participate in all the political activities that were occurring in the aftermath of the EZLN uprising. With some initial financing we were able to start the first workshops on women's rights. In 1994 we held the first state indigenous women's forum, which we called: "Let us speak of our customs, know our rights." In this forum, the members of J'pas Joloviletik took the central organizing role. In this first forum there were 200 women of J'pas Joloviletik, the Independent Organization of Indigenous Women (OIMI), and women from Amatenango del Valle who later organized into two pottery cooperatives. The meeting was wonderful. The women participants began to question "customs," as they called them, especially the practices and values that made them unhappy, that they saw as unfair.

At the same time, upon seeing the type of work that we were doing, the INI began to withhold my salary. For an entire year they did not pay me in order to pressure me to resign, but I refused. Along with other compañeras, I worked voluntarily. Once we began to receive outside financing, we were able to be paid again.

As for the training, the two representatives were trained in a few weeks. They learned to make deposits and withdrawals very quickly. There were no women who could speak Spanish fluently, but these two women managed to do so quickly. Soon they began to do accounting work. A few months later, we decided that it would be better to have an independent accountant, not one from the INI. With this step, we sought to resolve one of the key problems of the cooperative—the lack of financial reporting at the general assemblies.

The new accountant trained two representatives to keep their records of monthly expenses and sales. We stipulated that every six months the representatives would make financial reports to the general assembly. In this way, the members could rely on receiving the information that they needed at the assemblies. We also arranged for the office of the mestiza accountant to remain open to the representatives of every local weaving group, so that they could have access to all the financial information. In this way, the artisans could act on their own behalf regarding everything related to the financial situation of the co-op; K'inal Antzetik stopped taking responsibility for this.

Another change during this time was expanding the geographic focus of K'inal Antzetik from the Highlands, home since the early '80s to production cooperatives, to other regions of Chiapas.

A Division and the Birth of Jolom Mayaetik: 1995–1996

At the end of 1995, there was an increase in attacks on J'pas Joloviletik, among them a robbery of a large amount of textiles and money, much of it belonging to the women producers from San Andres Larráinzar. The robbery brought on our greatest crisis. Immediately after this assault, a general assembly was held in which representatives of the 9 townships and 23 communities met in order to discuss what was happening and how they wanted to continue as an organization. The women asked themselves: How is it that people (government people) could carry out this razing, this aggression? Why are they targeting poor women? What is the sense of attacking an organization in this way?

It is likely that the government was responsible for the attacks. During that time, two soldiers made "visits" to the cooperative offices. They came into the store precisely when I was not there, or when women of the co-op's advising team were absent. They searched the boxes of raw material and entered the bathrooms. We don't know what they were looking for. We also had anonymous telephone calls, which led us to think that the perpetrators were not government officials, but people from San Cristóbal de Las Casas who were linked to the governor. Once a caller told me, "If you don't stop working with your little Indians, it's going to be very bad for you. It would be better for you to quit." It is important to remember, that J'pas Joloviletik—like so many other organizations- was an important political resource for the INI and for the previous governor. The women of this cooperative, dressed in their traditional clothing, "adorned" all the gubernatorial visits to the communities and townships. For many years, the women were required to attend such visits, to wear their best clothes and to walk arm-in-arm with the INI official or state governor.

The December 1995 assembly was decisive for the future of the cooperative. The founding women analyzed what was happening in Chiapas, including the Zapatista armed uprising, the marches in support of this movement, and the workshops on rights, in which some of the members of the organization participated. Several of the women admitted to being afraid and not wanting to continue. They saw that "it is easier to go with the INI." To continue with this government institution assured them of keeping the store, since this location had been obtained through the INI. To have the store without paying any rent gave them a place to sell their products in the city. Through this government organization, they also had the possibility of attending national fairs, where they could also sell their products.

At the same time, the young women, mostly daughters of the founders, declared, "No. We want an independent path; we want to organize in another manner. To us, it is not only important to sell our crafts, but also to participate in the movement."

The young women's pronouncements signaled a process of division of the co-op between, on the one side, women in Zapatista support bases and women sympathetic to the EZLN (especially supporters of the PRD, the Party of the Democratic Revolution); and on the other side, women linked to the PRI and the state government. The young women saw the independent organization as a means to have access to information from outside of their communities and a context in which they could reflect on it; further, they were restless to participate politically. This movement was especially supported by two women from

San Andrés Larríainzar. Women from this township eventually made up the majority of the founding women of the new cooperative.

Returning to the subject of the division in J'pas Joloviletik, it is important to note a symbol in communities that created much confusion and distress among women co-op members. After the Zapatista uprising, it became common for people to place white flags outside their homes to indicate that they are not sympathetic with the Zapatistas. In fact, this act was imposed by the state government. When a woman put up her white flag, she marked herself as supporting the government. The act of flying white flags facilitated many rumors. The first rumor that began to circulate in San Andrés said that every house that had a white flag would not be attacked if there was shooting or bombing. This rumor caused people to fight amongst themselves and the group began to factionalize. Another element that also contributed to division among people was the presence of the Mexican Army. Women and their families saw the installation of military encampments, for example in San Andrés, as something "external" to the communities. People in the communities never saw or felt the soldiers as a "part" of them. Under this social stress, relationships between co-op members with different political commitments became strained.

These stresses led to the division of J'pas Joloviletik into two groups. Along with approximately 200 women, the consulting team left J'pas Joloviletik to form a new co-op, Jolom Mayaetik, Tzotzil for Tejedores Mayas (Mayan Weavers). This new cooperative appointed Lorenza Gómez from Jolxhic, Chenalhó as its first president. Under Lorenza's leadership, we shared a process of struggle and searching. We also endured intimidation and direct threats to the integrity of various women, including Lorenza. Lorenza finished her two-year tenure with Jolom Mayaetik and joined K'inal Antzetik as a consultant, in order to begin her own path. Later, the members of Jolom Mayaetik elected Rosalinda Sántiz Díaz as their next president.

Constructing this new cooperative has been difficult for many reasons, among them the threats and obstacles to marketing in a world that is increasingly more competitive. However, at the beginning of the this century, we can say that Jolom Mayaetik is one of the most important artisan cooperatives in Mexico. It does not limit itself to the marketing of products; it continuously connects itself to the social and political processes ongoing in Chiapas.

Some Challenges for the Future

Opening Spaces for Women

Working exclusively with women has held great meaning for me and has also brought many successes. The process has taken time, in part because it integrates education in women's rights into training in production processes and political processes.

Although my work has been primarily with women, we have never required that meetings be composed exclusively of women. As mentioned earlier, some men were present during the first meetings. After 1994, only women attended meetings. But in the following years, men began to return. These men were mostly Zapatista supporters who came to become informed about what was said in meetings, to learn what women were asking for, and to assist with the setup during a workshop or a video showing. We have never had a confrontation with any of these men. We tend to leave them alone as we continue giving the workshop or carrying on the meeting.

We also had to be very proficient achieving consensus, which was a goal of the women. In the pueblos, ejidos, and other communities, the people continue to build consensus, independent from external influence. This consensus is based on their own local values that respond to a community dynamic. In the process of arriving at consensus, the women engage in the process of autonomy, the appropriation of their productive, cultural, and social organizations. For example, when two men wanted to speak at a meeting, the women came to a consensus and said, "Yes, let them." But the women asked that the men speak at the end. Further, the participation of the men also had its advantages. Their presence in this type of process can be useful when the men take responsibility to help women keep their organizations functioning successfully. In local communities, even all–women's cooperatives welcome men's assistance in certain aspects of their work. A sense of collective responsibility is created as men and women acquire joint interests in each others' groups.[5]

Economic Profitability in Cooperatives

The economic profitability of cooperative work has been minimal. The crafts do not make the women who produce them rich, but they do give them the possibility of a certain sense of economic independence, for example, of being able to contribute something to their household. "It gives me money for my soap. It gives me money for my oil. It gives me money to buy my corn, even if it is a little," the women say. Providing a sustained source of income for women producers through cooperatives remains one of the most vexing problems for cooperatives.

The New Generations of Women

One of the challenges that the artisan cooperatives are beginning to face are the *maquiladoras* (factories) planned for Chiapas as part of the Mexican government's development project, Plan Puebla Panama. From the point of view of a young woman, one might ask: What is best, to continue as an artisan earning very little, or to work in a factory that, even if it does not pay well, provides a better income? The individual, familial, and group security that comes with a

---

[5]See Eber 1999 for a discussion of how women in a Zapatista baking co-op in Chenalhó are involving men in their work.

bimonthly salary is important to everyone, not only indigenous women. However, one might also ask: What will happen in factory work to the process of seeking collective autonomy, to a woman's capacity for "self-determination" learned in the heat of the social processes that have taken place at different levels in Chiapas?

Artisan cooperatives are not the same as they were in the 1980s. They are now more diverse in terms of age, ethnicity, and religious and political affiliations. Indigenous women's cooperatives are now full of young women. These young people have different concerns than older indigenous women. Many young women are migrating to the cities from the countryside. The number of young people leaving to search for work is impressive. At times it would seem that the younger people no longer desire to work collectively. Cooperatives face an uncertain future. Certainly, young people can formulate novel alternatives, but that requires a great deal of work, "ants' work," close, collective discussion and analysis.[6]

Autonomy of Indigenous Women and the Appropriation of Spaces

K'inal Antzetik has been responsible for the majority of the education and training projects in its work with indigenous women. Jolom Mayaetik and the other co-ops have received education and training. Yet, at the same time as we have provided training, we have been preparing the way for indigenous women to assume this work themselves, for them to control their own projects without consulting K'inal Antzetik. Some of Jolom Mayaetik's members are young women who have the capacity to initiate this type of new experience— that is—to continue and build on their own and to maintain relationships with foundations, multilateral agencies, and social organizations.

Questions about power have emerged as young women become leaders. For example: Should they use their power for personal gain or share it? Will they hold on to their power? Women leaders have seen examples of what it is means "to have power" or to be "leaders" in their own communities, for example, bilingual teachers and political leaders. These models of leadership focus on having power and not losing it, adding to it, not sharing it. I have seen this view of power in the women leaders also, perhaps because of the original model of power that they learned.[7] How to delegate power, how to share power? These are major problems to resolve.

---

[6]See Rebecca Rodriguez (2002) for a discussion of how young women are using artisan cooperatives to find alternative social worlds that enable them to remain single. Rodriguez conducted interviews with several single women members of Jolom Mayaetik and J'pas Joloviletik.

[7]In indigenous communities, women are also introduced to a view of power as a resource partly controlled by powerful spiritual beings who share it with humans for the benefit of all. Healers, midwives, and religious and political leaders articulate these ideas of power in the public arena.

Another concern that women face as more and more of them become leaders, is the future of women leaders after their terms of office end. Is it possible for these women to return to the ranks? How can they handle losing the social recognition that goes with representing a collective? Some women leaders have said that once they are no longer representatives, they feel "abandoned" or "isolated." These are understandable responses. Few possibilities for advancement and social recognition exist in the women's communities, compared to those that cooperatives provide.

In light of the prevailing pressures to seek, conserve, and increase power, the future of a cooperative of women that builds its autonomy and capacity for self-management on a daily basis is uncertain. At this writing, at the head of Jolom Mayaetik is Manuela Díaz Ruíz, a young woman, an excellent leader, who is capable of speaking in large forums in any part of the world. The past president, Rosalinda Sántiz Díaz, is now responsible for fund-raising for Jolom. Heading K'inal Antzetik, is Micaela Hernández, the Tzeltal women who has been fully incorporated into urban life, a space from which she supports Jolom Mayaetik in a committed manner. Jolom Mayaetik is currently building a Training Center for Indigenous Women, a physical, social, political, and cultural space where they can reproduce what they have learned, and train themselves in new areas, as well as make new openings for the younger generations that are experiencing important changes in their communities.

We, the mestiza and indigenous women of Jolom Mayaetik and K'inal Antzetik have entered a new phase, a phase of constructing new identities and organizational spaces. Indigenous women are opening new spaces of civil resistance based on concrete demands, such as fair markets for artisan products and alternatives to working in maquilas or migrating to big cities in the Mexico or the U.S. Organized mestiza feminists are stepping back to reflect on their experiences and to learn from them. We have learned to be more humble and in the process we have changed the manner in which we come together with other women for change. From the first years to the present, we mestizas have learned not to force processes on indigenous women. In this new phase, some mestizas prefer to continue working in the broader movement of indigenous women. Others choose to be involved in organizations that interrelate issues of gender, class, and ethnicity. In these organizations we reflect on our singular paths as mestizas whose lives intertwine with those of mestizos and indigenous women and men. In the process we are creating new organizational forms comprised of both men and women. We put our faith in the construction of civil resistance and the dream of creating new alternatives to struggle against globalization and neoliberalism.

19
Compañeras

**Translated by Christine Kovic
and Francisco Argüelles Paz y Puente**

Indigenous and peasant women commonly express their experiences organizing for social justice through song. "Compañeras" was written by the Catholic women of the Diocesan Coordination of Women (CODIMUJ) and is sung in Spanish at local and regional meetings of this group. Women of Jolom Mayaetik and K'inal Antzetik also sing it (see Yolanda Castro's chapter). The song describes the ways poor women work together as compañeras (friends or partners) to defend their dignity. It also affirms the value of women's work in the household. The tune of the song is "De Colores," a popular Mexican folksong.

Let us welcome, yes, we welcome
with pleasure and fondness all the compañeras.
That have come, that have come
to examine so many big problems.
And now, and now
we are going to be looking for a good solution.

Therefore we are
organized with our husbands and we must fight
to combat the oppressive class that always
devours our humble home.

We women, we women
we carry the water, we wash the clothes and make tortillas.
We prepare, we prepare our simple food,
we take care of children.

Yet no one, but no one
values our work, due to lack of love.
Men are big *machistas* because of this system of great oppression.
This individualist, neoliberal system today is
the cause of great destruction.

It is now, it is now
that we are able to value ourselves.

We discover that the children and all kinds of men depend on us.
If it wasn't, if it wasn't
for all our work, they just couldn't live.
Because we are the foundation
of the same class for all existence.
Because we are the foundation
of the same class for all existence.

20

 Learning Everything
I Can about Freedom

Testimony of a Social Worker and Popular Educator

DIANA DAMIÁN PALENCIA
Translated by María del Pilar Milagros Garcia

Life in Cristóbal Obregón, a Zoque community in Villa Flores, Chiapas,[1] evolved around each sowing season. My father would take my sister and me early in the morning to sow the land. We had to walk all the way to the piece of land my dad rented to plant tomatoes. I was 12 and my little sister was only 2. We helped our dad water the tomatoes and also shared our mom and dad's illusion to win the lottery one day. Being the eldest sister I had many obligations and responsibilities: I had to help with the household chores and I also had to do my homework. Everything had to be perfect.

The majority of children in my community did not go to school since the girls had to help with the housework and the boys had to help in the field. But my mom and dad believed in providing us with an education. Although my dad is Zoque from Villa Flores, his parents sent him to school in Mexico City where he met my mother, a mestiza from the city. They sent us to school because they were convinced that if we studied we would have the chance to live a better life. So, I attended school. In the afternoons I would gather with the other children in the center of the village to play. Late in the evening, we would run in the semidarkness watching some boys and girls secretly kiss. In my community young people were not allowed to kiss or touch.

My adolescence also flew by in the semidarkness, between secret letters and some hand-holding. A first kiss, a first feeling of love and desire stayed silent in the darkness awhile. But that silence ended when my mom found a letter from a boy declaring his love for me. She beat me so hard that I regretted even saying

---

[1]Villa Flores is located near the Pacific coast, in the eastern central part of Chiapas, two hours from the capital, Tuxtla Gutiérrez. Most of the Zoque inhabitants of the township, like my father, have lost their native language due to the heavy influence of mestizos and large landowners in the region. Spanish has been the lingua franca among the Zoques, poor mestizos, and native peoples from other parts of Chiapas who come to work on the many corn, cattle, and sugar-cane plantations in the region.

"hello" to him. It was a scandal. His mother also had a very low opinion of me. To her I was "crazy," "a tart." I was only 12 and I had "already chosen the wrong path," they told me.

I finished primary school. A junior high school had just opened in our village and I decided to continue on in school. I also continued having relationships with some young boys in my community. I had various secret boyfriends but, living in a small community, secrets always end up being daily gossip. My mom suffered because people used to say the worst things about me. My behavior was especially hard for my mother, because when she came to live in Cristóbal Obregón people called her *la güera de la ciudad* (the light-skinned woman from the city). Eventually the community accepted her, because she was the wife of a native man, but she still struggled to belong. I made a huge effort to get the best grades in school so that my parents would accept me and I would not be "just a problem." But my good grades did not count; my "crazy behavior" canceled out my academic successes.

At 17 I started having sexual relations with a steady boyfriend. He would arrive at my house and I would give in to have sex just to please him. I didn't like it. It bothered me. Yet, I thought he liked me best that way.

The situation at home became unbearable. My mom had to put up with recriminations because of me. Beatings were part of my daily routine. In my community, that was the only way to discipline children. Due to the problems I was causing, I had to leave. My parents sent me to Mexico City to live with my aunt. But I only stayed there a short time. I returned home and got pregnant from my boyfriend. At first, I was scared of the beating that awaited me when my parents learned that I was pregnant. But I was also happy because now I could lead a different life as a wife. I could be away from my house, out of Mom's and Dad's reach. On the other hand, I dearly loved my parents and siblings, who were like my own children. I left my house feeling hurt, but with the hope of freedom.

During the weekdays I lived in Tuxtla Guitiérrez where my husband worked and I went to school. On the weekends we would visit my community. But I didn't want to have much to do with my community because people did not accept my being different. If I had accepted their opinion of me, the rejection would have only hurt me more.

My married life lasted five years. I lived in Mexico City during part of this time. There I attended school and had all the housework to take care of, as well. I also had to take care of my daughter, Carolina, whom I loved long before she was born.

My husband followed my community's traditions in relation to gender roles. He still enjoyed all the privileges and freedom of men, but all I had was work, always work. My husband also drank heavily and beat me when he was drunk. He tried to stop drinking but he would always start back again. My family blamed me for marrying a man who would treat me so badly. Their lack of understanding only made my suffering worse. The violence and rejection reflected in my anemic, tired, and sad body. With all the work, violence, and feelings of rejection, the love I once felt for my husband turned into obligation, or maybe it had always been like that. I don't know.

In 1986 I began to study social work in Tuxtla Gutiérrez. Part of the course of study was doing internships. I chose to work with women in communities in highland Chiapas rather than in hospitals or in other institutions. In Cañitas, Ixtapa I gave talks on reproductive health. I began with basic workshops about how to prevent pregnancy through contraceptive methods. I also taught about infant care and how to prevent common illnesses. I used methods that I had learned in school, but little by little I began to change my approach as I realized that the methods that I was using didn't bear fruit. Through intuition and experience I changed my methods to ones that came from within the communities. In time I researched methods of teaching in books, too. But these didn't give me much help.

In 1989 I became involved in women's organizations where I observed the methods that they use. I attended all the workshops that I was invited to, but I was more of an observer than a participant; I wasn't conscious of gender at this time. I didn't know what it meant. I had barely heard about gender issues, and I wanted to learn. My own personal situation made me want to work with women who could listen, accompany me, and share solidarity. In 1990 in Tuxtla Gutiérrez I got involved with a group of women and men focusing on gender and reproductive health. The group members were well-prepared and I learned a lot from them.

It was at this time that I left my husband. My family turned their backs on me since I was still the bad daughter and the rebel. My daughter had to put up with offensive words from people in my community and from my family. They pointed at me as a bad woman and mother. My husband put all the blame on me. I chose to separate; he was the abandoned one, the victim.

I returned to Mexico City to live with my daughter. I was alone, and not well-organized. Yet, I was sure that the path I had chosen was the right one. I was willing to go anywhere and do anything to earn money to support my daughter. In Mexico City I became involved in a women's group, SIPAM, that pushed me to further research and systematize everything that had to do with women's health, including mental and reproductive health. I conducted research and interviews for a radio program in Education Radio, called, "*Dejemos de Ser Pacientes*" (Stop Being Patients). To be aired, my program had to be of excellent quality. I learned more in preparing radio programs than I did in school.

I returned to Chiapas at the beginning of 1994 and continued working with *campesino* and indigenous women, but in the border and jungle regions. I have been involved in more workshops, seminars, and courses than I can remember. Through my experiences and studies and daily life, I have developed new methods to work in reproductive health and in gender, working from women's traditions and local experiences. It is a great challenge. It is my life.

I also experienced another personal change and challenge: I truly fell in love. With my new love I wanted a different relationship, but I did not know what one was like. I sought freedom, even if I was scared of being alone, since I had always depended on someone. I did not know how to live otherwise. In retrospect, it has been a difficult experience to live in a different way, to have chosen a partner and to have lived with him the way I wanted.

Conducting Workshops on Gender

Since 1995 I have been working with FOCA (Formation and Training), a collective of women and men founded in 1995 based on common political, human, and social principles. We work in the context of popular and alternative education. We believe that women and men know a lot, but that they need to remember what they know. We believe that participatory workshops are the context in which all can learn what they know, but may have forgotten. We have redesigned the workshop plan and principles as a result of our experiences leading many workshops. We have learned not only through books and activism, but through a blend of many methods, including innovative lectures, direct work with campesino and indigenous populations, and talking with workshop participants about what they most like and how they learn best. From these experiences, we have learned to embrace differences and the importance of each person finding her or his own identity. In our work we focus on the concepts of unity and support. These two concepts help us search for common demands that unify us across our differences.

The first step in planning a workshop is to meet with people in communities and collaborate together on a plan. Nothing is imposed, nor prepared apart from this process. In the workshops with women, first we talk with the women in a planning meeting. We see what motivates them, if they want help to develop themselves, and what topics are most important to them. We make an outline of topics and a calendar. For example, I am responsible for reproductive health and women's overall health. According to what topic comes up on the calendar, I see if I can facilitate the workshop. If I can, I prepare my *carta descriptiva* (guideline of how to present the workshop), and indicate when to schedule it, and so forth. Then I prepare my materials for the workshop. The materials have to be well designed for educational purposes.

I present the materials in the context of a participatory workshop in which women can smell, feel, and touch the materials with their hands. I work from the lived experience of each woman. For example, if we work on the theme of women's bodies, we use modeling clay, crayons, natural clay, and we sculpt and draw our bodies, according to how we see ourselves and think of ourselves. At the beginning of the workshop we ask, "Who does your body belong to?" Women almost always answer that it is theirs. But in the course of the workshop they discover that it also belongs to their father, their mother, their brothers and sisters, their aunts, the priest in their community, the customs, God, among others. After so many owners nothing remains for them. After sculpting we talk about what our bodies are to each of us. We touch on traditions, religion, the family, self-esteem, empowerment, and recognizing our bodies.

We also explore how our bodies communicate without speaking. For example, we say with our mouth that we are well, but our bodies often say other things. In order to arrive at this awareness we create an exhibition of our clay bodies or our drawings of our bodies. The women tell each other how they see the bodies. We discover many things that we don't see at first. At times we cry, at times we laugh. Sometimes we embrace each other. We realize what we have in common and we value the differences between us.

We end the workshop by asking each woman to share what she has done for her body that day. This action moves us a lot, as it is a way to begin to care more for our bodies. We give the women homework to give a little love to their bodies each day. The women provide the examples of how to do this, for example: to laugh; to play; to go visit a doctor; to go out and walk a little to breathe in air deeply; to talk with some friends awhile; to look in a mirror and see themselves as beautiful; to take a bath in the river, enjoying themselves and looking under the water. Many ideas about how to be happier and healthier arise from the workshops.

At the end, participants evaluate the workshop, if it served their needs, what they didn't like, what they liked most, and how we could improve the next time. Finally, I write a report on the workshop. I use the evaluations and my report to make the next similar workshop better for everyone.

Workshop Themes

In workshops with women I have learned that relationships between women and between women and men are profoundly affected by three factors: (1) communication, (2) power, (3) and women's demands. I devote the remaining pages of this chapter to understandings about these three themes from popular workshops. Although I have separated the themes, in our workshops and in our daily lives the themes intertwine in complex ways.[2]

Communication

Communication between men and women has been a constant theme in workshops with indigenous and nonindigenous women. In their relationships with men, women make some of the same demands that indigenous people are making of the state, for example to have autonomy and equality. Although

---

[2]The following workshop proceedings lend additional insights on women organizing to transform gender relations in Central America: "Women's Outcry Against Violence and Impunity in Chiapas," Mercedes Olivera, Martha Figueroa, Adela Bonilla, et al. (San Cristóbal de Las Casas, November 25–26, 1999); "Gender Workshop" in Kuna Ayala, Panamá," Diana Damián (December 2000); International Gender workshop, "Ni Hombres ni Mujeres si no todo lo Contrario," Abelardo Palma, Diana Damián, Antonio Salgado, Luis Reyna, Javier Herrera (San Cristóbal de Las Casas, March 2000).

many social change organizations prioritize class struggle, in the workshops I have organized we encourage women to integrate their gender demands into those of their class.

Women's testimonies reveal their fear of talking about gender issues in their communities and organizations. Their fears are rooted in the fact that relationships with men, and by association, their communication with men, is often confrontational. Women are searching for ways to communicate what they want in such a way that men do not feel attacked. In the democratic indigenous peasant movements, men are often threatened when women talk about what they want or do not want, even if these men are sensitized to and conscious of women's demands throughout history. In rural and urban areas, women face discrimination for talking about equality between men and women and for starting communitarian popular work. Women's families and communities often argue that their ideas are not valid and that they come from outsiders.

Power

Power is a dominant theme in community workshops. It was also a major topic at international workshops on gender held in Chiapas and in Panama in 2000. In these diverse workshops we discussed the power in the communication that women establish and how to reconceptualize power in and on our own terms. The following distinctions have emerged:

"Power over" is the power that someone exerts over other people at a variety of levels and contexts. Political leadership provides an example of this kind of power. In many Latin-American countries, leaders have plunged women into poverty and have exposed us to discrimination, through their exercise of "power over." Religious leaders also exercise this kind of power. Many religious and political leaders have forced women into submission and have deprived us of the right to exercise our sexuality or to make our own decisions about marriage and maternity. In the workshop held in Panama we commented on the fact that Panama has a woman president, but one who is not conscious of gender issues. The majority of the women in the workshop agreed that having women leaders is not enough; women must have a gender and class consciousness.

In contrast to this kind of power, we discussed two other forms of power: "power to" is the power to communicate, to learn, to solve and to overcome problems, and to accept different abilities and knowledge; "power with" is the collective effort to overcome obstacles and to reach goals.[3] Examples of the latter forms of power are the achievements of organized movements in different states or countries. For example, the Zapatistas have articulated a conception

---

[3]For discussions of feminist reformulations of "power," see Janet Townsend et al. (1999) and Magdalena León (1997).

of leadership that they call *mandar obedeciendo,* to lead by obeying. This concept rejects the idea of leadership being about exercising power over people.

In organizations, women sometimes perpetuate "power over" styles of leadership without intending to. We sometimes fall into stark rivalry and arrogantly promote ourselves as redeemers. We talk about honesty and respect without being honest ourselves. We do not respect either the work or space of others. We prioritize public relationships in order to obtain security and acceptance. We call ourselves *jefa* (boss). We believe in the struggle for equal rights, but we compete with each other. We sow anguish and reap turbulence.

Women's groups can be important training grounds for women to find noncompetitive ways to express power and to avoid falling into patriarchal or matriarchal traps. These groups build in self-criticism and also help women be conscious of their "internal powers" based on self-acceptance and self-respect. Tapping internal power is a necessary complement to articulating power in political arenas.

Men's Responses to Women's Demands

Testimonies of women about their partners' responses to their demands for greater equality offer many insights on the challenges women face. Women married to husbands who are members of organizations that work in the area of gender are especially revealing. Many of these men work with leftist democratic organizations. They may identify as anarchists, Maoists, Trotskyites, communists, socialists, internationalists, masculinists, or pro-feminists, or they may not give themselves a label. Some of these men have been writing about masculinities or leading workshops on the subject. In their discourse, these men reflect on the privilege that they continue to enjoy as men, men's responsibility for violence toward women, and the benefits that feminism has brought both genders.

Men have made progress in relation to women's demands, but women express concern that in mixed workshops or meetings men often act like patriarchs, redeemers, or the only ones with something important to say. Men often correct women when they speak. In this oppressive context, women sometimes surrender to the men's power.

Concluding Reflections

Workshops on women and gender have helped advance women's understandings of their places in their societies and of the many obstacles they face to greater autonomy and equality with men. A severe obstacle women face is the legacy of never having been allowed to speak out freely or to say what they think without fear of reprisal. In Chiapas, women's words have not been valid; only men's words have carried weight.

Women also confront the obstacle to communicate with women from diverse social sectors, ideologies, and orientations to militancy. We have discovered that sharing a gender identity does not imply that we can communicate well. Workshops have helped us communicate the ways that we are different. We believe that demanding an identity of our own is important. At the same time, we also recognize many ways in which we indigenous, mestiza, Chiapanecan, and Mexican women are united. In our workshops we focus on the concept of unity and support and attempt to forge bonds based on common demands.

Sometimes women reinforce the patriarchal system through the ways we relate and communicate. We can be the worst inquisitors of other women, reproducing the very system and methods that men have used through history to marginalize women. We do this especially when we compete with other women and men. Competition between women is an especially painful issue for women in organizations in Chiapas. Although our discourse speaks of another way to communicate and exercise power, we find ourselves thinking that others' approaches are bad and ours are good. One way that we are confronting this contradiction and its divisiveness is to listen to each others' truths and stories, which are important to complete our own. In the process we find that other women feel hurt from being excluded or unrecognized for their unique contributions. We also need to be self-reflective, to raise our consciousness about oppression, and to value others' paths of self-expression. In this way we affirm that the personal is truly political. In the current context of war and confrontational political positions, each of us has her own story, experienced in her own sphere of life and work. Each person's story is a partial truth, but arrogance prevents us from recognizing the truths that come from the mouth and eyes of those whom we have already labeled as being incorrect.

Perhaps the greatest obstacle we face is to move beyond discourse to changing attitudes, beliefs, and behaviors at the most basic level. My work has taught me that communicating well and exercising power in a healthy way requires one to value our own and others subjective experiences, to strive for a unity between our minds and bodies, and to resist prioritizing public or political spaces over private ones.

What results have we had? I believe that as long as even one woman benefits from our workshops, the work is worthwhile. I am encouraged by how women in Chiapas are building themselves up from their inner selves. The women I have worked with share a strong capacity to overcome difficulties and to not give up. Our paths continue to be full of challenges. Yet, every day I tell myself, "I've spent all my life searching for freedom and finally I have it in my hands. What do I do now? I need to learn everything I can about it."

21

Song for International Women's Day, March 8, 1997

FLOR DE MARGARITA PÉREZ PÉREZ
Translated by Christine Eber

Flor de Margarita Pérez Pérez of San Pedro Chenalhó first heard the story of the 1911 Triangle Shirtwaist Company fire in New York City during a rally she attended for International Women's Day in 1996 in San Cristóbal de Las Casas. She wept as she heard about the 146 women who died in the fire because their managers had locked them in the building. Soon after returning home, she wrote a song commemorating the women's deaths that linked them to the struggles of women in Chenalhó.

Flor de Margarita's song illustrates the ways in which women in Chiapas are learning about the struggles of women across time and space and how they are letting these stories filter through their own into the oral traditions of their people. Her song transposes some of the experiences of women in Chenalhó with the Mexican Army onto the experiences of women textile workers in the United States who were oppressed by store managers and unfair labor laws, not by soldiers.[1]

Flor de Margarita sang this song with her 13-year-old son, Davíd, at an International Women's Day celebration in 1997 in the community of Oventic in

---

[1] In 1910 labor organizer Clara Zetkin declared March 8th to be International Women's Day. The day was founded to commemorate the struggles of women garment and textile workers in New York City to protest unfair working conditions and to establish a union. In the first demonstration, March 8, 1857, women workers protested low wages and a twelve-hour workday. In 1869 they formed their own union. On March 8, 1908, women in the needle trades in New York City organized a march, the "uprising of the 20,000." At this time, the women added women's suffrage and protests over child-labor abuses to their demands. Throughout the twentieth century, International Women's Day became an important celebration in socialist countries. In the United States its observance declined until the late 1960s when participants in the women's movement began to revive it. However, in the United States, Women's History Month has taken precedence over International Women's Day. Women's History Month was inaugurated in 1977 by schools in Sonoma County, California as a means to integrate women's history into public-school curricula.

the township of San Andres sakam ch'en de los pobres. Since the Zapatista uprising, Oventic has become a cultural, educational, and social center for Zapatista supporters in the Highlands.

—Christine Eber

March 8th, 1908 many women died,
because they asked for liberty and justice.
The bad government didn't like
how the women protested.

The bad government sent soldiers
to burn their factories,
where they worked,
the oppressed women.

They aren't animals,
those the army was sent to kill.

The bad government was like a blood-thirsty animal,
like a buzzard that eats dead people.
The Zedillo government is the same,
it wants to be a buzzard, too.

The government doesn't say clearly
if it will give peace, liberty, and justice.
It only deceives us and doesn't fulfill
its promises in the dialogues of San Andrés.

But we will not surrender.
We will continue going forward,
asking for justice,
men, women, and children.

We are not cowards,
not like the government.
The government feels strong
because it has guns, tanks and airplanes.
The government ignores the suffering of
the people holding hands to protect peace.

22

Hacía la Autonomía
Zapatista Women
Developing a New World

MELISSA M. FORBIS

We carry a New World, here in our hearts. That world is growing this minute.
—Buenaventura Durruti

In 1989, Mexico became the first Latin-American signatory of the International Labor Organization's Covenant 169 on Indigenous Culture and Rights. Three years later, on the Quincentennial of Columbus's "discovery" of America, President Carlos Salinas de Gortari legally recognized Mexico as a "pluricultural nation." These developments seemed to signify a move toward the full recognition of the existence and rights of Mexico's indigenous peoples. Yet, on January 1, 1994, a predominantly indigenous guerrilla army, the Zapatista Army of National Liberation (EZLN) rose up in Chiapas with a list of demands including land, health care, education, and justice.

The EZLN uprising, timed to the day that the North American Free Trade Agreement went into effect, was more than a brilliant act of propaganda by disgruntled *campesinos* (peasants) in ski masks. It was the product of years of planning, with roots in student, worker, and campesino organizing of the 1960s and '70s; liberation-oriented religious teachings; and centuries of indigenous resistance. Because of the uprising, the voices of Mexico's most marginalized and oppressed were being heard clearly for the first time on the national stage.

To the ruling *Partido Revolucionario Institucional* (PRI) and Mexican political establishment, these voices calling for democratization represented a direct threat to their economic restructuring program and the privatization of national resources. Indeed, the government's response to the 1994 uprising was military retaliation. A number of factors, including national and international pressure, mitigated this use of force. Despite that victory, coercion has remained a state strategy, with over 30 percent of Mexico's military stationed in Chiapas (Centro de Información y Análisis de Chiapas 1997:96), most of it in the areas with a sizable Zapatista presence.[1]

---

[1]Although President Fox promised to reduce the military presence in Chiapas, nongovernmental organizations such as CIEPAC, SIPAZ, and Global Exchange note that troops have been transferred and consolidated rather than removed.

When coercion failed to eliminate the rebellion—military incursion may have actually expanded Zapatista ranks—offers of projects and material goods followed. Conscious of past government practices, the EZLN rejected these kinds of offers as efforts to buy off their demands and to divide communities by not making equal offers to all. This kind of stalemate between gifts and force, with an emphasis on appeals for national unity and the "rule of law," continues.[2]

Soon after the uprising, the Mexican government asserted that the conflict in Chiapas was a localized problem. This attempt to disassociate the EZLN's demands from the larger context of international struggles against global capitalism and neoliberalism was unsuccessful.[3] Many leftists at home and abroad, disillusioned by post–Cold War geopolitics,[4] viewed the EZLN as a new force of insurrection in Latin America linking indigenous and campesino issues—a force made more notable due to the participation of indigenous women.[5]

On March 28, 2001, eleven years after the government's initial step toward the recognition of Mexico's diversity, *Comandanta* Esther, a rural woman from the margins of the nation, spoke in front of the Mexican Congress: "[It is] symbolic that it is I, a poor, indigenous and Zapatista woman, who would have the first word, and that the main message of our word as Zapatistas would be mine. . . . My voice comes to ask for justice, liberty, and democracy for the Indian peoples. My voice demanded, and demands, the constitutional recognition of our rights and our culture." With the backing of the Indigenous National Congress,[6] comprised of 360 organizations and communities from 18 states, Esther's words echo the continuing discontent of many of Mexico's indigenous peoples with the government's promises of multiculturalism and underscore the importance of women to the movement.

---

[2]In response to the creation of Zapatista autonomous townships, the Chiapas state government began a process of remunicipalization. It was an effort, in the name of "rule of law," to delegitimize the EZLN as representative of indigenous communities and to divide the population by creating new townships around current autonomous ones.

[3]It is clear that the conflict in Chiapas spills over national boundaries. One example is Mexico's status as a primary recipient of U.S. military aid in Latin America, receiving funds to fight the "war on drugs." However, this aid has also supported the militarization of Chiapas. For further information and an analysis of the global implications of militarization in Mexico, see Global Exchange, CIEPAC, and Cencos (2000).

[4]This disillusionment is frequently symbolized by the demise of the Sandinista revolution in Nicaragua.

[5]See Benjamin (1996 [1989]), Collier (1999), Harvey (1998), LeBot (1997), Nash (2001), and Stephen (2002) for a more in-depth historical overview. Also, see Tello Diaz (1995) for an alternative interpretation.

[6]The third National Indigenous Congress met from March 2 to March 4, 2001 just before the EZLN march's arrival in Mexico City. For the first time, the delegates accepted a proposed *"Mesa de Mujeres"* (a Women's Roundtable). Significantly, the main purpose of the Mesa was not to discuss "women's issues," but to discuss gendered views of the government's proposed "Law of Indigenous Rights and Cultures."

This chapter examines the perspectives of women of the Zapatista *bases de apoyo* (civilian support communities) on women's mobilization and indigenous autonomy. Since Zapatista women's daily lives and political mobilizations are framed by their participation in Zapatista-constructed autonomous townships (*municipios autónomos*), I briefly discuss the EZLN autonomy initiatives. I then touch on some of the national debates surrounding the issue of autonomy. Finally, I discuss women's participation in the movement and present their testimonies about the recent changes in their lives and communities.

The importance of the EZLN lies not just in its armed forces in the mountains but in the tens of thousands of men, women, and children of the *base*. A focus on elite understandings of the movement has ignored the ordinary people living in the communities in Chiapas. It is in these communities where the Zapatista agenda is being put into practice and social relations of power are being transformed. There has also been a tendency to analyze the EZLN as postmodern rebels using the internet as a site of resistance. This focus is important in understanding the movement's emphasis on identity politics and the power of the word, but says little about the reality of being indigenous in Chiapas—living without electricity and sanitation, much less telephones or computers. Viewing the Zapatistas as postmodern rebels denies them the agency that they have fought hard to create. This focus also suggests that the EZLN is the politico-military structure that issues statements, rather than the communities living in resistance.[7]

Lack of attention to the actions and lives of the members of the base also leads to a replication of static notions of indigenous subjectivity. Often research on identity politics has concentrated on indigenous rights activism at the national and international levels, and on movement leaders and intellectuals (Nelson 1999; Warren 1998). Rather than solely focusing on leaders, I center on the everyday actions and experiences of indigenous women in communities, but through their contextualization in larger fields of power.[8] In practice, the women of the Zapatista support communities are negotiating multiple identities: indigenous, Mayan, Mexican, campesina, revolutionary, community organizer, woman, wife, and mother within the specific context of their local autonomy projects. This chapter examines this complexity in the

---

[7]One of the results of this characterization has been the assumption that when *Subcomandante* Marcos is silent, so is the EZLN. For example, during the public silence of Marcos between February and July 1998, Zapatista communities issued over 40 communiqués, but the main perception of the media and the government was of the silence of the EZLN.

[8]A number of recent studies have paid closer attention to these processes incorporating analyses of nonelite understandings of indigenous women's agency and emerging political subjectivities (Eber 1999; Hernández Castillo 2001a; Nash 2001; Olivera 2001). Donna Haraway (1991) characterizes these as partial, subjugated knowledges.

context of autonomy, what it means to women of the base, and how understanding women's involvement can help us understand the challenge of the Zapatista movement and the roots of its sustainability.

Zapatista Autonomy

The practice and consolidation of autonomy is critical to the success of the Zapatista movement and is one of its greatest challenges to the Mexican state. The recognition of Mexico as multicultural was a move away from earlier assimilationist and antidemocratic policies, but this move came without offers of control over material resources or substantive changes in governance.[9] Within this context, the EZLN demand for indigenous autonomy has moved from the periphery to become the core issue in the ongoing conflict.[10] The long history of autonomy in Chiapas and Mexico is beyond the scope of this chapter, but I touch on the elements of the dual Zapatista initiatives—juridical and practical—and on key debates in Mexico on autonomy.[11]

In the context of peace negotiations, a juridical representation of indigenous rights, the so-called San Andrés Accords, was signed in February 1996 by the Mexican government and the EZLN. The San Andrés Accords was more than just an agreement between the government and EZLN—for many in Mexico, it represented the hope of building a new nation.[12] Although directly negotiated by the EZLN, the accords do not limit indigenous autonomy to a specific model. Part two of the accords states that:

> Autonomy is the concrete expression of the exercise of the right to self-determination, within the framework of membership in the National State. The indigenous peoples shall be able, consequently, to decide their own form of internal government as well as decide their way of organizing themselves politically, socially, economically, and culturally. Within the new constitutional framework of autonomy, the exercise of self-determination of indigenous peoples shall be respected in each of the domains and levels in which they are asserted, being able to encompass one or more indigenous groups, according to particular and specific circumstances in each federal entity. The exercise of autonomy of indigenous people will contribute to the unity and democratization of national life and

---

[9]In fact, just the opposite was occurring as President Salinas pushed a constitutional reform of Article 27 of the Mexican Constitution through Congress, paving the way for privatization of *ejidos* and formerly communal lands.

[10]Autonomy was not one of the original demands of the EZLN at the time of the uprising. However, during peace negotiations and discussions on indigenous rights and culture, the right to autonomy for indigenous peoples emerged as a central. See *Zapatistas! Documents of the New Mexican Revolution* (EZLN, 1994) for the development of the EZLN's discourse.

[11]For a history of movements for autonomy see Burguete Cal y Mayor (1995, 1999); Diaz-Polanco (1996, 1997a, 1997b); and Stavenhagen and Iturralde (1993) among others.

[12]The National Indigenous Congress, a grouping of indigenous peoples from all 32 states of Mexico, and civil society organizations helped draft the accords and participated in the negotiations as consultants.

will strengthen national sovereignty (EZLN-Mexican Federal Government 1996:2).[13]

Another key point in the document is the right to self-development; this means the participation of indigenous peoples in a process of development, which takes into consideration "their aspirations, needs, and priorities," with "indigenous woman" specifically mentioned as a priority for these projects (EZLN—Mexican Federal Government 1996:4).

The Mexican government refused to implement this "first step" toward creating a truly pluricultural nation. President Zedillo issued a revised version of the accords in December 1996, which was immediately rejected by the EZLN and even angered his own negotiators. The government's objection was that the San Andrés Accords constitutionalize favoring certain groups by according them a special status and privilege and, therefore, are racist. The government's position favors individual rights over collective rights and charges that granting specific rights to indigenous groups would result in Mexico's "balkanization." The accords remained in juridical limbo during Zedillo's tenure.

Heralded as a sign of the democratization of Mexico, Vicente Fox of the *Partido de Acción Nacional* (PAN) became president in December 2000. His election represented a historic shift in power. Shoftly after his inauguration, Fox made public comments in support of the San Andrés Accords. The EZLN march to Mexico City from February to March 2001 was an effort to pressure congress to pass the accords. However, in lieu of the existing agreement, congress drafted and passed a new Law on Indigenous Culture and Rights—a watered-down version of the existing document. Although the legislation was rejected by the states with high indigenous populations, the majority of state congresses approved it in August 2001 and it became law. There were a number of legal challenges to overturn the law, but Mexico's Supreme Court rejected the appeals in September 2002.

Although the EZLN's juridical efforts have been unsuccessful, there has been a unique and important advance in the form of de facto autonomy. In 1994, EZLN communities declared themselves "communities in resistance." During the following years, the EZLN and sympathizers founded 32 autonomous townships.[14] They set up an alternate system of territorial governance, complete with juridical and administrative functions, and control of local resources. These townships are part of a process; they are not homogeneous or exclusively indigenous, and all regions do not follow one model. Regardless of the differences between townships, the EZLN's autonomy project is establishing a new political order and transforming the relationship of communities to

---

[13]All translations of texts and interviews from the original Spanish are mine.
[14]This number has fluctuated over the years.

the state. But without the juridical backing of the San Andrés Accords, this process is open to attack.

Starting with the invasion of the *ejido* of Taniperla in April 1998, Chiapas's substitute governor Roberto Albores Guillén began the task of "dismantling" the autonomous townships and bringing them within "law and order." The prison of Cerro Hueco filled with people charged with the crime of "usurping government functions" for their participation in an autonomous township. In 2000, independent candidate Pablo Salazar Mendiguchía was elected governor of Chiapas. Salazar, a former PRI legislator who broke with his party position on the conflict in Chiapas, was widely touted as the man who would bring peace to the region. Although he has halted the policy of dismantling autonomous townships, militarization and violence continue.

Autonomy and Gender Debates

The demand for indigenous autonomy has been a hotly debated topic in Mexico. The bulk of the literature about indigenous autonomy focuses on its compatibility with the Mexican state; that is, on fundamental questions about the subject of the state, and whether collective rights are compatible with existing forms of governance and individual rights or whether they represent the possible dissolution of the nation-state (Burguete Cal y Mayor 1995, 1999; Díaz-Polanco 1996, 1997a, 1997b; Hernández Navarro 1995; Stavenhagen and Iturralde 1993). The discussions also center on possible models of autonomy, incorporating reflections from other experiences in Latin America.[15]

In most of this literature, gender is absent.[16] When gender does emerge, it is often employed to evaluate the possible negative effects of customary law. These discussions center on charges that customary law and indigenous traditions are patriarchal and will continue to oppress women if indigenous groups are granted autonomy. Therefore, the state must protect women by rejecting autonomy. This discourse has been supported by a number of prominent Mexican intellectuals and anthropologists such as Ignacio Burgoa Orihuela, Roger Bartra, and Enrique Krauze, sparking frequent debates in the newspaper *La Jornada.*

Other writers put forth a romantic view, which argues that indigenous autonomy and gender empowerment work seamlessly together since patriarchy and social conflict are the effects of colonization. They argue that once autonomy is achieved, indigenous peoples will once again live in "harmony" (León Portilla 1997:9). This position characterizes indigenous traditions as static, rooted in the past. It also fails to acknowledge the role played by capitalist

---

[15]In the case of Nicaragua, see Hale (1994).

[16]There are a few cases where the relationship between gender and autonomy has been evaluated (see Gutiérrez and Palomo in Burguete Cal y Mayor 1999). However, these accounts tend to be marginalized from the central discussions.

hegemony in creating and recreating the sociocultural realities of both indigenous traditions and capitalist modernity (Díaz Polanco 1997a:76). Further, this discourse is generally limited to advocating for cultural rights and divests indigenous peoples of claims to economic rights within the state. Although pro-autonomy, this romantic position dovetails with the realignment of state rule in Mexico, which promotes the discursive recognition of cultural difference, but without concurrent changes in rights regimes or material practices.

These debates are not just abstract, but play into various state strategies to undermine the demands for and the practice of autonomy. A number of these strategies have clear implications at the site of gender, building policies from the early part of the twentieth century. Indigenous women were targeted as agents of modernization, with women's bodies becoming a particular site of discipline and normalization. Those who study women in Chiapas have pointed out that assertions of collective rights based on local *usos y costumbres* (customs and traditions) are made problematic when those customs perpetuate the subordination of women (Chenault and Sierra 1995; Garza Caligaris 1999).

One emerging strategy of governance has deployed women's rights discourses in order to subvert Zapatista (and other indigenous) claims based on cultural difference. This strategy draws on the debates outlined in the foregoing and positions the state as guardian of women's interests, in order to oppose moves toward autonomy.[17] Patricia Espinosa, director of the government's National Women's Institute, lauded the same indigenous rights law of 2001 that was denounced by the majority of indigenous groups solely because it makes specific mention of women's rights, and is thus needed "to rescue them [indigenous women] from traditions and customs . . ."[18]

Other state strategies of rule include the incorporation of discourses of multiculturalism and rights (human, women's, constitutional, etc.) of nongovernmental organizations (NGOs), and transnational actors (Speed and Collier 2000). These emerging policies involve the recognition of some aspects of collective rights, such as cultural rights, provided they do not challenge

---

[17]There are other gendered strategies. One has been the deployment of military and paramilitary violence, aimed at punishing Zapatistas, especially Zapatista women. For example, women's meetings in the Central Highlands were taken to be a sign of Zapatista activity, positioning women as a special target of paramilitary violence before the Acteal massacre in 1997. Some researchers claim, "the Acteal massacre was the most violent of this series of aggressions; by murdering the women, they were intending to destroy a symbol of Zapatista resistance. The purpose was to 'kill the seed,' which those same paramilitaries shouted this past December 22 [1997]" (Garza Caligaris and Hernández Castillo 1998:60–61). Another has been the feminization of indigenous men, which implicitly recognizes men as the "leaders" of the EZLN and women as subordinate to their mandate.

[18]Quoted in an Interpress Service article by Pilar Franco, "Mexico: Indigenous Rights Bill Recognizes Women's Rights," from April 27, 2001.

basic regimes of power or displace the abstract individual as the national subject. In some cases, NGOs and feminist organizations have inadvertently supported these state strategies by prioritizing one right against another. However, these efforts have not been entirely successful due to the mobilization of indigenous women who are also publicly agreeing that usos y costumbres can be oppressive, but who maintain the right to change these traditions together with indigenous men in the context of their own communities, and not through state regulation.

The Revolution Before the Revolution

A product of the women's struggle within the EZLN was the Revolutionary Women's Law, accepted internally in March 1993 and made public on January 1, 1994.[19] It is a document elaborated by women of the base from all regions, with the input and help of the women of the military structure. The law codifies the points that women wanted to be part of the EZLN program such as their right to participate in decision-making, to education, to decide how many children they will have, and so forth (Rovira 1996:112). *Subcomandante* Marcos dubbed this process the "revolution before the revolution."

Unlike many guerrilla movements, the inclusion of issues important to women and the transformation of traditional gender roles were a part of the overall Zapatista strategy before the uprising. The EZLN developed in the sparsely populated Lacandon Lowlands or *Cañadas,* which began to be settled in the 1950s by people from the Central Highlands looking for arable land.[20] There was a second wave of migration in the 1960s and '70s spurred on by a nationwide government program, which brought mestizos in greater numbers to settle the jungle (Leyva Solano et al. 1997). The region received another influx in the 1980s, as refugees fled violence in neighboring Guatemala. Although the camps have been dismantled and many Guatemalans returned home, some remained settled in the region.

In the communities of the Cañadas, a different type of collective identity was forged by the juxtaposition of campesinos from different ethnic and regional groups, creating a type of frontier society. There was also a rupture in traditional gender relations as women were forced by necessity to take part in what had traditionally been men's tasks. "The collective identity present between the colonists in the canyon areas of the Lacandon jungle was the substance that wove the clandestine network of the EZLN together" (Leyva and Ascencio Franco 1996:171). I focus on women in this area to expand upon discussions about gender and indigenous autonomy.

Women's participation was an important part of Zapatista organizing. A number of texts focus on the *insurgentas* (women insurgents) and the equality

---

[19]See Box 1 in this book, p. 23.
[20]See Garza Caligaris et al. 1993 for a history from a woman's perspective.

being forged in the military camps in the mountains (Holloway and Peláez 1998; Kampwirth 2003; Lovera and Palomo 1997; Rovira 1996; Stephen 2002). About a third of the military members are women, including many holding high ranks (EZLN 1994:304). Although generally young, between 14 and 25 years old, the insurgentas played key roles in the taking of San Cristóbal, Ocosingo, and Las Margaritas on January 1,1994. The insurgentas have also been important role models to women of the base, who often sing *corridos* about them at public events.[21]

Before increased militarization restricted insurgentas' mobility, they frequently came down from the mountains to give talks to women in the communities. They spoke of their lives in the mountains and the changes that they were living—as one woman said, "a life more equal." They explained Revolutionary Women's Law and advocated for women's rights. When Major Ana María, military commander of the zone of Los Altos was asked if she thought community women would disapprove of her decision to take up arms, she said:

> No, to the contrary, they saw it positively. And many women, many, wanted to enter into the struggle but couldn't; because they were married or had children they couldn't leave. But here we don't only fight with the weapon: the women in the communities organized themselves; they do collective work, put on meetings to study, to learn something from books. And they help the Zapatista Army because their children, their siblings, and their in-laws formed the same army . . . And they make sure that they [the insurgents] have food in the mountains (Rovira 1996:107).

Ana María's words underscore the mutually supportive relationship between the insurgentas and the women of the base.

However, the women of the base have not received as much notice as the insurgentas, and although accounts of insurgent life are important, they have tended to be taken as a statement for all Zapatista gender relations.[22] This position elides critical differences between insurgent and community women. For the women of the base, others closer to home inspire them to become civilian leaders and participate in the political life of their communities. Some of them are public figures like Comandante Ramona, a small monolingual Tzotzil woman, who became a symbol of the strong indigenous woman, arriving in her red and white brocaded *huipil* (blouse) and black ski mask to the talks with the government in 1994. Others are the anonymous women in every community whose daily struggles are equally important.

However, these changes have not come without conflict and there has been a backlash against women's mobilization. Zapatista women, as the racialized gendered subjects of political practice, expose and challenge the normalizing

---

[21]The *corrido* is a type of ballad that relates a story. It has been popular in Mexico for well over 100 years. See Chapter 4 for a corrido about a woman killed at a protest.
[22]Notable exceptions are Lovera and Palomo (1997) and Rovira (1996).

and disciplinary mechanisms of the state *and* ethnic nationalist movements. Whether intending to bolster the hegemonic national project or subvert it, interventions designed to undermine women's organizing—including gendered state violence such as sexual harassment and malicious gossip in their home communities—are signs of the consolidation of new forms of patriarchy.

As biological and cultural reproducers, and gatekeepers of ethnic/racial/national boundaries, women serve as the embodiment of difference (Mani 1989; Mohanram 1999; Smith 1995; Stoler 1995; Yuval-Davis, et al. 1989). National and ethnic leaders' desire for racial and national homogeneity locates them similarly in the nation. "The bodies of women, literally and metaphorically, have been the raw material for: an official nationalism based in the myth of a homogenous and mestizo Mexico; an indigenous movement that founds its discourse in the revindication of its millenarian traditions and that considers women the transmitters par excellence of culture and; for a low-intensity war that values rape as a demobilizing strategy" (Hernández Castillo 1998: 128–129).

Some feminists have also critiqued the EZLN on the issue of gender. Reacting to the disparities that continue to exist in the communities, they have charged that the EZLN's gender politics is little more than discursive propaganda, and since there is no overt analysis of patriarchy, there can be no new forms of social relations (Rojas 1994, 1995a). Although correct in their assessment of the continued existence of certain patriarchal practices—certainly domestic violence has not been eradicated—these critiques often lack the empirical evidence to measure changes in either gender relations or women's empowerment.

Further, these critiques avoid discussion of issues of privilege, racism, and classism in Mexican society and remain focused on essentialist demands of rights for women as a universal group. The women of La Correa Feminista writing about the Indians [*sic*] say that ". . . they are like women: they are another group made invisible, silenced, punished, and oppressed. In many analyses of the situation of Indians, you could exchange the word 'Indians' for 'women' and [vice versa] and you wouldn't notice the difference" (Lovera and Palomo 1997:92). Nash (2001) refutes this idea of interchangeability by pointing out the differences between indigenous and nonindigenous women, and discusses the tradition of gender complementarity in communities, which is not compatible with liberal notions of equality.

It is this lack of attention to differences *between* women that allows Marcela Lagarde, in an effort to express her fundamental disagreement with armed struggle to simultaneously define *the* feminist position and outline how Zapatista women must change:

> It is essential that the rest of us women, who identify with feminism and feel empathy with the Zapatista cause, assert our righteous pacifist tradition, so that the

alternative imagined by them [the Zapatista women] for their emancipation abandon the path of destruction and death. War is not a liberatory path. It is necessary that we create an option together, one that is alive, universal, democratic, peaceful and liberating (Lovera and Palomo 1997:177).

Although Lagarde is a Zapatista supporter, she excludes Zapatista women from the possibility of feminism and presumes to know the path to their liberation. It is positions like this that postcolonial writer Gayatri Spivak takes to task, charging that ". . . much so-called cross-cultural disciplinary practice, even when 'feminist,' reproduces and forecloses colonialist structures" (1986:237).

For many Zapatista women, it is hard to imagine how the efforts they've made to fight multiple oppressions could be so easily dismissed. As Dalia, one of the two EZLN representatives to the Second Intercontinental Encounter for Humanity and against Neoliberalism in Spain in 1997 stated, "We, the women of the Zapatista communities, see that women struggle in other countries, but we see that they struggle for things that we sometimes don't understand. I want to tell you that the Zapatista women respect the thoughts of all of you" (Ejército Zapatista de Liberación Nacional 1997:98). The EZLN struggle for liberation is for the liberation of all women. But First World nonindigenous discourses often fail to recognize that the liberation of women in rural Chiapas is a process that must include all aspects of their identities, and the concurrent liberation of their men and children.

The *Base*: Site of Struggle

The women who are on the front lines of the day-to-day struggle are not in the mountains, but in the *milpa*.[23] They experience a triple oppression for being women, indigenous, and poor. Living in Chiapas, one of Mexico's poorest states, further marginalizes them. Infant mortality is about 65 out of 1000 children born in Chiapas and even higher in majority indigenous areas (Centro de Información y Análisis de Chiapas et al. 1997:31). When a woman is asked how many children she has, she'll frequently give a number and then explain how many of them are still living. In 1995, a government study reported that 37.5 percent of the population in Chiapas is illiterate. The number for men and women can be as high as 71.5 percent in heavily indigenous townships (Centro de Información y Análisis de Chiapas, et al. 1997:35).

This chapter focuses on women from communities of the autonomous townships of Francisco Gómez and 17 de Noviembre. These correspond to the official townships of Ocosingo and Altamirano, respectively, an area known as the Cañadas, or the canyons of the Lacandon Lowlands. Before 1994, there were few government institutions present and little infrastructure—a situation that has been characterized as *olvido* (oblivion) by the EZLN. Building

---

[23]*Milpa* refers to the fields farmed by peasants, traditionally planted with beans, corn, and a variety of squash.

and improving roads and providing electric service were used as pretexts for the military invasion of February 1995. Transport is scarce—one or two buses a day and some private traffic—and expensive in terms of the local economy. The nearest medical facilities can be as far as 12 hours away.

Since 1995, these townships have been involved in coordinated occupations of large landholdings, creating communities known as *Nuevo Centros de Población* (New Population Centers). These Nuevo Centros are a social experiment in creating exclusively Zapatista communities. These communities are not necessarily comprised of people from the same ejido, region, or indigenous group. They serve as a counterpoint to the claim that autonomy would lead to ethnic strife and forced homogeneity, or "balkanization."

I began formal research in this area in 1997, after noticing a disparity between what I was reading about the EZLN and gender relations and what I saw women and men in communities actually saying and doing.[24] I submitted a proposal to township authorities and received permission to interview; I conducted formal interviews between June 1997 and August 2001. I informed each woman that she could deny my request for an interview, but none did. In fact, several told me that it would be good for other women to hear their words and learn from them. The interviews were conducted in Spanish, my mostly fluent third language. For all but two of the women, it was also their second or third language and their fluency varied. On occasion women who could speak Spanish would decide to answer in Tzeltal or Tojolabal and have another woman translate.

Zapatista women have begun to change their lives and transform gendered relations of power within the framework of autonomy and self-government. For women, autonomy includes economic rights and the control of production, human rights, physical rights to their own bodies, and a sociocultural right to decide how they will structure their identities. In many ways, women's struggle within the EZLN is parallel to the overall struggle—it is about "equality," but with difference. Women's right to participate in public life and in the regional autonomy project is generally supported, but their personal autonomy can come with a price. The changes that strike most directly at traditional family life and women's roles within it are often the most difficult. In the following section, I focus on women's general views on "autonomy," and how this concept relates to their lives on personal and collective levels.

Women on Autonomy

Asking women directly about "autonomy" provided a variety of responses that quickly shifted from talking about autonomy as an abstract concept to talking

---

[24]This chapter is based on ethnographic data collected in structured and informal interviews from 1996 to 2001. The research also draws on my four years of experience living and working with the women of these communities on appropriate technology and health education projects. This research is ongoing and will become the basis for my dissertation in social anthropology.

about praxis—about what autonomy means for them personally and how they are implementing autonomy in their lives. Many women began their responses like Romelia,[25] a 48-year-old Tzeltal woman who said, "I have not been speaking in public for very long and I am afraid that I will give the wrong answer." Many women also told me that they were "for" autonomy, but that they didn't know what the "real (*mera*) autonomy was." Almost all of the women thought that the men had a clearer understanding of autonomy as a concept, but my conversations with most men didn't bear this out.

Carmen is a Tzeltal woman in her early thirties with four children. She has been involved in social movements since her teens and is the women's *respons-able* (representative, literally "person responsible") of her region and a political authority in the larger zone. She was one of the first women I met in Santa Rita, one of the larger villages of the autonomous township, when I was referred to her as the contact person for a possible project with women at another site. She told me:

> Sometimes we women don't know how to respond to what autonomy is. But later we figure out that we are doing autonomy by doing the things we do. We know we can speak; we are doing away with the fear, the shame. We can speak in assemblies. We are doing our work. It is there that autonomy is formed. Sometimes we don't know what autonomy is, but in our deeds, we are doing it. Sometimes we don't understand that, when people are asking us, but later we reflect and see that we are already inside of it, we are already doing it, but without recognizing what we are putting forth.

I asked Carmen, if she could give me comparative information about women's status in all of the EZLN territory. She said that she only knew her area and couldn't really comment on the work of others. However, she did go on to note that although Women's Commissions have been named since January 1, 1994 to oversee the political and productive work of women, she thought her area was the one where this process was most successfully underway.

My first visit to Dignidad was in the middle of the rainy season, driving for what seemed like hours down a muddy dirt road filled with livestock-swallowing potholes. Dignidad is among the oldest towns in its region and is sandwiched between two federal military camps, the closest only 200 yards away. On that trip, I met Lupe and her husband Roberto, both Tzeltal and in their late twenties. Lupe was working as a health promoter at the time. She said:

> We know very well about autonomy because we are now working in it. Now, we are not taking part in the [federal] government . . . we have our own authorities, an authority for our communities . . . The work that the township councils are doing is going more or less well and it's there that there is advance in the autonomy. And there are women doing the work together with the men. Not only the men have

---

[25]For security reasons, I have selected pseudonyms for the women interviewed and for their communities.

rights, but the women also have rights to have a *cargo*[26] and that is why the region put women on the councils, so that they could work together with the men.

Lupe continued, reflecting the responses of many women who did not separate a discussion of autonomy from what autonomy means for women and their participation:

> It was with the Zapatistas that we began to organize ourselves because we also began to see our suffering. Before we didn't know that we also had rights as women. But with our struggle, now we know that we also have the right to participate and to do all the things that the men do as well. If the men have rights, then we, too, have rights to participate. But we would not have seen this if we didn't have the Zapatista movement.

Aurelia was a midwife in her mid-60s living in the Nuevo Centro of Nueva Victoria.[27] Her family migrated to the area in the early part of the 1900s to work on plantations. She considered herself "formerly Tzeltal" since she could no longer speak the language. She and her family decided to leave the comforts of their old community to become part of a Nuevo Centro in 1995. Aurelia stated, "We are part of this, the autonomy, but we still don't know what it wants, what it says, we don't understand. We are *caminando*[28] in the Word of God, in the work, but more than this, we don't understand. Now we are meeting again to understand what autonomy is."

Aurelia began her work long before the uprising, participating in CODIMUJ, the coordinating group of women of the San Cristóbal Diocese.[29] Her husband, Rogelio—whose father spent a year fighting with Emiliano Zapata during the Mexican Revolution—is a regional deacon who encouraged her to work. He believes that if a man decides to become a catechist, his wife also has a right to a position if she wants one. "They should be *caminando* together equally," he asserted. Aurelia spent years walking up and down the canyon visiting groups of women and talking about women's rights. She said, "One needs to know what one's right is. . . . We have to see our rights to participate, to make things better, to do something. That's what it [autonomy] says, how we are going to organize ourselves. We were with [the Zapatistas] almost since the beginning, the women, too. Who is going to want to stay behind when they see

---

[26]Positions of responsibility, which are something one is named to, often based on talents or qualifications. The cargo system is part of an indigenous form of governance.
[27]Aurelia, one of my closest friends in Chiapas, died in February 2000. Over the course of several years, she visited the regional hospital in Altamirano a number of times complaining of headaches and vision problems. Each time she was given aspirin and sent away. In late December 1999, she suddenly became paralyzed. A group of religious visitors brought her to Mexico City where she was diagnosed with a massive brain tumor. Her husband brought her back to her *tierra* to die at home with her family.
[28]Literally "walking," used to mean participating and organizing.
[29]For information about CODIMUJ see Kovic's chapter in this book.

the men ahead of them? Whatever the men live through, we are also ready to fight. We are ready for everything, come what may."

Access to land on which to carry out projects represents a new type of opportunity to most of these women.[30] Carmen emphasized, "Women also have their collective land, which is a form of autonomy. They now have their own land and are doing projects and not only the men get to do projects." They are now learning to administer their projects and account for any funds involved. Organizing projects also involves learning or improving reading, writing, and math skills that were never taught to them (or to most men). These experiences translate into women's desires for their daughters to attend school and to learn as much as possible because it will move their personal and collective struggles ahead.

Many women focused on their work in collective projects. Rosa is a Tzeltal woman in her early thirties with three small children. She said that in her community, Zapata, the women now have collective work—in the milpa and horticulture, raising chickens and bread making. One of these projects is a community vegetable garden. The women were the ones who decided to buy seeds and organize the plot. She explained the project:

> We sell the vegetables cheaply to ourselves, but it's not done individually, it's done as a community. First, we organized to figure out the costs and we named a secretary to be in charge of the money. We name secretaries for all the projects. This is how we are caminando. We worry and think, what if there is no advancement in our work? So, we decided this is how we are going to work and we share what there is between us.

Rosa is also proud that many women left their homes to help build the *Aguascalientes*, the regional community center of the autonomous township. "Before the women didn't really work collectively and didn't know how. Now we know that the women in the communities can do something and are working together."

Rosa's neighbor Clara is a Tzeltal woman in her mid-forties who speaks Spanish and Tzeltal fluently. Clara had moved to the town of Altamirano with her husband who found work there. When she heard about the organizing, she wanted to join but had to prove herself. She told me that her mother was one of the first Zapatistas in their home community, but that "she kept her secret," not even telling Clara until later. After the uprising, her family decided to move to a Nuevo Centro to be with others in the movement. Her sister also lives in Zapata and works with her on collective projects.

---

[30]See the video *Mujeres Unidas* (Chiapas Media Project 1999) for another representation of the collective projects in practice. Made by indigenous videographers from the local communities, the video presents some of the same projects described by women in these interviews.

Clara is a health promoter and a regional organizer who went to Mexico City with the 1111 Zapatistas representing her community in September 1997 and on the *Consulta*, the EZLN plebiscite that sent 2500 men and 2500 women throughout Mexico in March 1999. She told me that before, "women were like chickens, locked up in the kitchen." They were only allowed to leave with men's permission. "Now, women are free to go to meetings to learn and the only thing stopping them is their own fear."

Clara, a mother of ten, remembers the exact day she began her organizing, as do many of the other women. The dates are remembered because they mark the moment that each woman was able to begin working for the benefit of her community. This represents a significant change in most women's lives. On her own initiative, Clara is recruiting women in other communities to become health promoters and to attend regional courses. She said, "The men and some of the women laughed at me for learning these [health] things. They thought that I was crazy. Although they may laugh, I am going to continue in the work that I've been given. All that I have in my heart, and all the information that I give, is offered to help my community. Now, they come to me when they are hurt and they see the value of my work. We women have to be strong."

Lucinda, Alicia, and Soledad are young Tojolabal sisters from Libertad, a remote Nuevo Centro. The first time I visited, there was no road—getting there involved taking a bus to a community across the canyon, hiking down a steep trail, crossing the hanging footbridge, and then climbing up the other side. I met Lucinda on that first trip and she laughed at what I thought was Libertad's remoteness. She pointed to a place almost at the ridge of the mountain behind us to show me their original community. For her, Libertad, with its good land was a dream come true, especially after the road was built the next month.

Although all three speak Spanish, they discussed my questions first in Tojolabal, and then Lucinda, who is one of the few women to have finished sixth grade, summed up the responses and answered in Spanish. Lucinda, the responsable for women's projects in the Tojolabal region of the township, told me that things have changed greatly for women since 1994.

> Before most women didn't go to meetings, the men wouldn't let their spouses leave, but now it's changing, we are all meeting together. Now we all have rights to participate and say what we want, men and women. But before the men didn't pay attention to us. The government said that women didn't have the right to participate and say things. And the men thought that way, too and didn't open spaces for us. We women were here in the kitchen and didn't want to leave to go to a meeting. But now it's not the same as before. There are some women who participate and know what autonomy is. They know how to work like the men, and now it's changing a bit. With those who are making the effort, it is changing a bit.

While I was visiting, Lucinda and her friend Rosa held a workshop on public health and hygiene. They are both health promoters in their late teens, although Lucinda is single and Rosa is married with three children. Lucinda's older brother jokes with her saying that he doubts that she'll ever get married, since it will be hard finding a man who is her equal. The two women travel hours to attend training courses on medicinal plants, supported by the other women who give them bus fare and a bit of extra money for snacks from the proceeds they earn selling their collectively planted corn.

This kind of work is new to them. Lucinda explained, "Before we didn't know how to work collectively, but now bit by bit, we are learning. Now we have collectives, we are working corn, beans, horticulture, these are pure collectives and the women are learning bit by bit. Because before we didn't know and now there is more or less something." After each course, they return, they gather the women together to explain what they learned and to talk about how they can put the training into practice in the community. Lucinda and Rosa are also managing the building of their own health center and are coordinating their projects with the male health promoters.

Women's health, especially reproductive health and family planning, is now a specific focus in these regions. Family planning is also now discussed positively in the communities, although not yet widely practiced. One problem is access. The Catholic Diocese pressured its constituents to only provide family planning to married couples—an act that drew fire from many Zapatistas and feminists, but which was eventually accepted by the communities. Women health promoters travel and give talks about how it is important for Zapatistas to plan their families, especially living with the threat of state violence.

Clara says, "We've already talked about many things with the women, like family planning and how you should do it. It's not obligatory, you don't have to stop forever, but you should take time. The women didn't all like it, but [things change] bit by bit. Some old women have knowledge of other ways." Although this is obviously an issue for men and women, it is most often women who must decide to take control and make these decisions. Some couples are waiting until their children are older to have more. But Aurelia told me that it is "still very few. But we are changing these customs bit by bit. You can't break everything at once, it takes time."

Chepita, a young newly married Tzeltal woman from Nueva Victoria, focused on the meaning of autonomy in terms of men's duties to support their wives. She explained:

> The men have the responsibility to look after the house if the woman leaves. They have the duty to take care of the children, to look for their food, to make it, to maintain them. Some men are doing this. They're doing this so that their wives can leave. And the wives of those who help leave. The men say they're ready to do this and that if the women don't leave, the men aren't responsible . . . but not all men help.

Maria also lives in Nueva Victoria. Her father is a health promoter and she followed his example, even doing some training in the town of Altamirano. I first met her while working on a project in the community. A man chopped his thumb with a machete and she stitched it, later explaining to me that one of the advantages of women health promoters is that they are often in the community during the day and not far away in the fields. She is in her mid-twenties and after remaining single longer than most women, she married an insurgent who had left the mountains to return to his community.

> Since the life there [in the camps] is more equal, at first he supported my work helping the people here. After I had my first baby, his mother told him that my place as a woman was here in the house to make him his food and take care of my son. He told her that I had an important cargo and that it was my right, but bit by bit he changed to bad thinking and began to forbid me from leaving the house because I had to make his food. I told him that I didn't need to ask his permission, but he threatened to leave me. It was this way for a long time, but I talked to my father and some of the women responsables and we had a community assembly. There we talked about this and he was told that he could not take away my right to serve my community. Then he came back to his clear thinking and asked me for my forgiveness.

Maria's story shows that the problems generated when personal and collective responsibilities come into conflict can have positive outcomes. However, women who do participate and leave their houses to organize often have to contend with gossip and jealousy in their communities upon returning. The charge that I've mostly commonly heard is that women go to regional courses and meetings to find other men, even though many of the courses are women-only and usually the training takes up all of their time, from waking to sleep. Rosita is a 17-year-old Tzeltal woman who spent time working and studying in a city three hours away. She said that every time she came home, "I would hear rumors about how I was going there to be with men and not to work and learn. It made me cry. My father told me to not listen and remember that I was doing important things, but I didn't like it [the rumors]." She finally decided to give up and married a young man from another community, so she could get away from the rumors undermining her work.

Even these kinds of personal choices can be contentious. The Revolutionary Women's Law states that women are now free to marry a person of their choosing, coming together as equals. This seems to be the case in the mountains, but the concept is not yet completely accepted by the base, where marriages are often still arranged. Aurelia tells me she knows some younger women who "found a partner and are just living together. Their parents aren't very happy but the young people are content." Juana, a Tojolabal woman in her thirties from San Andrés, says that where she lives "a girl can pick her own boyfriend. If the girl wants to marry her boyfriend, she's free to do so, even if her mother and father say no, she's still free to do so."

But if a couple decides to elope because they did not get permission from their parents or to avoid paying for the wedding, they may still be punished by their fathers and forced to marry. I happened to be in an adjacent building during such an incident. I asked the young women beside me to explain what was happening. They told me, a bit scandalized, that a couple that had eloped were being punished physically by their fathers. Rosita, who was clearly upset, said, "Some people can't think yet. One day they will be clear-headed (*claro*)."

Another contentious change is the ban on alcohol adopted by the EZLN, which was instigated by women of the communities. Since alcohol was usually involved in cases of domestic violence, women argued that a ban was a positive and necessary step toward curbing abuse. In the cases that still happen, women can apply the Revolutionary Women's Law. Sometimes just the threat is enough. Aurelia told me about one man in Nueva Victoria who beat his wife. "His wife came to us and complained, so we got the women together and went to his house to witness his wife publicly denounce him." When the women showed up, "He took off running." Aurelia says the couple reconciled and that he never hit her again. Other women told me similar stories from their communities.

The punishment for a man who beats his wife is a night or two in the Zapatista "jail" and a fine, but the punishment doesn't necessarily stop the behavior. Vicente holds no cargos, but his wife, Adela, is a regional authority who traveled north during the Consulta. He decided to support his wife and her organizing work by taking care of the home when she is gone. Right before she left for the Consulta, he hit her "because she had no decent shoes to wear." Adela had him brought before the local authorities and things were subsequently worked out.

I was saddened when he told me about the incident because I know how much he supports her work, but I wasn't surprised. We'd had extended conversations about domestic violence over the years. He would ask me, "Why is it wrong to hit her if she doesn't do what she is supposed to? How else will things get done?" For Vicente, autonomy means that men and women have the right to participate and serve their community, but they also have the responsibility to fulfill their roles at home. He said that gender equality means "she [his wife] also has the right to hit me, if I don't do what I am responsible for," although in the end he would say that violence isn't the answer.

Domestic violence is not always dealt with and underscores the tension between the rights of the individual and the good of the collective. If the man holds a regional cargo or is a community leader, his behavior may be excused. Cecilia and her husband Alberto were both respected regional organizers from Santa Rita. He was violently jealous of her work and fear of his beatings forced her to give up her organizing responsibilities. Although Alberto was punished a few times, he was never relieved of his duties because he was a good organizer. For women, the choices aren't as simple as just packing up and leaving to find another place or another partner. Even if a woman wants to leave, family relationships and material necessity often tie her to her husband. Eventually Cecilia began organizing again, but only on a limited basis and with Alberto.

Juana told me that in San Andrés, if a man and woman have conflicting cargos "the community decides who will get to do the cargo; it can't be both. Who will make the tortilla? Who will take care of the house? It is our custom that someone take care of these things." However, it is not automatically the man who gets to retain his position. She said that if the community sees "how we are participating in the struggle, how we suffer, put up with hunger and thirst in order to do our work, then they value what we are doing."

Sustainable Resistance

Women play a crucial role in sustaining the autonomy project on a day-to-day basis. Until now, the government has taken a paternalistic stance and has underestimated the power of the women of the base. Government functionaries assumed that indigenous women would sell out their struggle for a new stove, a sack of corn, and a kilo of beans. Clara said "they tried to trick us with their hand-outs. I'm not going to go to them and give up for a bit of rice or *maseca* (dried cornmeal for making tortilla). They're trying to kill us." Some women and men do give up, but the majority stay on and fight.

Women have also been on the frontlines protecting their communities from military incursions. When soldiers tried to enter the autonomous townships in January 1998, women decided to organize and defend their communities. The government falsely accused the EZLN of manipulating them. Women from communities of the autonomous township of 17 de Noviembre, sent a collective communiqué on January 28, 1998 about the incursions. They stated, "We asked that they [the soldiers] go back. We told them that not only the men have the right to speak, that the women also have the right to speak and that they should respect our word" (Autonomous Township of 17 de Noviembre 1998:10). Carmen said, "We sent the men off because when the army came in 1994, they took three of our men and killed them.[31] So, we told the men to go hide and we got sticks and chased the soldiers out. They were so scared that they were slipping in the mud. We asked them if they would treat their mothers and fathers this way."

Although women do fear attacks by PRI men, paramilitaries, and soldiers, many talk about how they are ready to die for their cause. Lupe explained what it is like living next to a military base and having to walk by the soldiers to gather firewood or go to her family's fields:

> The soldiers still bother us; it's the same up to this day. Some women are afraid because they don't know how to respond. The soldiers more or less know me by now because, for my part, I'm not afraid of them just because they have weapons. When we go to gather firewood, they want to take our picture. And I tell them that I don't want them to take my picture, I tell them no and I berate them.

---

[31]This case has been brought before various human rights bodies.

She was also one of the thousands of women to march in San Cristóbal de las Casas on March 8, 2000 and participated in the takeover of the government radio station, Radio Uno. At first, the station director wouldn't let them in, but she said that when they threatened to push the door down, he opened it. Afterward, she said he was "very polite. He gave us the studio and we broadcast our message to all the women and men, and then we left."

On one occasion, Aurelia told me, "After the conflict, I stayed at home because I was no longer able to leave. Because the army is going around watching what we do and where we go, everything. It was then that I became afraid and because I didn't have anyone to accompany me. I was alone and I stopped because I was afraid that they would grab me. So I stayed without work." However, she went on to talk about her participation in public demonstrations, "It's not important where the demonstration is—in Ocosingo, in Cuxulja, in Altamirano—we always go to the demonstrations. I went to San Cristóbal when they raped the nurses,[32] we went there to demonstrate."

On January 12, 1998, police in Ocosingo fired randomly into the crowd during a peaceful public demonstration against militarization and the Acteal massacre. Guadalupe Méndez López, a 38-year-old woman taking part in that march, was assassinated and has become a symbol of the struggle of indigenous women. Women often sing a *corrido* about Guadalupe at public events in these regions of Cañadas.[33] Aurelia was there that day. She told me that when the shooting began, she ran and jumped into a ditch, cutting herself on barbed wire. Her son was frantic because he couldn't find her. When he did, he began to cry, thinking that she had been shot. "He told me that I shouldn't go to the demonstrations anymore, that it was too dangerous. But I told him that I had to, that once you are caminando, you can't give up."

Conclusion

The praxis within communities of the base shows how diverse forms of resistance and political practice engage and contest wider intersecting systems of power and representation. The political subjectivity of Zapatista women is grounded in their experiences living as women, indigenous, and poor in Chiapas, Mexico. Listening to the voices of women of the base underscores the multiple and relational nature of their identities and helps us recognize the significance of "feminisms that may go by other names" (see Visweswaran 1994).

The EZLN regional autonomy project is now intrinsically linked with women's (and men's) personal autonomy. Women participate in the autonomy project on two levels. One is collective; they are part of the larger struggle

---

[32]On October 4, 1995, three nurses taking part in a vaccination campaign were raped in a heavily militarized zone of Chiapas.
[33]The *Corrido* is in Part 1, Chapter 4.

and work for the advancement of their vision regionally and nationally. The second level is personal; they are creating autonomy at home in their relationships with other men and women in the community. For Zapatista women, autonomy secures their right to difference but also to change the traditions that have excluded or oppressed them. They are rejecting an indigenous essentialism that demands that they hold onto their traditions in a static fashion.

However, their demands cannot be reduced to individual rights for women; rather they are grounded in an understanding of "women's rights" that can often be consistent with claims to "collective rights." Zapatista women are not struggling to be the same as men—in a Western fashion—but they do demand the right to decide how they will structure their lives within the larger community. They are not completely discarding traditional gender roles, but they are actively changing gendered power relations.

As participants in a movement to create a new relationship to the state, Zapatista women embody a complex position. They are not necessarily agents of modernization and as such, they challenge state strategies to subvert the movement. Their new politics of gendered resistance undermines the position that indigenous women must be protected from their patriarchal traditions and it disrupts counterclaims of the inherent gender equity of indigenous culture. Zapatista women refute the subordinate status accorded to them, giving voice to their own agency. It has not been an easy path, as the women are quick to point out, but it is the only one that leads to justice and dignity. As Carmen says, speaking to me as well as to her indigenous sisters, "We know that the struggle exists and takes time. We want the struggle to stay in the memory, not just of one woman, but of all women, so that they too can resist."

Bibliography

Abbassi, Jennifer and Sheryl L. Lutjens, eds. 2002. *Rereading Women in Latin America and the Caribbean: The Political Economy of Gender.* Boulder: Rowman and Littlefield.

Abu-Lughod, Lila. 2002. "Do Muslim Women Really Need Saving? Anthropological Reflections on Cultural Relativism and Its Others." *American Anthropologist* 104(3): 783–790.

———. 1993. *Writing Women's Worlds: Bedouin Stories.* Berkeley, CA: University of California Press.

Agee, James and Walker Evans. 1939. *Let Us Now Praise Famous Men: Three Tenant Families.* New York: Ballantine.

Aguilar Gómez, Delfina. 1998. *Rosa Caralampia: historia de una mujer tojolabal.* Xalapa, Mexico: DEMAC, CIESAS, Instituto Oaxaqueño de las Culturas, IVEC.

Aguilar Gómez, Delfina, Hermelindo Aguilar Méndez, and Juan Méndez Vázquez. 2001. *Voces de maíz: Relatos Tojolabales.* Comitán, Mexico: Centro de Investigaciones en Salud de Comitán.

Alexander, M. Jacqui and Chandri Talpade Mohanty. 1997. *Feminist Genealogies, Colonial Legacis, Democratic Futures.* New York: Routledge.

Alvarez, Sonia, Evelina Dagnino, and Arturo Escobar, eds. 1998. *Cultures of Politics/Politics of Cultures: Re-Visioning Latin American Social Movements.* Boulder, CO: Westview Press.

Aquino, María Pilar. 1998. "Latin American Feminist Theology." *Journal of Feminist Studies in Religion* 14(1): 89–107.

Arias, Jacinto. 1985. *San Pedro Chenalhó: Algo de su historia, cuentos y costumbres.* Tuxtla Gutiérrez, Mexico: Publicación Bilingue de la Dirección de Fortalecimiento y Fomento a las Culturas de la Subsecretaría de Asuntos Indígenas.

Autonomous Township of 17 de Noviembre. 1998. "Testimonio de las Mujeres del Municipio 17 de Noviembre, Chiapas." *El Tiempo* 53 (February 18–23): 7–12.

Balboa, Juan. 1997. "Prostitutión prolifera en zonas militares en Chiapas." *La Jornada,* January 27.

Barrios, Walda and Leticia Pons. 1995. *Sexualidad y Religión en Los Altos de Chiapas.* Tuxtla Gutiérrez, Mexico: Universidad Autónoma de Chiapas.

Bedregal, Ximena. 1994. "Reflexiones Desde Nuestro Feminismo." In *Chiapas, ¿y las mujeres, qué?* Vol. 1. Rosa Rojas, ed. Pp. 43–56. Mexico City: La Correa Feminista.

Behar, Ruth and Deborah A. Gordon. 1995. *Women Writing Culture.* Berkeley, CA: University of California Press.

Bellinghausen, Hermann. 2002. "Autonomía indígena, alternativa ante conflictos comunitarios en Chiapas, afirma investigador." *La Jornada,* May 4.

Benería, Lourdes. 1992. "The Mexican Debt Crisis: Restructuring the Economy and the Household." In *Unequal Burden: Economic Crises, Persistent Poverty, and Women's Work,* Lourdes Benería and Shelley Feldman, eds. Pp. 83–104. Boulder, CO: Westview Press.

Benjamin, Thomas. 1996 [1989]. *A Rich Land, A Poor People: Politics and Society in Modern Chiapas.* Albuquerque: University of New Mexico Press.

Bermúdez, Jesús Morales. 1995. "El Congreso Indígena de Chiapas: Un Testimonio." *América Indígena* LV(1–2): 311.

Bonilla, Adela. 1994. "Nuestro primer entusiasmo estrellándose con la realidad." *Correa Feminista* 15.

Boserup, Esther. 1970. *Women's Roles in Economic Development.* New York: St. Martin's Press.

Brown, P. 1981. "Language, Interaction and Sex Roles in a Mayan community: A Study of Politeness and the Position of Women." Ph.D. dissertation, The Australian National University.

Brown, Pete. 1997. "Institutions, Inequalities, and the Impact of Agrarian Reform on Rural Mexican Communities." *Human Organization* 56(1): 102–10.

Brusco, Elizabeth. 1995. *The Reformation of Machismo: Evangelical Conversion and Gender in Colombia.* Austin: University of Texas Press.

Burdick, John. 1993. *Looking for God in Brazil: The Progressive Catholic Church in Urban Brazil's Religious Arena.* Berkeley, CA: University of California Press.

Burguete Cal y Mayor, Araceli, ed. 1999. *México: Experiencias de Autonomia Indígena.* Copenhagen: IWGIA.

———. 1995. "Autonomía indígena: un camino hacia la paz." *Revista Memoria* 175 (March): 19–24.

Calvo, Angelino, Anna María Garza Caligaris, María Fernanda Paz, and Juana María Ruiz. 1989. *Voces de la historia: Nuevo San Juan Chamula, Nuevo Huixtán, Nuevo Matzam.* San Cristóbal de Las Casas, Mexico: DESM/CEI/UNACH.

Cancian, Francesca. 1965. "The Effect of Patrilocal Households on Nuclear Family Interaction in Zinacantán." *Estudios de cultura maya* 5: 299–314.

———. 1964. "Interaction Patterns in Zinacanteco Families." *American Sociological Review* 29(4): 540–550.

Cancian, Frank. 1992. *The Decline of Community in Zinacantán: Economy, Public Life and Social Stratification 1960–1987.* Stanford: Stanford University Press.

Castellanos, Rosario. 1962. *Oficio de Tinieblas.* Mexico City: J. Mortiz.

———. 1952. *The Nine Guardians: A Novel.* New York: Vanguard Press.

Castro, Gustavo. 2000. "Las fuerzas armadas en Chiapas." In *Siempre Cerca, Siempre Lejos: Las Fuerzas Armados en México.* Compiled by Global Exchange, CIEPAC, CENCOS. Pp. 109–135. Mexico City: Impretei.

Castro Apreza, Inés. 2000. "Mujeres indígenas en Chiapas: El derecho a participar." *Memoria* 139: 20–27.

Centro de Derechos Humanos Fray Bartolomé de Las Casas (CDHFBLC). 1999. *Presunta Justicia.* San Cristóbal de Las Casas, Mexico: CDHFBLC.

———. 1998(a). *Camino a la masacre: Informe especial de Chenalhó.* San Cristóbal de las Casas, Mexico: CDHFBLC.

———. 1998(b). *Esta es Nuestra Palabra: Testimonios de Acteal.* San Crístobal de Las Casas, Mexico: CDHFBLC.

———. 1996. *Ni Paz Ni Justicia: Informe general y amplio acerca de la guerra civil que sufren los Ch'oles en la Zona Norte de Chiapas.* San Cristóbal de las Casas, Mexico: CDHFBLC.

Centro de Información y Análisis de Chiapas (CIACH), Coordinación de Organismos No Gubermentales por la Paz (CONPAZ), and Servicios Informativos Procesados (SIPRO). 1997. *Para Entender Chiapas: Chiapas en Cifras.* Mexico City and San Cristóbal de las Casas, Mexico: CIACH, CONPAZ, and SIPRO.

Chanteau, Michel. 1999. *Las Andanzas de Miguel: La Autobiografía del padre expulsado de Chenalhó.* San Cristóbal de Las Casas, Mexico: Editorial Fray Bartolomé de Las Casas.

Chenault, Victoria and Maria Teresa Sierra, eds. 1995. *Pueblos indígenas ante el derecho.* Mexico City: CIESAS.

Chiapas Media Project. 1999. *Mujeres Unidas.* Chicago: www.chiapasmediaproject.org

Chojnacki, Ruth. 1999. "Retrato de un catequista: la religión liberadora y la comunitas en los Altos de Chiapas." *Nueva Antropología* 17 (56): 43–62.

———. 1995. "Indigenous Apostles: Notes on Maya Catechists Working the Word and Working the Land in Highland Chiapas." Paper presented at the Latin American Studies Association, September 30.

Centro de Investigaciones Económicas y Políticas de Acción Comunitaria (CIEPAC). 1998. "We Are Infested with Paramilitaries and Armed Groups." Two-part article. Bulletins Number 139 and 140. December 22 and 29. http://www.ciepac.org

———. 1997. "Forced Displacement: The Fingers Which Keep the Wounds Open." Chiapas El Día, Bulletin No. 135, November 7. http://www.ciepac.org

CODIMUJ. 1999. *Con Mirada, Mente y Corazón de Mujer.* Mujeres para el Diálogo and CODIMUJ.

Collier, George with Elizabeth Lowery Quaratiello. 1999 [1994]. *Basta!: Land and the Zapatista Rebellion in Chiapas.* Oakland, CA: Institute for Food and Development Policy.

Collier, Jane. 1974. "Women in Politics." In *Women, Culture and Society.* Lousie Lamphere and Michelle Rosaldo, eds. Pp. 89–96. Stanford: Stanford University Press.

———. 1973. *Law and Social Change in Zinacantán.* Stanford: Stanford University Press.

———. 1968. "Courtship and Marriage in Zinacantán, Chiapas, Mexico." New Orleans. Middle American Research Institute. Publication 25: 149–201.

Comisión Nacional de Derechos Humanos (CNDH). 1998. "Recommendation 1/98." Mexico City: CNDH. January 8.

Coordinación de Organismos No Gubernamentales por la Paz (CONPAZ), Centro de Derechos Humanos Fray Bartolomé de Las Casas (CDHFBLC), and Convergencia de Organismos Civiles por la Democrácia. 1996. *Militarización y violencia en Chiapas.* Mexico City: CONPAZ, CDHFBLC, and Convergencia.

Cruz Cruz, Petrona and Isabel Juárez Ch'ix. 1993. "La Desconfiada." *Mesoamérica* 23: 135–141.

Davis, Angela. 1981. *Women, Race, and Class*. New York: Random House.

De Olivera, Orlandina. 1998. "Familia y relaciones de género en México." In *Familias y relaciones de género en transformación: Cambios trascendentales en América Latina y El Caribe*. B. Smuckler, ed. Mexico City: Population Council-Edomex.

Denich, Bette. 1995. "Of Arms, Men and Ethnic War in (former) Yugoslavia." *Feminism, Nationalism, and Militarism*. Arlington: American Anthropological Association.

Díaz Polanco, Héctor. 1997(a). *Indigenous Peoples in Latin America: The Quest for Self-Determination*. Boulder, CO: Westview Press.

———. 1997(b). *La rebelión Zapatista y la autonomía*. Mexico City: Siglo XXI Editores.

———. 1996. *Autonomía regional: la autodeterminación de los pueblos indios*. Mexico City: Siglo XXI Editores.

Droogers, Andre, Gerrit Huizer, and Hans Siebers. 1991. *Popular Power in Latin American Religions*. Saarbrüken, Germany: Breitenbach.

Eber, Christine. 2001(a). "Buscando una nueva vida (searching for a new life): Liberation Through Autonomy in San Pedro Chenalhó, 1970–1998." *Latin American Perspectives* 28(2): 220–247.

———. 2001 (b). " 'Take my water': Liberation Through Prohibition in San Pedro Chenalhó, Chiapas." *Social Science and Medicine* 53(2): 251–262.

———. 2000 [1995]. *Women and Alcohol in a Highland Maya Town: Water of Hope, Water of Sorrow*. Austin: University of Texas Press.

———. 1999. "Seeking Our Own Food: Indigenous Women's Power and Autonomy in San Pedró Chenalhó, Chiapas, 1980–1998." *Latin American Perspectives* 26(3): 6–36.

Eber, Christine and Brenda Rosenbaum. 1993. " 'That We May Serve Beneath Your Flowery Hands and Feet' ": Women Weavers in Highland Chiapas, Mexico. In *Crafts in the World Market: The Impact of Global Exchange on Middle American Artisans*. June Nash, ed. Pp. 154–180. Albany: State University of New York Press.

Eber, Christine and Janet M. Tanski. 2001. "Obstacles Facing Women's Grassroots Development Strategies in Mexico." *Review of Radical Political Economics* 33: 441–460.

———. in press. "Women's Cooperatives in Chiapas: Strategies of Survival and Empowerment." *The Journal of Social Development Issues* 24(3).

Ejército Zapatista de Liberación Nacional (EZLN). 1997. "Ponencia que presenta la delegación del EZLN sobre la lucha de las Mujeres Zapatistas." (Dalia and Felipe, presenters). *Instituto de Investigaciones Económicas (UNAM) Chiapas Revista* 5: 97–99.

———. 1994. *Zapatista! Documents of the New Mexican Revolution*. Brooklyn: Autonomedia.

Ejército Zapatista de Liberación Nacional-Mexican Federal Government. 1996. *Propuestas conjuntas que el gobierno federal y el EZLN se comprometen a enviar a las instancias de debate y decisión nacional, correspondientes al punto 1.4 de las Reglas de Procedimiento*. San Andrés Larráinzar, Mexico.

Elson, Diane. 1992. "From Survival Strategies to Transformation Strategies: Women's Needs and Structural Adjustment." In *Unequal Burden: Economic Crises, Persistent Poverty, and Women's Work*. Lourdes Benería and Shelley Feldman, eds. Pp. 26–48. Boulder, CO: Westview Press.

Escobar, Arturo and Sonia E. Alvarez, eds. 1992. *The Making of Social Movements in Latin America: Identity, Strategy, and Democracy*. Boulder, CO: Westview Press.

Fallers, L. A. 1954. "Fashion: A Note on the 'Trickle Effect.' " *Public Opinion Quarterly* 5 (18): 314–321.

Farmer, Paul. 2002. "Structural Violence and the Assault on Human Rights." *Society for Medical Anthropology Newsletter*, January.

Fazio, Carlos. 1994. *Samuel Ruíz: El Caminante*. Mexico City: Espasa Calpe.

Fernández-Kelly, Maria Patricia. 1983. *For We Are Sold, I and My People: Women and Industry in Mexico's Frontier*. Albany: State University of New York Press.

Fernández Liria, Carlos. 1993. "Enfermedad, familia y costumbre en el periférico de San Cristóbal de Las Casas." In *Anuario 1992*. Tuxtla Gutiérrez, Mexico: Gobierno de Chiapas.

Flinchum, Robin. 1998. "The Women of Chiapas." *The Progressive*. March: 30–31.

Flood, Marielle. 1994. "Changing patterns of interdependence: the effects of increasing monetization of gender relations in Zinacantán, Mexico." *Research in Economic Anthropology* 15:145–173.

Fortuny Loret de Mola, Patricia. 1989. *Religión y sociedad en el sureste de Mexico*. Cuadernos de la Casa Chata 165. Mexico City: CIESAS del Sureste.

Freyermuth Enciso, Graciela. 2001. "The Background to Acteal: Maternal mortality and birth control, silent genocide?" In *The Other Word: Women and Violence in Chiapas Before and After Acteal*. Aída Hernández Castillo, ed. Pp. 57–73. Copenhagen: International Work Group on Indigenous Affairs.

————. 2000. "Mujeres de humo: Morir en Chenalhó durante la maternidad." Ph.D. dissertation, UNAM, Mexico City.

————. 1999. "Matrimonio, violencia doméstica y redes de apoyo: factores constitutivos de riesgo durante la maternidad. El caso de Chenalhó, Chiapas." In *Género y salud en el sureste de México*, Vol. 2. Esperanza. Tuñón, ed. Mexico City: Ecosur/Consejo Estatal de Poblacion en Chiapas/Fonda de Poblacion de la ONU.

————. 1996. "Morir en Todos Santos." In *Catorce estampas de mujeres mexicanas*. Diana Lucía Alvarez Macías, ed. Mexico City: Menciones DEMAC.

Freyermuth Enciso, Graciela, Anna María Garza, and Gabriel Torres. 1997. *Campaña en contra de la muerte materna: Porque damos la vida tenemos derecho a ella*. San Cristóbal de Las Casas, Chiapas: Grupo de Muieres de San Cristóbal de Las Casas (COLEM).

Freyermuth Enciso, Graciela and Mariana Fernández. 1995. "Migration, organization and identity: The Women's Group case in San Cristóbal de Las Casas." *Signs* 20: 970–995.

Freyermuth Enciso, Graciela and Gabriel Torres. 2001. *Historias, comité por una maternidad voluntaria y riesgos en Chiapas*. Chiapas, Mexico: ACASAC.

Friedel, David, Linda Schele, and Joy Parker. 1993. *Maya Cosmos: Three Thousand Years on The Shaman's Path*. New York: Quill.

Friere, Paulo. 1973. *Pedagogy of the Oppressed*. New York: Seabury Press.

Gallagher, Eugene. 1990. *Expectation and Experience: Exploring Religious Conversion*. Atlanta: Scholars Press.

García de León, Antonio. 1985. *Resistencia y utopia*, vols. 1 and 2. Mexico City: Ediciones Era.

Garma Navarro, C. 1987. *Protestantismo en una comunidad totonaca de Puebla*. Mexico City: INI.

Garrard-Burnett, Virginia and David Stoll, eds. 1993. *Rethinking Protestantism in Latin America*. Philadelphia: Temple University Press.

Garza Caligaris, Anna María. 1999. "El Género Entre Normas en Disputa: San Pedro Chenalhó." MA thesis. UNACH, San Cristóbal de Las Casas, Mexico.

Garza Caligaris, Anna María and Rosalva Aída Hernández Castillo. 1998. "Encuentros y enfrentamiento de los tzotziles pedranos con el Estado mexicano: Una perspectiva histórico-antropológica para entender la violencia en Chenalhó." In *La Otra Palabra: Mujeres y violencia en Chiapas, antes y despues de Acteal*. Rosalva Aída Hernández Castillo, ed. Pp. 39–62. Mexico City: CIESAS, COLEM, CIAM.

Garza Caligaris, Anna María and Juana María Ruíz Ortiz. 1992. "Madres solteras indígenas." *Mesoamérica* 23: 67–77.

Garza Caligaris, Anna María and Sonia Toledo. 2002. "Mujeres, agrarismo y militancia." In *Chiapas: La Perspectiva de las investigadoras*. Maya Lorena Pérez Ruiz, ed. Mexico City: UNAM.

Garza Caligaris, Anna María, María Fernanda Pas Salinas, Juana María Ruíz Ortiz, and Angelino Calvo Sánchez. 1993. *Sk'op antzetik*. San Cristóbal de Las Casas, Mexico: Centro de Estudios Universitarios, Universidad Autónoma de Chiapas.

Giménez, Gilberto, ed. 1996. *Identidades religiosas y sociales en Mexico*. Mexico City: IIS-UNAM.

————. 1988. *Sectas religiosas en el sureste: aspectos sociodemográficos y estadísticos*. Mexico City: SEP/CIESAS, Cuadernos de la Casa Chata no. 161.

Global Exchange. 1998. *On the Offensive: Intensified Military Occupation in Chiapas Six Months Since the Massacre at Acteal*. San Francisco. On-line publication at http://www.global exchange.org/campaigns/mexico/OntheOffensive.html

Global Exchange, CIEPAC, and CENCOS. 2000. *Always Near, Always Far: The Armed Forces in Mexico*. San Francisco. On-line publication at http://www.ciepac.org

Glusker, Susannah. 1998. "Women Networking for Peace and Survival in Chiapas: Militants, Celebrities, Academics, Survivors, and the Stiletto Heel Brigade." *Sex Roles* 39 (7/8): 539– 557.

Gobierno del Estado de Chiapas. 1995. "Plan Estatal de Desarollo, 1995–2000." Tuxtla Gutiérrez, Mexico: Talleres Gráficos del Estado.

Gómez Cruz, Patricia and Christine Kovic. 1994. *Con un pueblo vivo en tierra negada: un ensayo sobre los derechos humanos y el conflicto agrario en Chiapas, 1989–1993*. San Cristóbal de Las Casas, Mexico: Centro de Derechos Humanos Fray Bartolomé de Las Casas.

Gossen, Gary. 1999. *Telling Maya Tales: Tzotzil Identities in Modern Mexico*. New York: Routledge.

————. 1994. "From Olmecs to Zapatistas: A Once and Future History of Souls." *American Anthropologist* 96(3): 553–570.

————. 1974. *Chamulas in the World of the Sun: Time and Space in a Maya Oral Tradition*. Prospect Heights, Ill: Waveland Press.

Greene, Graham. 1984 [1939]. *The Lawless Roads*. New York: Penguin.

Greenfield, Patricia. 1972. "Cross-Cultural Studies of Mother-Infant Interaction: Toward A Structural-Functional Approach." *Human Development* 15: 131–138.

El Grito de la Luna (Document from the Workshop on the Rights of Women in Our Customs and Traditions). 1994. *Ojarasca* 35/36: 27–31.

Guiteras-Holmes, Calixta. 1961. *Perils of the Soul: The Worldview of a Tzotzil Indian.* Chicago: University of Chicago Press.

Hale, Charles R. 1994. *Resistance and Contradiction: Miskitu Indians and the Nicaraguan State, 1894–1987.* Stanford: Stanford University Press.

Haraway, Donna Jeanne. 1991. *Simians, Cyborgs, and Women: The Reinvention of Nature.* New York: Routledge.

Harvey, Neil. 1998. *The Chiapas Rebellion: The Struggle for Land and Democracy.* Durham: Duke University Press.

———. 1994. *Rebellion in Chiapas: Rural Reforms, Campesino Radicalism, and the Limits to Salinismo.* San Diego: Center for U.S.–Mexican Studies.

Harvey, Neil and Chris Halverson. 2000. "The Secret and the Promise: Women's Struggles in Chiapas." In *Discourse Theory and Political Analysis.* David Howarth, Aletta J. Norval, and Yannis Stavrakakis, eds. Pp. 151–167. Manchester: Manchester University Press.

Haviland, John. 1977. *Gossip, Reputation and Knowledge in Zinacantán.* Chicago: University of Chicago Press.

Hefner, Robert, ed. 1993. *Conversion to Christianity: Historical and Anthropological Perspectives on a Great Transformation.* Berkeley, CA: University of California Press.

Hernández Castillo, Rosalva Aida, ed. 2001(a). *The Other Word: Women and Violence Before and After Acteal.* Copenhagen: International Working Group on Indigenous Affairs.

———. 2001(b). *Histories and Stories from Chiapas: Border Identities in Southern Mexico.* Austin, TX: University of Texas Press.

———. 1998. "Construyendo la utopía: Esperanzas y desafíos de las mujeres chiapanecas de frente al siglo XXI." In *La otra palabra: Mujeres y violencia en Chiapas, antes y despue de Acteal.* Rosalva Aída Hernández Castillo, ed. Pp. 125–142. Mexico City: CIESAS, COLEM, CIAM.

———. 1997. "Between Hope and Adversity: The Struggle of Organized Women in Chiapas Since the Zapatista Uprising." *Journal of Latin American Anthropology* 3(1): 102–120.

———. 1994a. "Reinventing tradition: the women's law." *Akwekon Journal* 18(1): 67–70.

———. 1994b. "Dicen su Palabra." *Ojarasca* 35/36: 27–31.

———. 1992. "Entre la victimización y la resistencia etnica: revision critica de la bibliografía sobre protestantismo en Chiapas." *Anuario del Instituto Chiapaneco de Cultura.* Tuxtla Gutiérrez: Gobierno de Chiapas.

———. 1989. Del tzolkin a la atalaya: los cambios en la religiosidad en una communidad Chuj-K'anhobal de Chiapas. In *El enfoque antropológica de la religión.* A. Fabregas, ed. Cuadernos de la Casa Chata 162. Mexico City: CIESAS del Sureste.

Hernández Castillo, Rosalva Aída and Olivia Gall. N.d. "Una Historia desde las Mujeres: El papel de las campesinas indígenas en las rebeliones coloniales y postcoloniales de Chiapas."

Hernández, Gloria, Adela Hernández Reyes, and Salvador Mendiola. 1994. "Guerra y Feminismo." In *Chiapas, ¿y las mujeres, qué?* Vol. 1. Rosa Rojas, ed. Pp. 57–65. Mexico City: La Correa Feminista.

Hernández Navarro, Luis. 1997. "Mil veces más verde que el gris de la teoría." *Ojarasca*, supplement of *La Jornada* 5 (September):3–5.

———. 1995. *Chiapas: la guerra y la paz.* Mexico City: ADN Editores.

Hidalgo, Onécimo. 2000. "Paramilitarización en Chiapas." In *Siempre Cerca, Siempre Lejos: Las Fuerzas Armados en México.* Compiled by Global Exchange, CIEPAC, CENCOS. Pp. 137–155. Mexico City: Impretei.

Hidalgo, Onécimo and Gustavo Castro. 1999. *Población Desplazada en Chiapas.* San Cristóbal de Las Casas, Mexico: CIEPAC and Consejería de Proyectos.

Holloway, John, and Eloína Peláez. 1998. *Zapatista!: Reinventing Revolution in Mexico.* London: Pluto Press.

Howard, Philip and Thomas Homer-Dixon. 1996. "Environmental Scarcity and Violent Conflict: The Case of Chiapas, Mexico." Occasional Paper, Project on Environment, Population and Security. American Association for the Advancement of Science and the University of Toronto.

Human Rights Watch. 1998. *A Job or Your Rights: Continued Sex Discrimination in Mexico's Maquiladora Sector.* www.hrw.org

INEGI /Instituto Nacional de Estadística, Geografía e Informática. 1993. *Cuaderno Estadístico Municipal de Tuxtla Gutiérrez, Estado de Chiapas.* Tuxtla Gutiérrez, Mexico.
———. 1990. *XI Censo de Población y Vivienda.* Mexico City.
Jacorzynski, Witold J. 2000. "En busca del paraíso perdido." *Estudios Sociológicos de El Colegio de México.* 18:52 (85–124).
Johnson-Odim, Cheryl. 1991. "Common Themes, Different Contexts." In *Third World Women and the Politics of Feminism,* Chandra Talpade Mohanty, Ann Russo, and Lourdes Torres, eds. Pp. 314–327. Bloomington, IN: Indiana University Press.
Kampwirth, Karen. 2003. *Women and Guerrilla Movements: Nicaragua, el Salvador, Chiapas, Cuba.* University Park, PA: Pennsylvania State University Press.
Keck, Margaret and Kathryn Sikkink. 1998. *Activists beyond Borders: Advocacy Networks in International Politics.* Ithaca: Cornell University Press.
Kellogg, Susan. N.d. *Weaving the Past: A History of Latin America's Indigenous Women.*
K'inal Antzetik. 1995. *Mujeres indígenas de Chiapas: Nuestros derechos, costumbres y tradiciones.* San Cristóbal de Las Casas, Mexico.
Komes Peres, María, with Diana Rus and Salvador Guzmán. 1990. *Bordando milpas.* (in Tzotzil and Spanish). San Cristóbal de Las Casas, Mexico: Instituto de Asesoría Antropológica para la Región Maya.
Kovic, Christine. 2003. "The Struggle for Liberation and Reconciliation in Chiapas, Mexico: Las Abejas and the Path of Non-Violent Resistance." *Latin American Perspectives.*
———. 2001. "Para Tener Vida en Abundancia: Visiones de los derechos humanos en una comunidad católica idígena." In *Los Derechos Humanos en Tierras Mayas: Política, representaciones y moralidad.* Pedro Petarch and Julián López García, eds. Pp. 273–290. Madrid: University of Compultense.
———. in press. *Walking With One Heart: Indigenous Rights and the Catholic Church in Highland Chiapas.* Austin: University of Texas Press.
Lacy, Sara. 1976. "Antel." Bachelor of Arts Honor Essay presented to the Department of Anthropology, Harvard University.
Lagarde, Marcela. 1994. "Hacia una nueva constituyente desde las mujeres." In *Chiapas, ¿y las mujeres, qué?* Vol. 1. Rosa Rojas, ed. Pp. 66–71. Mexico City: La Correa Feminista.
Laughlin, Miriam. 1989. "To Cure the Sadness." *The New Renaissance* 10(2): 42–47.
———. 1987. "Happiness." *Arizona Quarterly.* 43(4): 313–330.
———. 1982. "A Very Special Affair." *Crosscurrents* 2 (3).
———. 1981. "A Day in Jail." *Arizona Quarterly* 37 (2): 127–136.
———. 1980. "The Compromise." *Arizona Quarterly* 36 (3): 217–239.
Laughlin, Robert. 1963. "Through the Looking Glass: Reflections on Zinacantán Courtship and Marriage." Ph.D. dissertation, Harvard University.
Laughlin, Robert M. and Carol Karasik, eds.1996. *Mayan Tales from Zinacantán: Dreams and Stories from the People of the Bat.* Washington, D.C.: Smithsonian Institution Press.
Leacock, Eleanor. 1979. "Women, Development, and Anthropological Facts and Fictions." In *The Politics of Anthropology: From Colonialism to Sexism Toward a View from Below.* Gerrit Huizer and Bruce Mannheim, eds. Pp. 131–142. The Hague: Mouton.
Le Bot, Yvon. 1997. *Subcomandante Marcos: El sueño zapatista.* Barcelona: Plaza & Janés.
Leon, L. 1987. "Artisan Development Projects." *Cultural Survival Quarterly* 11(1): 49–52.
León, Magdalena, ed. 1997. *Poder y empodermiento de las mujeres.* Bogatá: Tercer Mundo Editores.
León Portilla, Miguel. 1997. "Autonomía Indígena." *La Jornada* August 8:9.
Leyva Solano, Xóchitl and Gabriel Asencio Franco. 1996. *Lacandonia al Filo del Agua.* Mexico City: CIESAS.
Leyva Solano, Xóchitl, Gabriel Ascencio Franco, and Luis Aboites. 1997. *Colonización, cultura y sociedad.* Chiapas: Universidad de Ciencias y Artes del Estado de Chiapas.
Linn, Priscilla Rachun. 1976. "The Religious Office Holders of Chamula: A Study of Gods, Rituals and Sacrifice." Ph.D. Dissertation, Oxford University.
Lovera, Sara and Nellys Palomo, eds. 1997. *Las alzadas.* Mexico City: Comunicación e Información de la Mujer.
Lutz, Catherine. 2002. "Making War at Home in the United States: Militarization and the Current Crisis." *American Anthropologist* 104(3): 723–735.
MacCormack, Carol and Marilyn Strathern, eds. 1980. *Nature, Culture and Gender.* Cambridge: Cambridge University Press.

Mani, Lata. 1989. "Contentious Traditions: The Debate on Sati in Colonial India." In *Recasting Women: Essays in Indian Colonial History*. K. Sangari and S. Vaid, eds. Pp. 88–126. New Brunswick, NJ: Rutgers University Press.

Marcos, Sylvia. 1997. "Mujeres Indígenas: notas sobre un feminismo naciente." *Cuadernos feministas* 1 (2): 13–17.

Marín, Carlos. 1998. "Acteal, 22 de diciembre." *Proceso* 1113 (March 1): 6–11.

Martin, David. 1990. *Tongues of Fire: The Explosion of Protestantism in Latin America*. Oxford: Basil Blackwell.

McClusky, Laura. 2001. *"Here Our Culture Is Hard": Stories of Domestic Violence from a Mayan Community in Belize*. Austin: University of Texas Press.

MacEoin, Gary. 1996. *The People's Church: Bishop Samuel Ruíz of Mexico and Why He Matters*. New York: Crossroad.

McClintock, Anne. 1993. "Sex Workers and Sex Work." *Social Text* 7: 1–10.

Medina, A. N.d. "El Paraje y La Familia en Tenejapa." San Cristóbal de las Casas, Mexico.

Melel Xojobal. 2002. *Rumbo a la calle: El trabajo infantil, una estrategia de sobrevivenica*. San Cristóbal de Las Casas, Chiapas: Melel Xojobal.

Miranda Arteaga, Laura. 1998. "Características de la violencia doméstica y las respuestas de las mujeres en una comunidad rural del municipio de Las Margaritas, Chiapas." MA thesis, El Colegio de la Frontera Sur, San Cristóbal de Las Casas, Mexico.

Modiano, Nancy. 1973. *Indian Education in the Chiapas Highlands*. New York: Holt, Rinehart, and Winston.

Mohanram, Radhika. 1999. *Black Body: Women, Colonialism, and Space*. Minneapolis: University of Minnesota Press.

Mohanty, Chandra. 1988. "Under Western Eyes: Feminist Scholarship and Colonial Discourses." *Feminist Review* 30: 61–88.

Mohanty, Chandra Talpade, Ann Russo, and Lourdes Torres, eds. 1991. *Third World Women and the Politics of Feminism*. Bloomington, IN: Indiana University Press.

Moksnes, Heidi. 2003. "Mayan Suffering, Mayan Rights: Faith and Citizenship among Catholic Tzotziles in Highland Chiapas, Mexico." Ph.D. Dissertation in Social Anthropology, Göteborg University, Sweden.

Molyneux, Maxine. 1986. "Mobilization without Emancipation: Women's Interests, the State, and Revolution." In *Transition and Development: Problems of Third World Socialism*. Richard Fagen, Carmen Diana Deere, and José Luis Coraggio, eds. Pp. 280–302. New York: Monthly Review Press.

Morris, Walter F., Jr. 1991. "The Marketing of Maya Textiles in Highland Chiapas, Mexico." In *Textile Traditions in Mesoamerica and the Andes: An Anthology*. M. B. Schevill, J. C. Berlo, and E. B. Dwyer, eds. Pp. 403–433. New York: Garland.

———. 1987. *Living Maya*. New York: H.N. Abrams

Mullings, Leith. 1997. *On Our Own Terms: Race, Class, and Gender in the Lives of African American Women*. New York: Routledge.

Nash, June. 2001. *Mayan Visions: The Quest for Autonomy in an Age of Globalization*. New York: Routledge.

———. 1997. "The Fiesta of the Word: The Zapatista Uprising and Radical Democracy in Mexico." *American Anthropologist* 99 (2): 261–274.

———. 1993. "Maya Household Production and the World Market: The Potters of Amatenango del Valle, Chiapas, Mexico." In *Crafts in Global Markets: Changes in Artisan Production in Middle America*. June Nash, ed. Pp. 127–154. Albany: State University of New York Press.

———. 1973. "The Betrothal: A Study of Ideology and Behavior in a Maya Indian Community." In *Drinking Patterns in Highland Chiapas*. In Henning Siverts, ed. Pp. 89–120. Bergen: Norwegian Research Council for Science and the Humanities.

———. 1970. *The Eyes of the Ancestors: Belief and Behavior in a Mayan Community*. Prospect Heights, IL: Waveland Press.

———. 1964. "The Structuring of Social Relations in Amatenango." *Estudios de Cultura Maya* 4: 335–359.

Nash, June and Maria Patricia Fernández-Kelly. 1983. *Women, Men, and the International Division of Labor*. Albany: State University of New York Press.

Nash, June and Helen Safa, eds. 1985. *Women and Change in Latin America*. South Hadley, MA: Bergin & Garvey.

Nathan, Debbie. 1999. "Work, Sex and Danger in Ciudad Juárez." *NACLA Report on the Americas* 33 (3): 24–30.

Nelson, Diane M. 1999. *A Finger in the Wound: Body Politics in Quincentennial Guatemala.* Berkeley, CA: University of California Press.

O'Brian, Robin. 1997. "Maya Market Women's Sales Strategies in a Stationary Artesanía Market and Response to Changing Gender Relations in Highland Chiapas, Mexico." East Lansing, MI: Working Papers on Women in International Development.

O'Donnell, Kate. N.d. "Poco a Poco: Women Weaving Social Justice in Chiapas."

Olesen, Thomas. 2002. "Long Distance Zapatismo: Globalization and the Construction of Solidarity." Ph.D. dissertation. Department of Political Science, University of Aarhus, Denmark.

Olivera, Mercedes. ed. 2001. *Identidades indígenas y género.* San Cristóbal de las Casas: CONACYT-UNACH.

———. 1998. "Acteal: Los efectos de la Guerra de Baja Intensidad" *La Otra Palabra: Mujeres y Violencia en Chiapas, antes y despues de Acteal.* Rosalva Aída Hernández Castillo, ed. Pp. 114–124. Mexico City: CIESAS, COLEM, CIAM.

——— 1995. "Práctica feminista en el movimiento Zapatista de Liberación Nacional." In *Chiapas, ¿y las mujeres, qué?* Volume 2. Rosa Rojas, ed. Pp. 168–184. México, D.F.: La Correa Feminista.

Ong, Aihwa. 1988. "Colonialism and Modernity: Feminist Re-Presentations of Women in Non-Western Societies." *Inscriptions* 3/4: 79–93.

Ortiz, Teresa. 2001. *Never Again a World Without Us!: Voices of Mayan Women in Chiapas.* Washington, D.C.: Epica Books.

Ozorak, E. 1996. "The Power, but Not the Glory: How Women Empower Themselves through Religion." *Journal for the Scientific Study of Religion* 35(1): 17–29.

Past, Ambar, ed. 1997. *Conjuros y ebriedades: Cantos de Mujeres Mayas.* San Cristóbal de Las Casas, Mexico: Taller Leñateros.

Pérez Enríquez, María Isabel. 1994. *Expulsiones Indígenas: Religión y Migración en tres municipios de los Altos de Chiapas: Chenalhó, Larráinzar y Chamula.* Mexico City: Claves Latinoamericanas.

Pérez Tsu, Mariano. 2000. "Conversaciones interrumpidas: Las voces indígenas del mercado de San Cristóbal." Introduced and translated by Jan Rus. In *Democracia en tierras indígenas: Las elecciones en Los Altos de Chiapas (1991–1998).* Juan Pedro Viqueira and Willibald Sonnleitner, eds. Pp. 259–267. Mexico City: El Colegio de México, CIESAS, and Instituto Federal Electoral.

Physicians for Human Rights. 1997. *Health Care Held Hostage.* Mexico City. December.

Pozas, Ricardo. 1962. *Juan the Chamula.* Berkeley, CA: University of California Press.

Price, Sally H. 1966. "I was Pashku and my husband was Telesh." *Radcliffe Quarterly* 50: 4–8.

Ramírez, Jesús. 1997. "Mapa de la contrainsurgencia." *Masiosare* (Supplement to *La Jornada*). January 13.

Ramírez Cuevas, José. 1998. "Militarización en Chiapas: Un Soldado por Familia." *Masiosare:* Supplement to *La Jornada*, January 25.

Reiter, Rayna, ed. 1975. *Toward an Anthropology of Women.* New York: Monthly Review Press.

Rivera Farfán, Carolina. 1998. "La diaspora religiosa en Chiapas, notas para su estudio." *Chiapas: El factor religiosa.* Mexico City: Revista Academica para el Estudio de las Religiones.

Roberts, Bryan. 1978. *Cities of Peasants: The Political Economy of Urbanization in the Third World.* Beverly Hills: Sage.

Robledo Hernández, Gabriela. 1987. *Disidencia y Religión: Los expulsados de San Juan Chamula.* Thesis. Mexico City: Escuela Nacional de Historia y Antropología.

Rodriguez, Rebecca. 2002. "Young Maya Women Weavers in Cooperatives: Staying Single in Chiapas." Masters thesis. Department of Sociology and Anthropology, New Mexico State University.

Rojas, Rosa. 1994. *Chiapas, ¿y las mujeres, qué?* Vol. 1. Mexico City: La Correa Feminista.

———. 1995(a). *Chiapas, ¿y las mujeres, qué?* Vol. 2. Mexico City: La Correa Feminista.

———. 1995(b). "De la Primera Convención Nacional de Mujeres a la Consulta Nacional del EZLN." in *Chiapas, ¿y las mujeres, qué?* Vol. 2. Rosa Rojas, ed. Pp. 3–70. Mexico City: La Correa Feminista.

Rosaldo, Michelle Zimbalist and Louise Lamphere. 1974. *Women, Culture, and Society.* Stanford: Stanford University Press.

Rosenbaum, Brenda. 1993. *With Our Heads Bowed: The Dynamics of Gender in a Maya Community.* Albany, NY: Institute for Mesoamerican Studies, State University of New York.
———. 1991. "Con nuestras cabezas inclinadas: mujer, sociedad y cultura en una comunidad maya tzotzil." Ph.D. dissertation, State Univeristy of New York, Albany.
Ross, John. 2000. *The War Against Oblivion: The Zapatista Chronicles 1994–2000.* Philadelphia: Common Courage Press.
Rostas, Susanna. 1999. "A Grass Roots View of Religious Change Amongst Women in an Indigenous Community in Chiapas." *Bulletin of Latin American Research* 18 (3): 327–341.
———. 1987. "From Ethos to Identity: Religious practice as resistance to change in a Tzeltal community, Tenejapa, Chiapas, Mexico." D. Phil. thesis, Sussex University.
Rostas, Susanna and Droogers, Andre. 1993. *The Popular Use of Popular Religion in Latin America.* Amsterdam: CEDLA.
Rovira, Guiomar. 1996. *Mujeres de Maíz.* Mexico City: Ediciones Era.
Ruíz Garcia, Samuel. 1993. *Carta Pastoral: En Esta Hora de Gracia.* Mexico City: Dabar.
Rus, Diane. 1997. *Mujeres de tierra fría: Conversaciones con las coletas.* Tuxtla Guitierrez, Mexico: Universidad de Ciencias y Artes de Chiapas.
———. 1990. "La crisis económica y la mujer indígena: El caso de Chamula, Chiapas." San Cristóbal de Las Casas, Mexico: Instituto de Asesoría Antropológica para la Región Maya.
Rus, Jan. 1995. "Local Adaptation to Global Change: The Reordering of Native Society in Highland Chiapas, Mexico, 1974–1994." *European Review of Latin American and Caribbean Studies* 58 (June): 71–89.
———. 1994. "The 'Comunidad Revolucionaria Institucional': The Subversion of Native Government in Highland Chiapas, 1936–1968." In *Everyday Forms of State Resistance: Revolution and the Negotiation of Rule in Modern Mexico.* Gilbert M. Joseph and Daniel Nugent, eds. Pp. 265–300. Durham: Duke University Press.
Rus, Jan, Shannon Mattiace, and Rosalva Aída Hernández Castillo, eds. 2002. *El movimiento Zapatista en Chiapas: La gente indígena y el estado.* Copenhagen and Mexico City: The International Work Group on Indigenous Affairs and El Centro de Investigaciones Superiores en Antropología Social.
———. 2001. "Introduction: The Indigenous People of Chiapas and the State in the Time of Zapatismo: Remaking Culture, Renegotiating Power. *Latin American Perspectives* 28 (2): 7–19.
Rus, Jan and Robert Wasserstrom. 1981. "Evangelization and Political Control: The SIL in Mexico." In *Is God an American?* S. Hvalkof and P. Aaby, eds. Pp 163–172. London: Survival International.
Russell, Philip. 1995. *The Chiapas Rebellion.* Austin: Mexico Resource Center.
Ruz, Mario. 1992. *Savia india, floración ladina: Apuntes para la historia de las fincas comitecas (Siglos XVIII y XIX).* Mexico City: CONACULTA.
Safa, Helen. 1998. "Women's Social Movements in Latin America." In *Crossing Currents: Continuity and Change in Latin America.* Michael Whiteford and Scott Whiteford, eds. Pp. 139–148. Upper Saddle River, NJ: Prentice Hall.
Sampaio, Anna. 2002. "Transforming Chicano/a and Latina/o Politics: Globalization and the Formation of Transnational Resistance in the United States and Chiapas." In *Transnational Latina/o Communities: Politics, Processes, and Cultures.* Carlos G. Vélez-Ibañez and Anna Sampaio, eds. Pp. 47–71. New York: Rowman & Littlefield.
Santana Echeagary, María Eugenia. 2001. *Las mujeres organizadas de la diocesis de San Cristóbal de Las Casas: De la lucha por su dignidad al empoderamiento.* MA Thesis. ECOSUR.
Sántiz Gómez, Maruch. 1998. *Creencias de nuestros antepasados.* San Cristóbal de Las Casas, CIESAS, Centro de La Imagen, and Casa de Las Imágenes.
Schlosser, Eric. 2001. *Fast Food Nation: The Dark Side of the All-American Meal.* Boston: Houghton Mifflin.
Scott, James. 1990. *Domination and the Arts of Resistance: Hidden Transcripts.* New Haven: Yale University Press.
———. 1987. *Weapons of the Weak: Everyday Forms of Peasant Resistance.* New Haven: Yale University Press.
Simonelli, Jeanne and Duncan Earle. N.d. "The Irrational Efficiencies of Planned Globalization: Alternative Development and Plan Puebla Panamá in Chiapas."
Sipaz (International Service for Peace). 2002. "The Challenges for Peace and Reconciliation in Chiapas." *Sipaz Report* 7 (1): 4–7.

Siskel, Suzanne E. 1974. "With the Spirit of a Jaguar: A Study of Shamanism in Ichinton, Chamula." B.A. Honors Thesis, Anthropology Department, Harvard University.

Siverts, Henning, ed. 1981. *Stability and Change in Highland Chiapas*. Occasional Papers 4. Bergen, Norway.

———. 1973. *Drinking Patterns in Highland Chiapas: A Teamwork Approach to the Study of Semantics through Ethnography*. Bergen, Norway: Universitetsforlaget.

Siverts, Kari. 1993 " 'I did not marry properly': the meaning of marriage payments in Southern Mexico." In *Carved Flesh/Cast Selves: Gendered Symbols and Social Practices*. Vigdis Broch-Due, Ingrid Rudie, and Tone Bleie, eds. Pp. 225–236. New York: Berg.

Smith, Carol A. 1995. "Race/Class/Gender Ideology in Guatemala: Modern and Anti Modern Forms." *Comparative Studies in Society and History* 37(4): 723–49.

Speed, Shannon and Jane F. Collier. 2000. "Limiting Indigenous Autonomy in Chiapas, Mexico: The State Government's Use of Human Rights." *Human Rights Quarterly* 22(4): 877–905.

Spivak, Gayatri. 1986. "Imperialism and Sexual Difference." *Oxford Literary Review* 8:225–240.

Stavenhagen, Rodolfo and Diego Iturralde, eds. 1993. *Entre la ley y la costumbre*. Mexico City: Instituto Indigenista Iberoamericano.

Steele, Cynthia. 1994. "'A Woman Fell into the River': Negotiating Female Subjects in Contemporary Mayan Theatre." In *Negotiating Performance: Gender Sexuality, and Theatricality in Latin/o America*. Diana Taylor and Juan Villegas, eds. Pp. 239–256. Durham: Duke University Press.

Stephen, Lynn. 2002. *Zapata Lives! Histories and Cultural Politics in Southern Mexico*. Berkeley, CA: University of California Press.

———. 1998. "Gender and Grassroots Organizing: Lessons from Chiapas." In *Women's Participation in Mexican Political Life*. Victoria E. Rodríguez, ed. Pp. 146–166. Boulder, CO: Westview Press.

———. 1997. *Women and Social Movements in Latin America: Power from Below*. Austin: University of Texas Press.

———. 1996. "Democracy for whom? Women's grassroots political activism in the 1990s, Mexico City and Chiapas." In *Neoliberalism Revisited: Economic Restructuring and Mexico's Political Future*. Gerardo Otero, ed. Pp. 167–186. Boulder, CO: Westview Press.

———, ed. and translator. 1994. *Hear My Testimony: Maria Teresa Tula, Human Rights Activist of El Salvador*. Boston: South End Press.

———. 1991. *Zapotec Women*. Austin: University of Texas Press.

Stephen, Lynn and James Dow, eds. 1990. *Class, Politics, and Popular Religion in Mexico and Central America*. Washington D.C.: The Society for Latin American Anthropology.

Stephens, John Lloyd. 1949. *Incidents of Travel in Central America, Chiapas, and Yucatan*. New Brunswick: Rutgers University Press.

Sternbach, Nancy, Marisa Navarro-Aranguren, Patricia Chuchryk, and Sonia Alvarez. 1992. "Feminisms in Latin America: From Bogota to San Bernardo." In *The Making of Social Movements in Latin America: Identity, Strategy, and Democracy*. Arturo Escobar and Sonia Alvarez, eds. Pp. 207–239. Boulder, CO: Westview Press.

Stoler, Ann Laura. 1995. *Race and the Education of Desire: Foucault's History of Sexuality and the Colonial Order of Things*. Durham: Duke University Press.

Stoll, D. 1990. *Is Latin America Turning Protestant?* Berkeley, CA: University of California Press.

———. 1982. *Fishers of Men or Founders of Empire*. London: Zed Press.

Sullivan, Kathleen. 1998. "Religious Change and the Recreation of Community in an Urban Setting Among the Tzotzil Maya of Highland Chiapas, Mexico." Ph.D. Dissertation, City University of New York.

Tello Díaz, Carlos. 1995. *La rebelión de las Cañadas*. Mexico City: Cal y Arena.

Tinoco, Rolando, J. Parsonnet, and D. Halperin. 1993. "Paraquat Poisoning in Southern Mexico: A Report of Twenty-five Cases." *Archives of Environmental Health* 48 (2): 78–80.

Thompson, E.P. 1967. "Time, Work-Discipline and Industrial Capitalism." *Past and Present* 38: 56–97.

Townsend, Janet, Emma Zapata, and Marta Mercado. 1999. *Women and Power: Fighting Patriarchy and Poverty*. London: Zed Press.

Traven, Bruno. 1952. *La rebelión de los colgados*. New York: Knopf.

Trinh, T. Minh-ha. 1989. *Woman, Native, Other*. Bloomington, IN: Indiana University Press.

Tsing, Anna L. 1993. *In the Realm of the Diamond Queen: Marginality in an Out-of-the-Way Place*. Princeton, NJ: Princeton University Press.

Turner, Paul. 1979. "Religious Conversion and Community Development." *Journal for the Scientific Study of Religion*. 18(3): 252–260.

Turner, Victor. 1982. *From Ritual to Theatre*. New York: PAJ Publications.

Van der Haar, Gemma and Carlos Lenkersdorf. 1998. *San Miguel Chiptik: Testimonios de una comunidad tojolabal*. Mexico City: Siglo Veintiuno Editores.

Van der Veer, Peter. 1995. *Conversion to Modernities: The Globalization of Christian Modernities*. New York: Routledge.

Vargas-Cetina, Gabriela. 1999. "Flexible Looms: Weavers' Organizations in Chiapas, Mexico." *Urban Anthropology* 28 (3–4): 299–325.

Viqueira, Juan Pedro. 1995. "Chiapas y sus regions." In *Chiapas: Rumbos de otra historia*. Juan Pedro Viqueira and Mario Humberto Ruz, eds. Pp. 19–40. Mexico City: Universidad Nacional Autónoma de México Ciudad Universitaria.

Visweswaran, Kamala. 1994. *Fictions of Feminist Ethnography*. Minneapolis: University of Minnesota Press.

Wali, Alaka. 1974. "Dependence and Dominance: The Status of Women in Zinacantán." B.A. Honors Essay presented to the Anthropology Department, Radcliffe College.

Walker Bynum, Caroline. 1984. "Women's Stories, Women's Symbols: A Critique of Victor Turner's Theory of Liminality." In *Anthropology and the Study of Religion*. Robert Moor and Frank Reynolds, eds. Pp. 105–125. Chicago: CSSR.

Warren, Kay B. 1998. *Indigenous Movements and Their Critics: Pan-Maya Activism in Guatemala*. Princeton, NJ: Princeton University Press.

Weinberger, Bill. 2000. *Homage to Chiapas: The New Indigenous Struggles in Mexico*. New York: Verso.

Werner-Brand, Karl. 1992. "Aspectos cíclicos de los nuevos movimientos sociales: fases de crítica cultural y ciclos del nuevo radicalismo de las clases medias." In *Los Nuevos Movimientos Sociales*. Dalton, Russel J. and Mandfred Kuecher, eds. Valencia, Spain: Ediciones Alfons el Magnanim.

Wilk, Richard. 1997. *Household Ecology: Economic Change and Domestic Life among the Kekchi Maya in Belize*. Dekalb, IL: Northern Illinois University Press.

Wilson, Carter. 1995 [1972]. *A Green Tree and a Dry Tree: A Novel of Chiapas*. Albuquerque: University of New Mexico Press.

———. 1966. *Crazy February: Death and Life in the Mayan Highlands of Mexico*. New York: Lippincott Co.

Womack, John. 1999. *Rebellion in Chiapas: An Historical Reader*. New York: The New Press.

———. 1998. "A Bishop's Conversion." *Doubletake* 4 (1): 26–39.

Yuval-Davis, Nira. 1998. *Gender & Nation*. Thousand Oaks, CA : Sage.

Yuval-Davis, Nira, Floya Anthias, and Jo Campling. 1989. *Woman-Nation-State*. New York: St. Martin's Press.

Contributors

Ruperta Bautista Vázquez was born in the Antiguo Valle del Hueyzacatlan, currently known as San Cristóbal de Las Casas. Her parents are Tzotziles from the highland community of Huixtán. Her principal literary interests are poetry, narrative, and theater. She studied social anthropology at the Autonomous University of Chiapas.

Inés Castro Apreza is a researcher with the Centro de Estudios Superiores de México y Centroamérica (CESMECA) of the University of Arts and Sciences in Chiapas. Formerly she was director of research at the Women's Institute in Chiapas. She is recipient of a grant from the Consejo Latinoamericano de Ciencias Sociales y Sarec-Sida for an investigation titled, "Indigenous Citizenship in Chiapas: How Women and Men Experience Conflict, Violence, and Justice" (in press).

Yolanda Castro Apreza was a founding member and coordinator of K'inal Antzetic (Land of Women), with headquarters in Chiapas. She has worked with indigenous women of a number of regions in Chiapas—including the Highlands, the Lancandon rain forest, and the Northern Zone—since 1988. She specializes in advising handicraft cooperatives. In the last two years, she has worked with the movement of *sociedad civil* (civil society) in the Coordinadoras de Contacto por la Consulta Zapatista, which supports the EZLN.

Diana Damián Palencia was born in Villa Flores, Chiapas. She has been active in the women's movement since 1988 and has worked as a social worker, activist, and popular educator in the nongovernmental organization Formación y Capacitación (FOCA) and the Colectivo de Educación Popular in Las Margaritas, Chiapas. She is a contributor to the books *Pasiones en torno al aborto* and *The Other Word: Women and Violence Before and After Acteal.* In 2002, Damián received a MacArthur grant to study the impact of sexual and reproductive rights on Maya communities.

Christine Eber is an anthropologist in the Department of Sociology and Anthropology at New Mexico State University in Las Cruces, New Mexico. Since the mid-1980s she has been studying gender, religion, and social movements in Chiapas, focusing on the township of San Pedro Chenalhó. She is author of *Women and Alcohol in a Highland Maya Town: Water of*

Hope, Water of Sorrow. She also writes poetry and fiction based on her research and assists women in weaving cooperatives of highland Chiapas to sell their products through fair-trade networks.

Graciela Freyermuth Enciso, researcher and past coordinator of CIESAS-Sureste, has carried out various research projects in the areas of health and gender. She has published three books and various articles on Guatemalan refugees, indigenous medicine, medical anthropology, and gender. She worked in San Pedro Chenalhó from 1988–1990 with the Organization of Indigenous Doctors of the State of Chiapas (OMIECH) on a project about indigenous medicine, and in 1995–1996 coordinated the project "Maternal Death in Chenalhó" with Anna María Garza. Her Ph.D. dissertation "Mujeres de humo: Morir en Chenalhó durante la maternidad" (UNAM 2000) has been awarded numerous prizes.

Melissa M. Forbis is a political activist and doctoral student of anthropology at the University of Texas. Her current research focuses on indigenous rights and gender in Chiapas, Mexico. She worked with a nongovernmental organization on appropriate technology and health education projects in Chiapas for four years. She is also a documentary photographer and has an MA in visual anthropology from Temple University.

Pilar Gil Tébar teaches anthropology at the University of Huelva, Spain. Her book *Caminando en un solo corazón: Las mujeres indígenas de Chiapas* is based on her 1994–1995 research with Tzeltal women in the township of Oxchuc. She has begun a new research project with single mothers who are recent migrants to the city of San Cristóbal de Las Casas.

Patty Kelly received her Ph.D. in anthropology from City University of New York Graduate Center. Her dissertation, "Prostitution, Morality, and Modernity in Chiapas, Mexico," was funded by a grant from the American Association of University Women. She has taught anthropology at John Jay College of Criminal Justice in New York City.

Christine Kovic is an assistant professor of anthropology at the University of Houston–Clear Lake. Since 1993, she has conducted research on the issues of indigenous rights and religion in Highland Chiapas. She collaborated with the Center for Human Rights Fray Bartolomé de Las Casas from 1993–1995, and conducted fieldwork with indigenous Catholics in one of the many colonias that surround the city of San Cristóbal de Las Casas. A forthcoming book on human rights and the Catholic Diocese of San Cristóbal will be published by the University of Texas Press.

June Nash is Distinguished Professor Emerita of anthropology at the City College and Graduate Center of the City University of New York. She has conducted ethnographic research in Chiapas since the 1950s. She is author of a number of books, including *We Eat the Mines and the Mines Eat Us* (Columbia University Press, 1979). Her most recent book is *Mayan Visions: The Quest for Autonomy in an Age of Globalization* (Routledge, 2001).

Margarita Pérez Pérez is a midwife and traditional healer from San Pedro Chenalhó. She was one of the early members of OMIECH, a traditional doctors' and midwives association in highland Chiapas.

Flor de Margarita Pérez Pérez is a founding member of two weaving cooperatives and a bakery cooperative in San Pedro Chenalhó. After the Zapatista uprising, she assisted women refugees in and around Polhó, Chenalhó to develop their weaving skills and to market their weavings. In 1999 she was one of the Zapatista delegates from her township to travel to Oaxaca to participate in the consultation on the San Andrés Accords.

Gabriela Patricia Robledo Hernández has a Ph.D. in ecology and sustainable development from El Colegio de la Frontera Sur. She is a professor in the Rural Development Program of the Universidad de Chapingo in San Cristóbal de Las Casas. She is currently collaborating with Dr. Jorge Luis Cruz Burguete of the Colegio de la Frontera Sur on a research project on the commercial sexual exploitation of children in four cities of Chiapas. The topic of her dissertation is religious change and households in Highland Chiapas. Since 1980 she has studied the migration resulting from the religious expulsions in highland communities.

Susanna Rostas teaches social anthropology and is a research associate in the Department of Social Anthropology at the University of Cambridge, England. She worked in Chiapas from 1980 to 1983 for her Ph.D. on ritual, ethos, and identity, and subsequently on religious change from 1987–1988 and has an enduring interest in the area. Her publications include The Popular Use of Popular Religion in Latin America, edited with André Droogers (CEDLA 1993). Recently she has worked in Mexico City, with the Concheros who perform a ritual circle dance. Her book on this subject will soon be published.

Heather Sinclair, a midwife and health educator, was a human-rights observer in Chiapas during 1996–1997 where she visited the Northern Zone and later lived in a Peace Camp. At home in the U.S., she helped form the Paso del Norte Chiapas Solidarity Committee in El Paso, Texas and has been involved in community organizing around issues of fair trade, environmental and human health, garment sweatshop conditions, immigrant abuse, and solidarity with democratic movements in Mexico and Colombia. She lives with her daughter in El Paso.

Shannon Speed is an assistant professor of anthropology at the University of Texas, Austin. She is currently working on a book based on fieldwork conducted in Chiapas, Mexico, from 1996–2001. Speed worked as Coordinator of Global-Exchange Chiapas in 1996–1997, and has been an adviser to the Red de Defensores Comunitarios por los Derechos Humanos since 1999. Her interests include human rights, indigenous rights, gender, globalization, and activist research.

Glossary

Key
Sp.—Spanish
Tz.—Tzotzil

Las Abejas: The Bees. An organization of Tzotzil-Mayas dedicated to nonviolent resistance in the highland township of Chenalhó; full name, Civil Society The Bees (Sp.).

Acteal: A community in the township of San Pedro Chenalhó where 45 members of Las Abejas (The Bees) were massacred while praying in a chapel on December 22, 1997.

autonomous township: A community or township that has established an alternate system of territorial governance, with local control of juridical and administrative functions and resources; concentrated in areas with strong Zapatista influence.

campesino: A peasant, a person who cultivates the land for subsistence (Sp.).

cargo: Work that is carried out for the benefit of one's community. Literally, a burden or duty, e.g. performed by the sponsor (cargo-holder) of a traditional festival (Sp.).

catechist: Catholic lay leader. In the Diocese of San Cristóbal de Las Casas, catechists prepare people for the sacraments and serve as religious leaders in their communities.

caxlan: A nonindigenous person, Mexican or foreign (Tz.).

Ch'ol: A Mayan language and the ethnic group that speaks this language.

civil society: Citizen groups outside the formal government who attempt to change the political process.

CODIMUJ (Diocesan Coordination of Women): A network of hundreds of grassroots women's groups linked through the Catholic Diocese of San Cristóbal de Las Casas.

Coleto: a Ladino living in San Cristóbal; derives from the pigtail (*cola*, literally "tail") or hank worn by Spanish colonists, especially bullfighters in the eighteenth century (Sp.).

colonia: Neighborhood or unregulated urban settlement, for the most part located on the outskirts of a city (Sp.).

compañera/o: Companion or friend (Sp.).

Catholic Diocese of San Cristóbal de Las Casas: Comprised of 41 townships in eastern Chiapas; under the leadership of a single bishop. From 1960 to

2000 the Bishop of the Diocese was Samuel Ruíz Garcia. The current bishop is Felipe Arizmendi.

EZLN (*Ejercito Zapatista de Liberación Nacional*) (Zapatista Army of National Liberation): An insurgent group that publicly emerged on January 1, 1994 with demands for justice, liberty, and democracy (Sp.).

headtown: cabecera (Sp.) Administrative center of a township.

INI (National Indigenous Institute): An organization of the Mexican federal government responsible for implementing policy in relation to indigenous peoples.

Iloletik: Traditional healers, literally "ones who see" (Tz.). Singular, ilol.

indigenous: In Chiapas indigenous describes individuals who identify with a distinct cultural group characterized by one or more of the following attributes: a language different from the national language; an economic system oriented mainly toward subsistence; a moral attachment to ancestral territories and their resources; and social and political institutions distinct from those of the dominant Mexican culture.

Liberation Theology: A form of Catholic theology first developed in Latin America in the 1960s. It asserts that the poor are the preferred subjects for the revelation of the Word of God; involves a rereading of the Bible from the perspective of the oppressed.

low-intensity warfare: A military strategy to counter popular organizations by instilling fear through misinformation and psychological and military tactics.

Maya: A cultural group that traces its roots to the ancient Mesoamerican civilization whose territory extended through contemporary Mexico, Belize, Guatemala, Honduras, and El Salvador.

mestizo: A person of mixed Spanish and indigenous blood; Mayas use this term interchangeably with *Ladino* to describe a nonindigenous Mexican (Sp.).

milpa: A plot of land cultivated with corn and beans and often squash and chile (Sp.).

NGOs: Nongovernmental, civil organizations independent of national governments.

North American Free Trade Agreement (NAFTA): Treaty between the Mexican, U.S. and Canadian governments designed to integrate the three economies.

PAN (*Partido Acción Nacional*) (National Action Party): Right of center party in Mexico (Sp.).

PRD (*Partido de la Revolución Democratica*) (Party of the Democratic Revolution): Left of center party in Mexico (Sp.).

PRI (*Partido Revolucionario Institucional*) (the Institutional Revolutionary Party): Centrist party that governed Mexico from 1929–2000 (Sp.).

paramilitaries: Armed groups of civilians.

peace camps: Name given to the physical presence in rural communities of outside observers who serve as both witnesses and deterrents to military abuses.

peso: basic unit of Mexican currency. In 2002, 10 pesos equaled about $1.00 (Sp.).

Plan Puebla Panama (PPP): An international development project aimed at expanding infrastructure and creating export-processing zones in the American Isthmus.

pox: A homemade rum produced from sugar cane juice (Tz.).

pozol: A drink made by grinding corn kernels and mixing them with water. (Sp.) matz' (Tz.).

San Andrés Accords: Agreements signed in February 1996 during peace talks between the EZLN and federal government that redefine and expand specific cultural, territorial, and political rights for indigenous peoples. The Mexican congress approved a watered-down version of these accords in 2002.

San Cristóbal de Las Casas: A mestizo-dominated city in highland Chiapas. Jovel (Tz.).

San Juan Chamula: A highland Tzotzil township (commonly referred to as Chamula).

San Pedro Chenalhó: A highland Tzotzil township located north of San Juan Chamula (commonly referred to as Chenalhó).

Tojolabal: A Mayan language and the ethnic group that speaks this language.

tortilla: A flat pancake made of maize; staple of Mayan diet (Sp.). vaj (Tz.).

Tuxtla Gutiérrez: State capital of Chiapas.

Tzeltal: A Mayan language and the ethnic group that speaks this language.

Tzotzil: A Mayan language and the ethnic group that speaks this language.

Zapatista support base: Civilian groups composed of men, women, and youth who provide material and moral support to EZLN combatants and participate in Zapatista programs and consultations about EZLN actions.

Zoque: An indigenous ethnic group in the northern region of Chiapas.

Index